MUNICH

FLOWERS OF MANCHESTER

A Manchester United

Anthology

JOHN LUDDEN

Photos are courtesy of Tracey Malone (Thank you!)

"It is the object of life to build. When I knew the worst of Munich I understood at last that to pray for death as I had done was wrong and cowardly. I knew somehow I must succeed again for the sake of those who died."

Matt Busby

SIXTY SIX YEARS SIXTY SIX SEASONS

For Manchester United supporters the snow from that Munich runway
has never really stopped falling. The following is an anthology of
work I have done over the years on the Busby Babes and the crash,
plus a section at the end for people to express their own feelings and
memories.

INTRODUCTION
THE SAN SIRO (Part One)

Milan. Wednesday 14th May 1958.

In the end it was men against boys. As the *San Siro* stadium hailed a famous 4-0 victory and a place in the 1958 European Cup final against Real Madrid, the beaten Manchester United players in their white shirts cut a sorry sight leaving the celebratory scenes erupting across the Milanese terraces and pitch. Not surprisingly for this was professional football and they were playing for the highest stakes, meaning no mercy shown by the home side AC Milan. The *Rossoneri*. The disaster at Munich was regarded by them a terrible tragedy, but it was not their tragedy. The crash that had decimated the English opponents just three months previously saw them say prayers for the Mancunian departed, but their desire to grind them into the *San Siro* turf was never affected. The loss of so many great players meant there could only ever be one ending to Manchester United's season. The boys wearing the United badge who took to the field at the *San Siro* were not so much a sad reflection of those lost amid the snow, ice and blood of that southern German runway. More a broken mirror smashed into a thousand and one pieces. The assistant coach Jimmy Murphy remained on the touchline, swearing, letting fly a hail of abuse at the Milanese behaviour throughout the match and at the final whistle. A lone policeman grabbed Jimmy and ensured he made it to the relative safety of the United dressing room before being lynched! Outnumbered by tens of thousands, riotous home supporters armed with rotten fruit and bottles of urine that had rained down throughout on the Mancunians. Such might have appeared unfair odds, but Jimmy Murphy was up for it. For he had been holding it all in. A Welsh firebrand. A powder keg of emotion. An unexploded grenade left over from the remnants of Munich. This man who had performed miracles to keep Manchester United in existence. Suddenly, the season was over, the fuel that had helped Jimmy Murphy rage against a ravenous Grim Reaper in their midst had run dry. So, Jimmy raged and ranted till the tears in Milan fell for his golden apples lost. A short period of time when the Busby babes took flight. What the late Sir Bobby Charlton back then christened "Paradise" had turned into Purgatory. The following is a testament of those years.

CHAPTER ONE
KILMARNOCK

"None of the youngsters in the side had let me down at Kilmarnock, so I decided to back them, come what may. Six of the side I selected were under twenty-one, but I knew that they would go on developing with experience, into just as big star performers as the Johnny Carey era, which was now coming to an end of six glorious years for Manchester United."

Matt Busby

The Ayrshire town of Kilmarnock was home to the first collection of work by the legendary poet Robert Burns in the Scottish Dialect. They were published there by John Wilson in 1786. The town was also the founding home of the Scotch whiskey brand *Johnny Walkers*. During the winter of October 1953, many say it was also the place where the Busby Babes first began to hatch. Where the lighting exploded out the bottle! Saturday 24th October 1953. In the Kilmarnock FC home programme priced at 3d against Forfar Athletic, there was an announcement for a forthcoming match on the Wednesday night.

MANCHESTER UNITED

"We inaugurate our floodlighting season on Wednesday 28th October, with a visit from Manchester United. I would appeal to all supporters to come to this game and help to make it a success. We have heard so long that if we could get a good team, we would get the crowd. Here is an opportunity to show your appreciation to Matt Busby's boys for their visit to Kilmarnock. I know you will enjoy the evening. The kick-off is 7.30. We hope to have another English team in a fortnight's time. For the above game season ticket holders may purchase their own seat. (5\). Tickets are on sale at Rugby Park."

Meanwhile, that same Saturday afternoon, 230 miles away, a gloomy looking Manchester United manager was not a happy man. Although Matt Busby had just seen his team beat a poor Aston Villa

1-0 at Old Trafford, with a goal twenty-minutes from time by Johnny Berry. A cross from Harry McShane, (father of actor Ian McShane), the performance had been dire. United had won only four of their opening fifteen games. It was terrible form. A crowd of 32,104 had also been far from impressed. One report back then really stuck the knife in! "How can football sink so low in this game? You expect £15 a week footballers to serve up something better than this, which was the season's worst performance!" Busby's immediate reaction was United appeared stale and in desperate need of new blood. It had been two seasons since the last title and the feel for an air of change could not escape his thinking. The old guard, loyal and long serving stalwarts were still fine players. But the likes of the no nonsense, courageous centre-half Allenby Chilton, the devastating centre-forward Jack Rowley of the thunderous shot. The non-stop running and skilful promptings of inside-left Henry Cockburn. The creative, sublime touches and clever finishing of inside-forward Stan Pearson, and the play anywhere, adaptable full-back John Aston could not go on forever. Age is every footballer's greatest enemy. Legs go. Busby's magnificent FA Cup and League winning Captain "Gentleman" Johnny Carey had already left at the end of the previous season to go and manage Blackburn Rovers. Following Carey's departure United's new Captain was Roger Byrne. Busby would use the upcoming friendly match against Kilmarnock to give an opportunity for a few youngsters to show their stuff. None more so than Duncan Edwards. He had already been handed a first team debut then sent back to Jimmy Murphy to perfect. Secretly, Duncan was both men's pride and joy, a talent, a powerhouse of a boy just turned seventeen that same month. Big Dunc was ready to be unleashed! Busby once compared of how himself and Jimmy Murphy worked on their prodigy was like a sculptor starting with just a mound of marble, until he carved away to produce a statue of beauty and wonder.

In Scotland, the Manchester United party stayed at idyllic Troon on the Ayrshire West coast, handing their manager ample opportunity to grab a round of his beloved golf on its magnificent courses. Also giving Busby time to ponder the coming, changing times set to fall upon the United team sheet. Two youngsters, the adaptable Jackie Blanchflower and the explosive inside-forward Dennis Viollet were brought in. Duncan Edwards would start on the bench. In friendly matches substitutes were allowed to be used. Happily, for the home

side, the trumpet call for more support in the previous Saturday's programme worked a treat, as 16,000 supporters turned up at Rugby Park. Although most were probably only there to see for themselves Matt Busby's legendary reds from Manchester! On a side-note, the original Kilmarnock programme proclaiming that Manchester United were coming to play at Rugby Park, now stands unique, as come the following Wednesday there was no actual programme printed.

United opened the scoring after just three-minutes when Henry Cockburn lobbed the Kilmarnock goalkeeper Jimmy Brown from twenty-yards. Shortly after Cockburn was injured and forced to leave the pitch. His replacement jumped straight up off the United bench and was ready to go. Onto the field of play at left-half came a fired up Duncan Edwards! Although heavily outclassed Malky Macdonald's brave side never stopped running and made opportunities of their own. The *Killie* forward Tommy Henaughan smashing in a shot that forced the United keeper Jack Crompton to push round his post. Yet, despite their efforts it was not long before Edwards was completely running the show! The visitors created a host of chances but proved wasteful, until on thirty-minutes when the red's centre-forward Tommy Taylor pounced to grab a classy, second rounding Brown to finish. As the second period wore on United continued to create playing some delightful football, as Jimmy Brown at times playing the visitors on his own! With Kilmarnock not giving up it proved a splendid contest. Crompton also pulled off two more fine saves from the Killie's inside-left Willie Harvey and left-winger Matt Murray. But it was to be United who struck next when the electric Dennis Viollet swooped to make the score 3-0, five-minutes from time. There had been clear signs throughout the game of the young Viollet forging what could be a devastating partnership with Tommy Taylor. As for Duncan Edwards? His appearance on the field had galvanised United. He was everywhere pushing the reds forward, tidying up at the back, dominating the middle of the pitch. *Killie* supporters watched on in disbelief. Who was this kid whose left-half position seemed to act only as a launching pad!

Matt Busby in his own words: "We'd played a friendly game in Kilmarnock on the Wednesday, following a 1-0 win over Aston Villa, but I wasn't happy, I wasn't satisfied about it and we played this match, I put a lot of these young boys in and we won 3-0. I remember the following day walking along the golf course thinking we won 3-0, but what was the strength of the team? This went on for a couple of days. All of a sudden I said: "Right, I'm going to put them all in!" And that was against Huddersfield the following Saturday. I think we played three of the championship side and eight new players. It was a big decision, but sometimes you have to face these things, it worked out the right way!"

The Team for Huddersfield. Wood, Foulkes, Byrne, Whitefoot, Chilton, Edwards, Berry, Blanchflower, Taylor, Viollet and Rowley.

A 0-0 draw was earned against a third placed Huddersfield Town team that had lost just once in ten matches. United should have won late on when Tommy Taylor put a barnstorming Duncan Edwards clear through on goal, only for him to shoot narrowly wide! This apart Edwards had produced a virtuoso showing. Following there was a headline in the Manchester Evening Chronicle that read:

"Bouncing Babes Keep All Town Away!"

Within the next three games they thrashed Cardiff City 6-1 away, and took apart Stanley Matthews FA Cup holders Blackpool 4-1 at Old Trafford in a stunning performance. An awesome Duncan Edwards by far the man of the match, despite a glorious hat trick from the on-fire Tommy Taylor! Matt Busby handed Edwards the difficult role of marking the brilliant Blackpool playmaker Ernie Taylor, and his young colt simply swamped him, whilst at the same time totally dominating the match itself. He was five-foot ten, twelve stone, six pounds with legs like oak tree trunks and thighs that opponents bounced off like running into concrete. He was Duncan Edwards.

The evolution at Manchester United had begun. A new era, a new United, one bloodied from the creche. Just two seasons later 1955-56,

Manchester United were crowned First Division champions once more with a team forever to be immortalised as the Busby Babes. "When we won the title in the 1955-56 season by a whopping eleven points from Blackpool and Wolves, the average age of our lads was twenty-three. Don't forget these lads were the forerunners for English teams in Europe. Manchester United were on a crusade and we had a wonderful spirit of adventure."
Jimmy Murphy

CHAPTER TWO
REACH FOR THE SKY

The journey began on Tuesday 11th September 1956. Manchester United flew to Belgium taking on RSC Anderlecht in the first qualifying round of the European Cup. The Belgian champions were managed by an Englishman, the 45-year-old ex-Blackburn Rovers and Northampton Town goalkeeper Bill Gormlie. The arrival of the English champions had electrified Brussels being advertised locally as **"Le Grand Match International en Nocturne!"**
The game would be played at the wonderfully, picturesque *Parc Astrid* stadium, so different to the broken down, antiquated English grounds the United players were used to performing in.

The Teams.

RSC (Royal Sporting Club) Anderlecht. Week, Matthys, Culot, Lippens, De Koster, Vanderwilt, De Dryver, Jurion, Dewael, Mermans and Vandenbosch.

Manchester United. Wood, Foulkes, Byrne, Colman, Jones, Blanchflower, Berry, Whelan, Taylor, Viollet and Pegg.

In front of 35,000 pumped-up, roaring Belgian spectators the visitors produced a mature, battling performance winning 2-0. Matt Busby had warned his players beforehand they could only be fully judged by playing against the best of the European elite, but Anderlecht, despite giving United a decent game were ruthlessly put away in devastating style. The capacity crowd in Brussels had been so eager to see their lads test themselves against an English side for the first time, but the occasion turned out to be a stroll in the *Parc* for the Busby Babes. United dominated the contest for large periods and deservedly took the lead through the Fallowfield born, 24-year-old, lightning-quick Dennis Viollet's, blistering, long-range drive after twenty-five minutes. A Mark Jones clearance found Eddie Colman, who in turn set up Viollet to rifle home past the Anderlecht keeper Felix Week. Despite going behind the hosts never lay down and come the second-half were handed the opportunity to equalise from the penalty spot after Jones fouled their Captain. The hugely, experienced 30-year-old Jeff Mermans. The golden boy of Belgian football nicknamed The *Bomber*. With Merman's at the helm Anderlecht had dominated the Belgium First Division for years, but now to level the tie up stepped the Anderlecht international midfielder Martin Lippens, only to strike the ball against Ray Wood's post! Incidentally, Busby paid £6000 Darlington for his ever-reliable goalkeeper. An absolute steal. After a period of more intense pressure by the Belgians, the game was wrapped up fifteen-minutes from time when United broke out and from a superb David Pegg cross, Tommy Taylor leapt high to smash a header home past Week. 2-0! Whilst the visiting Mancunians celebrated a job well done at the full-time whistle, United fans at home desperately waited for news as to how their team had gone on, and it finally came to them through a BBC-10.pm radio bulletin. Those were the days!

The travelling Guardian journalist Donny Davies was gushing in his praise of the English champions. "If one wants to feel British and proud of it, travel around with Manchester United. The reverence with which their players are received in Belgium stems from the detailed knowledge of the club's achievements."

The following day there was strong rumours that the Football League were intent on pressing United to withdraw from the European Cup on the basis of possible fixture congestion, but Matt Busby was adamant and blunt with his retort. "We intend to go on," he told the newspapers journalists. "The decision has been made." Busby was not prepared to be bullied by the rantings of the authoritarian Alan Hardaker, just because he refused all demands to doff his cap.

"We do not fear a congestion of fixtures. We have at least eighteen players who can play in the first team without noticeably weakening it. Also, the experience gained in competition against the finest clubs in Europe will be invaluable to my young players. After England's last two failures in the World Cup, (1950 and 1954) alone, demands that the continental challenge should be met, not avoided." Hardaker's incessant rants at Manchester United that participating in the competition would affect their League form were proving to be abject nonsense as the following Saturday they took apart the newly promoted Sheffield Wednesday, 4-1. Goals from Johnny Berry, Tommy Taylor, Dennis Viollet and Billy Whelan delighting a 48,000 Old Trafford crowd. United were electric, Eddie Colman was inspirational and Johnny Berry's brilliant diving header was the best of the four. One of the older players by three years Berry was already training to be a physiotherapist for when he retired. The home team simply ran the legs off their Yorkshire opponents. Hardaker must have winced when the score came through, but he was by no means ready to give up the sniping. Beware a truly, arrogant man scorned.

CHAPTER THREE
SWAN LAKE IN FOOTBALL BOOTS

"What makes a Manchester United player is skill, fitness and character. And the most important of these is character."
Matt Busby.

Two weeks later RSC Anderlecht came to England attempting to turn around their 2-0 deficit. The game would take place at Manchester City's Maine Road, due to the floodlights still not fully ready to be switched on at Old Trafford. It was a painfully slow and expensive process costing £40,000 from GEC. Four pylons, each 160 feet high, holding fifty-four floodlights. Until they were erected and set to go, City loaned United their ground on agreed terms of £300, or 15% of the gate money in each game. Brotherly love maybe, but there was still a tidy sum to be made out of their neighbours.

The Manchester Evening News greeted RSC Anderlecht to the Rainy city with the headline. **"Soyez les bienvenus! et que la meilleure equipe remporte la Victoire!" ("May the best team win!")**
Manchester United were about to unleash hell on an unsuspecting RSC Anderlecht!

The Teams.

Manchester United. Wood, Foulkes, Byrne, Colman, Jones, Edwards, Berry, Whelan, Taylor, Viollet and Pegg.

RSC Anderlecht. Week, Gettemans, Culot, Hanon, De Koster, Vanderwilt, De Dryver, Vandenbosche, Mermans, Dewael and Jurion.

Wednesday 26th September 1956. Four days on from beating Manchester City 2-0 in front of a 53,751, crammed Old Trafford, goals from Dennis Viollet and Liam Whelan settling the derby, United turned up at Moss Side watched this time around by a 40,000 crowd, and romped home by an astounding 10-0, against the poor, unsuspecting Belgians! A brittle Anderlecht were quite literally left wondering what the hell had hit them and collapsed like a pack of cards. With Duncan Edwards available once more after a toe injury, and free from his National Service duties for a while as an ammunition storeman, (Army number 23145376). Edwards was the only change from Brussels in place of Jackie Blanchflower. United produced a jaw-dropping performance. On a pitch flooded with sprawling pools of water, the Manchester rain forever incessant the Babes ran riot. It was like Swan Lake in football boots!

Their play at a rapier pace, eye-catching and bewildering. The ball was not so much passed around the Anderlecht shirts more pinged, struck like on a pinball machine. At the time Bobby Charlton was doing his National Service with the Royal Army Ordnance Corps, but managed to make the game from an Army camp in Nesscliffe near Shrewsbury to watch his pals. All he can remember saying to himself as the tally mounted was: "Unbelievable! The lads who played that night did with a power and a majesty quite stunning. Especially when you consider the age of the team…They were just kids?"

The goal-scoring list read like the end of a Hollywood movie credit.

Dennis Viollet, four.

Tommy Taylor, three.

Liam Whelan, a brace.

Johnny Berry with one.

All making the magical number ten.

Despite Viollet's four goal haul and Taylor's hat-trick, the undoubted star of the evening, the one who tortured and destroyed the Anderlecht defenders to create the vast majority of the goals was the United left-winger David Pegg. A Yorkshire lad, Pegg was born in the village of Highfields, north of Doncaster. He Joined United at fourteen and was tipped by many to succeed the great "Preston Plumber" Tom Finney. By then nearing the end of his international career in the England team. Originally spotted by United's northern scout Norman Scholes, Pegg's father Bill was a miner, a no nonsense character determined that his son should get the best deal. Bill met with all the clubs who wanted to sign David with always one question and a typical Yorkshire, straight forward attitude. "Tell me straight and no rubbish, what do you think of my son's prospects?" Most he saw straight through and sent on their merry way, but when he spoke to Matt Busby, Bill met a man like himself. No fool for false words. "Bill, Your son with reasonable luck will be successful as a professional footballer." David Pegg was off to Manchester United! It was the type of night for Pegg when everything he attempted just came off. A once in a career "Saturday Night at the Palladium" take a bow performance, as Pegg effortlessly switched wings causing the Belgians equal havoc on each. Indeed, such was his immense contribution the last moments were spent with grateful teammates trying desperately to gift him a much-deserved goal, only for the ball, tired of hitting the Belgian net refusing to go along.

10-0! Come the final whistle, the sporting, if devastated Anderlecht team clapped Manchester United off the pitch. A wonderful gesture considering the humiliation they must have been feeling. Across the delirious, soaked and wooden Maine Road terraces, rain-sodden Mancunians handed their boys a rousing, standing ovation. They were already quite taken by the grand sounding notion of this European Cup. The savage ten-goal slaughter reverberated across Europe, for RSC Anderlecht were a proud club and deemed by no one as an easy touch. This was a truly outstanding European team. Their Captain Jeff Mermans spoke afterwards to Tom Jackson of the Manchester Evening News. He appeared still reeling and in shock at what had befallen them. "Why do they not pick the whole of this side for England? There is not a single excuse we can offer for our humiliating defeat. We gave of our best, but it was just not good enough against what must rate as one of the finest club teams in the world. We have played against the best of Hungary, France, Italy and Russia, no one has ever beaten us like that. Even at 6-0 they just kept running and running." Billy Whelan was in fact Irish, but Merman's point was well made! Even the referee Welshman Mervyn Griffiths was taken aback by the cold-eyed determination of Busby's young colts to not let Anderlecht off the leash. "I have never seen football more deadly in execution." The man himself, a beaming, exuberant Matt Busby failed to hide his excitement at seeing his young side play in such a beautifully, devastating fashion. "It was the finest exhibition of teamwork from any side I have ever seen, club or international," he gushed. "It was simply near perfection. I can never hope in the rest of my lifetime to see anything better than this." That long, gone night at Maine Road as the heavens opened, despite him quite miraculously never making the score sheet will always though belong to David Pegg.

Four days later Manchester United travelled to Highbury with only one change from the side that had annihilated Anderlecht. Ronnie Cope for the injured Mark Jones. In front of the Gunner's highest crowd of the season, 62,479, United won 2-1 with first-half goals from Johnny Berry and Liam Whelan. The home side grabbed one back after the interval with a dubious penalty, but ultimately the Red Devils deserved to win a cracking match! The Babes looked unbeatable and just to ensure the conveyor belt was still in fine order, the following week saw an 18 year-old boy from the north-east, Ashington, make his League debut called Bobby Charlton! On Saturday 6th October 1957, against Charlton Athletic at Old Trafford, Bobby scored twice in a 4-2 victory. Another golden apple had dropped from the tree and this one was truly special.

CHAPTER FOUR
BLOODY MISTAKES

Wednesday 17th October 1956. The European campaign continued for the Busby Babes, when the newly crowned West German champions Borussia Dortmund came to Manchester.

The Teams.

Manchester United. Wood, Foulkes, Byrne, Colman, Jones, Edwards, Berry, Whelan, Taylor, Viollet and Pegg.

Borussia Dortmund. Kwiatkowski, Burgsmuller, Sandmann, Schlebowski, Michallek, Bracht, Peters, Preissler, Kelbassa, Schmidt and Kapitulski.

 A huge Maine Road crowd of 76,598 witnessed a blistering first-half showing from Busby's youngsters, as they carried on in the same vein of form that blew away RSC Anderlecht. An outstanding 3-0 interval lead was established by the reds. Borussia's golden-satin shirts found themselves chasing shadows and were being handed a hiding that threatened to seriously rival the one served out to the Belgians in the previous round. Two goals from Dennis Viollet, a striker of such clinical precision whose partnership with the powerful Tommy Taylor, was simply far too much for Dortmund. They tore apart the Germans. Viollet was exceptional. The third came unexpectedly from the panicking defender Wilhelm Burgsmuller, who after being hassled and harried by the box of tricks David Pegg contrived to put the ball in his own net. Only the bravery and heroics of the Dortmund goalkeeper Heinz Kwiatkowski wearing a green jersey borrowed off fellow countryman, Manchester City's Bert Trautman, managed to keep the score-line down to just three. Half-time arrived and deafening cheers rang out from the Maine Road terraces in appreciation of yet another superb Manchester United performance. Their boys had taken to this competition like a duck to water. It appeared for many supporters this European Cup held no fears. However, such thoughts would swiftly change as Borussia responded to their angry coach's Helmut Schneider's dressing down to finally show their true colours and teach these cocky English champions a priceless lesson. No doubt buoyed and thinking the job was already done United eased off in the second period, and were made to pay a heavy price. The first-half heroics faded fast as the Germans came roaring back to snatch two late goals. Both were defensive errors, one of them a true rarity from the Captain Roger Byrne. When instead of just kicking clear he tried to chest the ball down and found himself robbed by Dortmund's flying winger Helmut Kapitulski, who then slammed the ball past Roy Wood. Dortmund's best player was their Captain Alfred Preissler. He terrorised the United defence in the last twenty-minutes. The silky Preissler strolling through to grab a vital, late second leaving the home crowd worried and shocked. No longer could the European Cup be viewed easy picking. No longer was it like shooting ducks in the fair. Borussia Dortmund were suddenly back in the tie with a real fighting chance to finish off Manchester United on home soil. Afterwards, a baited and clearly annoyed Roger Byrne unusually bit at the gathered news hacks. Byrne was asked if he thought his error would prove crucial? "Yes, of course it was a silly mistake!" he snapped. "But don't you lot ever make bloody mistakes?" Suddenly, the red side of Manchester had been awoken to the troubles and trepidations of European football. Amid the glamorous names, the unfamiliar faces, the dangers of the unknown had surfaced. The Busby Babes, whom only a short time previously appeared a certainty for the quarter-final stage, now faced a battle to survive in the competition on German soil.

CHAPTER FIVE
SKATING ON THIN ICE

Wednesday 21st November 1956. At Borussia Dortmund's stadium, the *Rota Erde,* Manchester United were forced back to defend for their lives against a ninety-minute onslaught from the proud German champions.

The Teams.

Borussia Dortmund. Kwiatkowski, Burgsmuller, Sandmann, Schlebowski, Michallek, Bracht, Peters, Preissler, Kelbassa, Schmidt and Niepieklo.

Manchester United. Wood, Foulkes, Byrne, Colman, Jones, McGuinness, Berry, Whelan, Taylor, Edwards and Pegg.

On a dreadful, bone-hard surface resembling more an ice rink and watched by 44,450 spectators, including 7,000 British servicemen stationed in the Ruhr valley, United found themselves besieged. The home side came at them in waves and the different manner in which Dortmund created an abundance of chances, only to then invent entirely new ways to miss them had their fans agonising throughout, and the Mancunians profoundly grateful. The marvellously gifted Captain Preissler, wearing an unfortunate hairnet was an ever-present thorn in the visitor's defence. He possessed the ability to skate over the icy ground. To truly compound United's on-field problems the container holding the rubber studs that would have replaced their normal ones had mysteriously disappeared on the day of the match. Whether German mischief-making or simple carelessness was to blame, it represented big problems for trainer Tom Curry, as he struggled to find replacements. Thus the United players were forced to take to the field wearing unsuitable studs on a pitch that felt more concrete than grass! Somehow, laced with huge doses of good fortune, big hearts, bags of courage and a refusal to be beaten Busby's team fought out a 0-0 draw to see them through. A performance of such guts and grim determination it surprised even their manager, who admitted he feared the worst after the Germans' late flurry of goals back in Manchester. A stupendous, goalkeeping masterclass from a tracksuit-bottomed Ray Wood, including two world class saves in the opening minute from point blank range proved critical, whilst a wonderful Captain's performance from Roger Byrne marshalling his troops around the penalty area, more than made up for the first-leg error. Centre-half Mark Jones was equally immense, as was a towering Duncan Edwards breaking up countless attacks and refusing to bow down as United buckled, rocked but never truly broke. With the astonishing Edwards crashing into tackles showing great calm and immense presence for just a 20-year-old when on the ball, United stood their ground. As the game strove to a dramatic climax even the German fans began to applaud this young English lion of a player. Of all their "Golden Apples" though neither would ever admit publicly it, the boy from 31 Elm Road on the Priory estate in Dudley, was Busby's and Jimmy Murphy's most dazzling pearl in a collection of priceless diamonds. On his day unplayable Duncan Edwards was already an established England international and amongst the finest young players in Europe. In the dying moments Dortmund saw a penalty appeal waived aside when Bill Foulkes clearly handled inside his own penalty area. Luckily for Foulkes and United it was on the referee's blind side and as the stadium roared out in disapproval the game finally ended. A severe struggle for the reds. Afterwards, Dortmund's Preissler was heavily disappointed but generous in defeat as he praised and made a prediction about his English opponents. "In England, Manchester swamped us with incredible football. Here in Germany they have fought like tigers. They will win the European Cup."

With this United team it really was a case of the Alexander Dumas Musketeer call to arms of "All for one!" A fine example of this occurred after the match when the players were allowed by Busby to go to a nearby hostelry for a few beers after a tough evening against the Germans. Suddenly, a stranger punched the keeper Ray Wood at the other end of the bar from where Mark Jones was stood. He simply put his pint down, walked over and smacked the offender on the chin knocking him clean out before returning back to finish the beer, as if nothing had happened! The boy from the Yorkshire pit town of Wombwell near Barnsley, where a talent for football saved him from a job down the mines was not having that done to a teammate.

The game against Dortmund was one of the rare occasions Wilf McGuinness and Duncan Edwards played together in the first team. A fine player who could easily command a regular place at any other First Division club, but like so many others at Old Trafford, Wilf never dreamt of moving elsewhere. Even though the task in front of him to somehow shift his mate out of the Babes line-up was one few ever believed possible. A typical example of Wilf's commitment to the Manchester United cause, and the genius of Jimmy Murphy came on his debut at home to Wolverhampton Wanderers, on Saturday 8th October 1955. The game itself was a classic with the reds winning 4-3 from a last minute strike by Tommy Taylor, but our story is set mostly in the United dressing room beforehand. The day before Duncan Edwards had gone down with flu meaning Wilf got the call he had been waiting for all his life from Matt Busby.

"You're playing Wilf son."

At just 17-years-old he would make his first team debut against the Wolves. An hour before the game whilst sitting nervously in the dressing room, a smiling Jimmy sat himself down next to his latest golden apple. "Tell me how you got into the first team Wilf lad?"

"By listening to you Jimmy."

"Did I ever tell you I hate black and gold Wilf?"

"I hate black and gold too Jimmy!"

"Good lad," replied the preacher.

"Now today you're up against their brilliant inside forward Peter Broadbent. I want you to mark him tightly Wilf."

"Yes Jimmy."

"The reason being Wilf, is because this man wants to pinch money from your dear old mother May's purse."

"Sorry Jimmy, I don't understand?"

"Well. Broadbent will be doing his utmost best to stop you Wilf. To stop you earning a win bonus, money you could give to your Mother. He's going to try and pull every dirty trick in the book to do this!"

By now Wilf is clearly fuming. "I get it now Jimmy!"

By the time Jimmy had finished with Wilf, he stood ready to quite literally rip poor Broadbent's head off, who was actually a really decent guy. An extremely fair, not to say rising star of the First Division. But, for the still gullible Wilf, Jimmy had painted a picture in his head of the Wolves man as a low down, thief in the night!

When on the pitch warming up beforehand in the kick about, word was passed to Peter Broadbent that the United kid marking him today was making his debut. Typical of Broadbent he headed over to Wilf offering his hand for good luck.

'Eff off you thieving bastard!" came the reply! Much to Broadbent's utter shock! Job done by Jimmy Murphy. Wilf McGuinness got stuck into Broadbent, United won and Wilf's mum got her money! In the dressing afterwards Jimmy put an arm around his latest golden apple to break through into the magic land of the first team. "Well done Wilf lad. I'm proud of you, and your dear old mother will be proud of you too!"

The following Saturday after the Dortmund game Manchester United fought out a compelling 2-2 draw away at White Hart Lane against Tottenham Hotspurs. Their closest rivals to the title. Fielding the same side as in Germany, the reds came roaring back from being 2-0 down at half-time to drew level with goals from Johnny Berry and then Eddie Colman firing home in the 88th minute from a Duncan Edwards run and cross. Another one in the eye for Alan Hardaker.

CHAPTER SIX
GO ON BILLY LAD, HIT IT!

The 1956-57 season saw a Manchester United team reared from the crèche by Matt Busby and Jimmy Murphy, fighting on all footballing fronts in an attempt to attain the previously, unthinkable treble. The League, the FA Cup and the European Cup. It was deemed impossible, the rantings of a madman to even suggest such could be achieved. Especially when it was announced United's opponents in the European Cup quarter-finals were to be the crack Spanish champions Athletic Bilbao.

 Formed in1898, by gangs of migrant British miners and shipyard workers, they were renowned as a fantastic football team. The European fever was really beginning to take hold within Manchester, and it was around this time, late 1956, that the magic word "Treble" began to be heard. It was the writer Tom Jackson of the Manchester Evening News, who first wrote about the possibilities of United doing the unprecedented threesome. It was an arduous enough task to do the Double, not achieved since before the turn of the century by Preston North End, but the Treble? A third trophy simply too far and out of reach. One too many. Many learned, football experts at the time were not giving Busby's young team much hope against such vaunted, Spanish opposition over two-legs. One that on home soil had ripped the title from the imperial grasps of *The Blond Arrow,* Alfredo Di Stefano's, beautifully talented orchestra of stars at Real Madrid. They being the first holders of the European Cup. In Manchester, however, nothing was being deemed beyond United. They loved and believed in their boys. With the Busby Babes illuminating a depressed, grim city still suffering the devastating effects of Hitler's Luftwaffe. A fire-charred landscape of skeletal buildings and rubble-filled wastelands, there was a belief they could pull it off. Away in Bilbao for the first-leg, if United could somehow stay in the tie and not get slaughtered then back home with a Mancunian full throated roar screaming them on all bets could well be off.

The previous season deep in northern Spain, the defiant Basques had taken to the streets in frenzied celebrations, as against all odds their team of hearts Athletic Bilbao, had pipped General Franco's favourite toy Real Madrid, to claim the Spanish championship. Unprecedented scenes of delight erupted throughout their homeland. It was a fierce outburst of pride from a place that had suffered unspeakable crimes during the wretched civil war in the thirties. The carnage and horror of the destruction of Guernica forever etched in the souls of the Basque people. Franco had claimed to have conquered the region and brought it to heel, but he was never able to dampen the Basques' unquenchable, thirst for freedom and revenge. Athletics' Bilbao's most prized asset was their man-mountain of a central defender, 27-year-old Jesus Garay. Without an equal in Spain, it was the hugely, inspirational Garay more than any other player responsible for the title being paraded in the *San Mames* stadium. Winning their domestic League placed Bilbao into the European cup with holders Real Madrid, and after defeating Porto in the opening round they were drawn against the great Hungarian champions Honved.
One of the great European ties duly unfolded.
On 29th October 1956, the players of Honved, one of the favourites for the European Cup, left their capital Budapest for a short tour prior to the away-leg against the Spanish champions Athletic Bilbao. These footballers formed the vast majority of their proud nation's *Magyar* international side. Five days later came the news that Soviet tanks had moved into the Hungarian capital and the player's families remained still trapped in the blood and chaos of an uprising being dealt with in brutal manner by the Soviet Union. Budapest-a firestorm of street battles and dead bodies piled high for barricades. The provisional government had been ruthlessly set aside and thousands of frightened refugees were surging towards the border. For the Captain Ferenc Puskas and his colleagues anxious for news of their families, the following few days were grim. Not surprisingly they went down fighting 3-2 in Bilbao, and no one seemed sure where the second-leg would take place, if ever at all. In this confused atmosphere the players arrived in Madrid where Puskas learned that his wife and

daughter had reached the Austrian frontier safely after a long journey on foot. Negotiations with Bilbao continued on whilst letters from the Hungarian FA demanded Honved's return or face a two year ban. It was even reported around this time by the BBC that Puskas had been killed in the fighting. All was chaos. Some of the younger players wanted to go home, but the club's three most famous names, Puskas, Sandor Kocsis and Zoltan Czibor ruled the roost, and they held firm for the moment. Honved continued to play a number of friendlies in Europe to pay bills and stay match-fit. Including a monumental 5-5 draw with a select Madrid team made up of players from both Real and Athletico. Here was where Puskas caught the eye of the Madrid supremo Don Santiago Bernabeu, who decided that very evening after watching the wonderful, still "Galloping Major" despite overweight and touching thirty-one, to take a most magnificent punt.

Finally, a second-leg was arranged to take place at the *Heysel* stadium in Brussels, where the Hungarians arrived carrying money in paper bags. There on 12th December, Honved ran into more trouble. They were a goal down within five-minutes and then trailed 3-1 after Czibor was forced to take over in goal from the injured keeper Farago. But in a glorious finish with the Honved footballers playing out of their skins, a last hurrah to a golden age the head of Kocsis and the glorious, left-peg of Puskas levelled the game at 3-3. But this was not enough to save the tie. A last minute effort by their Captain struck the underside of the crossbar, and with that it was over. Athletic Bilbao were through, but it had been a wonderful effort by the Hungarians. Cue then after such a classic battle the draw against Manchester United. One hardly filling the mighty Basques with dread. Rumours had reached Bilbao of these much talked about Busby Babes, but they were a side who had taken on and beaten the might of Real Madrid and Barcelona on home soil, then seen off the great Hungarians in the European Cup. What fears could a handful of mere boys from the northern English city of Manchester hold?

However, the ultra-professional Basques were not about to take any chances. The Sunday before they took on United in the first-leg they played nine reserves in a 2-0 defeat at Barcelona. But there was a reason for such supposed madness. With the possibility of a semi-final place at stage it was a god given opportunity to spear Franco in the full glare of a watching world, taking off him his beloved Real Madrid's European Cup. Such meant they simply could not afford to slip up against United. The Basques viewed the Mancunians as a difficult challenge, but one hardly likely to give them sleepless nights.

Monday 15th January 1957. On a freezing, ice-cold, frosty Manchester morning, the Dakota aircraft ferrying United to Spain for their quarter-final first-leg against Athletic Bilbao, via Bordeaux for refuelling was caught in a ferocious snowstorm. The journey was to be terribly rough and the aircraft found itself tossed about like a rag doll in the heavy turbulence. Mark Jones and Liam Whelan were both violently sick. It was a three hours plus trip and for most of the time the Dakota shuddered violently, rocking from side to side. There was great fears on board of the troubled aircraft tumbling from the skies. After refuelling in Bordeaux, still the storms raged, lightning bolts illuminating the portholes as they crashed down onto a raging Atlantic ocean. All the time an atmosphere of impending doom existed. As the aircraft approached the Basque mountains the passengers cut a fraught sight. The Dakota nosed forever onwards. The party by that time could see the dark, foreboding mountainous cliffs that etched out into the sea. Finally, along the coastline a much welcome entrance to Bilbao, although the flight would hardly improve inland.

Since taking off at Ringway airport Duncan Edwards had sat quietly alone turning a worrying grey! An apprehensive Edwards was not the best of travellers at any time and was violently sick throughout the journey. Bill Foulkes earned the wrath of his shivering team mates by falling asleep with his gangling legs resting on the heater unknowingly switching it off! When awoken from slumber, Foulkes faced an inquest more resembling a mid-air lynching! From that day on earning the nickname of "Popular Bill!" After twenty-minutes of sheer torture flying over the airport waiting to land and to everyone's great relief, Captain Riley began the descent. As the Dakota dipped its wings the views from the passenger's portholes were of hundreds of small fishing boats covered in snow resting peacefully in Bilbao harbour. Like some idyllic scene from a Christmas card. Making his wary path downwards Riley struggled badly to locate any sign of the runway, for little did he know that the airport had been shut down only hours before due to the treacherous weather. It had only been when a member of the British Consul spotted the aircraft circling that a call was made and the runway swiftly re-opened, thus averting a possible disaster. As the chaos ensued on the ground in the air it reached almost tragic-farce proportions when Riley was reduced to tannoying the passengers asking them if they could see anything of note out of their portholes? Hardly a reassuring question for the already, pensive Mancunians? Amid the turbulence, racing hearts and sweating brows, Manchester United finally arrived with an almighty bump on Basque soil. The landing caused a showering sea of snow and ice to engulf the aircraft as it came to a fearful, screeching halt on a deserted field with no terminal buildings. Watched only by two bored airport officials from a broken-down old customs shack.

With the United players so familiar of holiday posters back in Manchester advertising *"Sunny Espana!"* Their first experience of Spain as the Dakota's doors were wrenched open was to reveal the previous forty-eight hours of the blizzard. A shut-down airport all but obliterated by a raging sea of snow and a ferocious rain storm.

Bill Foulkes recalled: "My impression of Spain being sun and sand were based on holiday posters at railway stations, so I was surprised that it was freezing!" None expected more the blast of sunshine on his face than Eddie Colman. As Colman stepped onto the treacherous, snow-slush filled runway of a deserted airport and black skies above, he turned around to the rest of his teammates, smiling wide declaring: "Caramba! This is just like Salford!"

More drama ensued on board. The tension of the rocky flight proved far too severe for the 75-year-old Manchester United chairman Harold Hardman, causing him to suffer a minor stroke. Immediately on disembarking Hardman was rushed to hospital missing the game, but recovered sufficiently to be allowed home later with the rest of the party. Arriving at the hotel Walter Crickmer was less than impressed with their local chefs. The food never suited the United players and Tommy Taylor was ill with stomach problems after eating some fried rice. Although he kept quiet until after the match. On visiting the stadium and witnessing the pitch, a drenched, quagmire of spattered mud and melting ice, Matt Busby and Jimmy Murphy were convinced the game would have to be postponed. Busby despaired, he was caught between the lunacy of attempting to play football on a swamp or having points deducted by the Football League, led by its Chairman Alan Hardaker gunning for him and United.

"A competition for wogs and dagos," claimed Hardaker, who threatened large fines and point deductions if United failed in any of their obligations to the League. It was a bitterness inflamed by an organisation not used being told to "Mind your own business." They had picked on the wrong man. Busby was not the sort for such "Johnny Foreigner" small mindedness. So, it was come the Bilbao game he urged against any postponement, if necessary his Red Devils would play the match in Wellington boots to ensure their ridiculously tight schedule was adhered to. On meeting with the highly, respected German referee Albert Dusch. A former Kaiserslautern goalkeeper, the United management and Bilbao officials both agreed with huge reservations that the quarter-final should go ahead. This despite Dusch dropping the ball on the surface and it nearly sinking! Busby was quietly fearful regarding the opposition for Athletic were a class apart from anything his lads had ever faced. They had lost only one home match in three years putting even the imperial Real Madrid in their shadow on home soil. He knew the real battle for the European Cup would begin in the shadow of the Basque mountains at the *Estadio San Mames*. Named after an unfortunate Christian who was thrown to the lions by the Romans. Happily, the heavens smiled on the fortunate Mames when the lions refused to eat him! Now, in Mames' sacred footsteps, Manchester United hoped for similar luck. For so far in the European Cup they had learned fast after quite literally exploding into the competition against RSC Anderlecht, and to a lesser extent Borussia Dortmund.

United's fitness worries over Duncan Edwards's sickness eased as the game grew closer with the player hardly surprisingly declaring himself available for selection. Never had Edwards' inspirational presence and all-round prowess been required more than in the intimidatory, blood-curdling atmosphere of the place the locals christened *La Cateda*. Here was where the Basque came to devour their opponents. A coliseum. With the large, ebullient figure of Herr Dusch overlooking the toss the two team Captain's Agustin Gainza and Roger Byrne shook hands. Kick-off grew ever closer. Byrne later describe the pitch as: "The worst I have ever seen." Finally, in spear-like driving rain and amid a lashing snowfall of biblical proportions, with 45,000 screaming, fanatical Basque supporters yelling for Mancunian blood. All seemingly wearing traditional black berets and armed with the same coloured umbrellas! Like a scene lifted from some magical but mysterious dark Basque forest. Athletic Bilbao were in no mood to lose against the Busby Babes with so much at stake.

The Teams.

Athletic Bilbao. Carmelo, Drue, Canito, Mauri, Garay, Etura, Arteche, Marcaida, Merodio, Uribe and Gainza.

Manchester United. Wood, Foulkes, Byrne, Colman, Jones, Edwards, Berry, Whelan, Taylor, Viollet and Pegg.

With Bilbao in their red and white stripes and Manchester United in change colours of all-blue, the game began. Almost immediately United went close to taking the lead. Dennis Viollet worked himself an opening before letting fly, only to see his shot stick like glue in the mud on the goal-line with the goalkeeper Carmelo Cedrun beaten. Wasting little time the fortunate Cedrun booted the ball back down pitch where United defender Mark Jones struggling in the wretched conditions lost possession. As Jones chased desperately back Athletic striker Jose Luis Arteche showed blinding pace and smashed a low

effort past a diving Ray Wood. The *San Mames* erupted!
Viollet recalled his unlucky, early close call: "I had a chance when the
score was 0-0, and I shot past the goalkeeper, only for the ball to stick
in the mud on the line. They then went straight down the other
end to score and at half-time Matt blamed me!" It was the beginning
of a nightmare first-half for the visitors in which Bilbao ripped them
to pieces. An audience baying for goals saw their appetites sated twice
more as the rapier-like Arteche and his equally dangerous partner in
crime Ignacio Uribe, indulged themselves causing mayhem in the
Mancunian defence. It was clever, incisive football played at
breakneck pace by the Basques that proved far too good for Busby's
side, and they were deservedly 3-0 up at the interval threatening many
more. It appeared a mis-match. The realities of European football at
the highest level clear to see as the much vaunted English champions
were being outclassed. Battles all over the field being lost, it appeared
that only Tommy Taylor in a merciless duel with Jesus Garay was just
about holding his own. Christened the *"Smiling Executioner"* by the
Daily Herald journalist George Follows, Taylor had fought and
scrapped for every ball, not always winning, in fact many times being
hacked, kicked and even punched by Garay for his trouble. There was
no rules as behind the referee's back it resembled a free for all! Yet,
the Barnsley boy, the lad signed by Matt Busby after nine good
scouting reports and a special recommendation from former United
Captain Johnny Carey. Finally bought for £29,999, so not to be tagged
with a £30,000 transfer fee. Taylor gave Garay good as he got. They
bred hard lads in the mining town of Barnsley. So far for the
Mancunian visitors it had been a terrible time in Bilbao, but it was a
calm, at least on the outside Manchester United manager who spoke
to his shattered, mud-caked players in the dressing room at half-time.
Busby and Murphy's fears regarding the outstanding quality of the
Basques had proved correct during an opening forty-five minutes that
had resembled men against boys. But Busby assured them in
measured tones that Athletic Bilbao were not supermen, and if they
just played their normal game chances would present themselves.
Whereas Jimmy Murphy let fly to remind the players of just who they

were there representing. Of the people back in Manchester sat waiting desperately for news of their progress. Busby and Murphy was the perfect double act. Every morning back in England before training the Welshman would attend mass, but when fire and brimstone was required on the training pitch players would feel the lash of Murphy's acid tongue with a language hardly ever heard in the hushed, holy halls of the Vatican! Together he and Busby worked a treat.

Within eight-minutes of the second-half restarting it was 3-2! Manchester United came out blazing, none more than Duncan Edwards. Jimmy Murphy's adopted son! Edwards ploughed and raked his way through the Basque mud urging his team mates forward with him and for the first time in Bilbao, United started to play like the devils on their shirt demanded. They hit back three-minutes after the break when the tenacious Taylor momentarily escaped his menacing shadow Garay to finish off Dennis Viollet's pass. Mancunian hopes were rekindled. Suddenly, the Basques were rocking and shortly after Viollet swooped in typical manner to add a second from close range flicking out a foot to divert the ball past Carmelo. 3-2, Game on! Ignoring Busby and Murphy's frantic, touchline pleas to calm down, United continued to sweep forward in search of a sensational equaliser. The game became stretched, far too stretched for the visitors and the Basques hit back from a corner when their left-winger Armado Merodio crashed home a fourth. 4-2! As a fraught United defence looked on in despair matters turned infinitely worse when Arteche shot past Wood from six-yards to restore their three-goal lead. Bilbao were rampant once more! The manager and his assistant's pleas from the side-line had gone unheard. At 5-2, this quarter-final was over. Manchester United were being put to the sword.

Five-minutes remained when United's languid, tall, beguiling Irishman Liam "Billy" Whelan carved himself his own personal notch in the short but tragic glorious history of the Busby Babes. The Dublin-born Whelan was a devout Roman Catholic whose faith remained the most important article in his life above everything. He was a young man who counted many priests amongst his closest friends, and who once told off United apprentice Nobby Stiles for swearing in a five-a-side training game! This was the same Liam Whelan back in 1954, who was a member of the Manchester United youth side competing in the inaugural Blue Star youth tournament in Switzerland. Amongst his team mates Duncan Edwards, Eddie Colman, David Pegg and an even younger Bobby Charlton. After a disappointing 0-0 draw with the local Blue Star side in the opening match the young reds swiftly got a feel for the competition going on to win it. A 4-0 victory in the final playing Blue Star again came mostly courtesy of a Duncan Edwards hat trick. Matt Busby deciding just to ensure they won the trophy he played Duncan at centre-forward! Following this United had two highly prestigious friendlies before returning home to Manchester. Firstly, against a Berne select eleven thrashing them 9-2 with a scintillating Billy Whelan scoring five! Next was yet another comprehensive victory for the United boys thrashing the Swiss national youth side 4-0 in their national stadium. People's eyes were being opened, just who were these lads from England playing football in a manner so enthralling? None more than the intrigued officials from the legendary Brazilian club Santos in Switzerland on their own tour, who appeared especially taken by the wonderfully, talented Whelan. His skill and technique more the beaches of Rio in origin than the backstreets of Dublin! One official asked if he was part Brazilian? They even enquired about signing Whelan, only to be given short shrift by United officials telling them to forget it! Originally recommended by legendary scout Billy Behan to United whilst playing for the League of Ireland's Home Farm, the gangling Whelan was amongst one of Busby's most precious jewels. At first sight an unlikely, awkward footballer, when on the ball, Billy Whelan came alive with a wonderful poise, balance and an eye for goal. Now, receiving a pass in his stride from Duncan Edwards, Whelan headed towards the Basque penalty area. On the side-lines with nerves exhausted and hearts racing Busby, Murphy and the entire United bench were screaming at him to pass to an unmarked Tommy Taylor, only for Whelan, ankle-deep in mud to take a different path. Suddenly, as if he could read his player's mind Busby whispered within earshot of Jimmy Murphy: "Go on Billy lad, hit it!"

Taking aim Whelan spotted an opening letting fly a swerving shot that flew past Carmelo into the top corner! A lifeline grasped by the boy from Dublin who with one moment of instinctive brilliance had dragged his club back into the European Cup. At 5-3, the game ended with both sides knowing all was still to play for. Jimmy Murphy was in awe of the Irishman's strike. "If a Brazilian had scored that goal it would have been acclaimed a world beater." As for the boss? Matt Busby was equally impressed as his Welsh sidekick. "Billy seemed to be going so terribly slowly, beating this man, then that man, meandering on. Finally, he reached the penalty area and had that defence in a rare tangle before scoring a brilliant goal!" Few held Liam Billy Whelan in higher esteem than his fellow Irishman and soon to be teammate Harry Gregg. "People should not be deceived by the picture of Billy as a quiet lad. He was a real charmer, but on the field he was gold. He seemed to ghost past players as opposed to beating them for speed. A genius in my opinion." Despite Whelan's late wonder-strike it had to be acknowledged Manchester United were at times horribly outplayed by the finest side they had ever faced. Bill Foulkes was left in awe by one particular Athletic player. "Bilbao had the best centre-half I'd ever seen. Jesus Garay. He was so good that he kept Tommy Taylor quiet for most of the game and I'd never seen anybody do that. No one."

That same evening at the Carlton hotel in Bilbao, the Basque hosts put on a splendid reception which was enjoyed by all. Now the football guns had been lowered all could relax temporarily until battle recommenced in Manchester. Speeches were cheered and applauded, many drinks were shared amongst the players and staff of both sides. Tommy Taylor and Jesus Garay got on gloriously well! Hard to imagine only a few hours previously they were kicking large lumps of Basque mud out of each other! The following morning even a bigger task now faced the Mancunian party. Getting home. The United party and press corps arrived at Bilbao airport which remained snowbound. A lack of foresight by the aircrew meant the Dakota had been left stranded outside through the blizzard as the one airport hangar was already full. Captain Riley took one look at the thick covering of ice and snow on the wings and decided flying home that day was out of the question. This meant almost certainly they would be stranded in Spain for another day or so, if not more. Riley spoke to Matt Busby explaining that unless the snow and ice was removed off the fuselage then it would be impossible to attempt a take-off. The airport had few facilities and no staff available to help. Putting it bluntly Riley explained to all if they wanted to get home that night it would be down to themselves to do the job. So, it was that the footballers of Manchester United and the travelling pressmen got stuck in!

"Operation Snow Shift!" Named by the radio officer, a man called Potter. Johnny Berry remembers vividly the desperation of just how important it was to get home. "It was far from sunny Spain, believe me. We thought we'd just be stuck there, but Matt was worried what would happen if we were not back for Saturday's League match. He had us all sweeping the snow off with long brooms, and eventually we got to leave." Busby later admitted as much.

"I could well imagine the repercussions if we failed to turn up at Hillsborough." There exists a poignant photograph of the players and the Press men, shovels, spades, brooms and scrapers in hand. Another of Bill Foulkes and David Pegg actually stood next to the fuselage posing with brooms held on their shoulders.

A haunting epitaph of what was coming.

With an important away League match the following Saturday against Sheffield Wednesday, Busby could ill-afford the possibility of returning late and being docked points by a vindictive Hardaker, who must have been praying for such a scenario to occur, so he could wreak revenge against Matt Busby. United just had to get home. All hands were drafted in by the manager to ensure the aircraft was made airworthy. With Captain Riley taking charge everybody helped to make the aircraft flight worthy. Finally, after four hours of toil and Riley duly satisfied, they headed on board. The Dakota taking the Busby Babes home to Manchester, rose rather half-heartedly into the still snow-lit Basque sky. As they reached the sea, the plane had a close run in with the Spanish coast's huge, steeping cliffs. "That was a close thing!" shouted Johnny Berry, whilst watching worryingly through his porthole window. The flight was not to be without further strife and incident for on approaching a refuelling spot in Jersey, they encountered a severe gale, one that caused the Dakota to dip frighteningly. Then, as the pilot opened up his throttle with the runway in sight they shot over and bounced ominously upon the ground to land with a nerve-shattering thump. After a truly, harrowing journey Manchester United finally made it back home, but the fraught-edged perils of early air travel had been experienced at first hand. Lessons clearly needed to be learned, but tragically in time not taken aboard. Sometimes the Grim Reaper required just a little patience, so would bide his time and return shortly to visit Manchester United Football Club.

CHAPTER SEVEN
THE MANCUNIAN MIRACLE

Manchester. A northern English city. Where pride and passion came from the soul not a birth right. Jews and Gentile, Irish, Scottish and Welsh, Italian, Catholic and Protestant all living in reasonable harmony. Drinking, cussing, laughing and arguing. John Lennon would later sing of imagining such a dream of living for today. A city hardly rich in diamonds and pearls, indeed still bomb-ravaged from World War Two. Smouldering, shattered buildings and craters, scattered-waste grounds. A sight not to behold, though open and welcoming to all. No more than to the Basque. At least off the pitch, for come one, come all, we would put the kettle on. Bring your best, keep your worst, for it never did to dare take Mancunians and Manchester United for granted. Athletic Bilbao, the proud Spanish champions arrived with a strut and rather, ignorant notion the tie was already over. The Basques had simply no idea what lay in wait for them.

With Old Trafford's floodlights still a month away from being ready, the European drama again moved across the city to Moss Side, for a game many United supporters of a certain vintage still regard as their club's greatest ever. It was an evening when red shirted heroes were required and none more than Tommy Taylor stepped forward. Time to go back now to a cold, misty February evening with 70,000 supporters roaring "UNITED!" towards the black, northern heavens. A strong, overwhelming smell of tobacco in the air, a light smattering of snow covering the pitch and a bitter freezing rain driving down. Manchester rain. A miracle was required, many prayers were being whispered on the terraces, but would these be enough?
Wednesday 6th February 1957.
It was a slow burner as the city of Manchester awaited with nervous anticipation throughout the day, the coming of the mighty Basques. Potentially United's last stand in the European cup. The build-up was

intense, the pressure unyielding, expectations amongst supporters rose as the kick-off drew ever closer for a miraculous recovery, beyond any fathomable footballing reason. People talked in factories, pubs, on buses and in shops of nothing else. Schoolboys fidgeted in class, their minds far away from maths and English as possible! As for Geography, they couldn't find their pencils! All counting the seconds down for that last bell to ring then off they would sprint home. Either for a quick tea then to the match or to listen on the radio. Scarf in hand. "Come on you reds!"

In an attempt to shelter the players away from this all-consuming, stifling atmosphere, Matt Busby had retreated to his favourite refuge of Blackpool's Norbreck Hydro hotel, where they were allowed to breathe. At the seaside he and Murphy planned the great escape. They were left with just one option. Attack and pray beyond the dark Mancunian skies that it would be their night under the hazy winter's glare of Maine Road's, floodlit moonbeams. The Athletic Bilbao coach, 57-year-old, silver-haired, former Barcelona manager Ferdinand Daucik, landed in England declaring it was almost insulting to suggest they could be eliminated. "No team on the planet can beat the Basque nation by three goals," the Czech insisted.

"At the very worst if things go wrong we will have to play off in Paris and just win there." Daucik had bought into the Basque mentality with all the intensity of a religious conversion, but also worrying delusions of invincibility. It was a dream to take away the European Cup off Franco's play-thing, but firstly Manchester United had to be dealt with. It came as a surprise because the Basque themselves were not of the sort to show such arrogance and disrespect to opponents, and so when a relaxed, smiling Athletic Captain Agustin Gainza, who whilst happily posing for photographers, made a 0 sign with his fingers after being asked if United still had a chance? Gainza shook his head. Amid others in the Athletic party there also existed an unhealthy air of over-confidence, as if the job had already been done. The previous Saturday was the Manchester derby with the reds winning 4-2 at Maine Road. They appeared in fantastic form with goals being spread amongst Edwards, Taylor, Viollet and Whelan. It had been a sensational showing by Manchester United, and Busby was quietly confident something extraordinary was set to occur against the Spanish champions. A little known fact is that very quietly Bilbao had contacted him in an attempt to prise the Scotsman away from Old Trafford, by offering the princely sum of five thousand pounds a year. Fortunately, as it turned out for United and their supporters, Busby thanked them, but then turned their offer down. Whether this was done to simply try and take his mind off the job in hand is unknown. The evening before the Bilbao players undertook a forty-five minute Ballet-style, training session on the Maine Road pitch. The Manchester City ground staff watched non-plussed as Athletic went through a series of subtle and delicate body-stretching exercises. This being totally alien to anything they had ever witnessed. The English football journalists who watched on from the grandstand sniggered quietly behind their notepads at these supposed, fierce Basque warriors. Not for the hacks this continental preparation/ unmanly display of finesse. One scribe wrote: "A slight smell of perfume lingered disconcertingly on the field!"

Cometh the hour no matter what Daucik claimed, hope sprung eternal in the hearts and minds of the 70,000 Mancunians as they crammed tight into Maine Road. Some paying high as £11 for a ticket. The demand was like never before seen. Indeed, United's Secretary Walter Crickmer claimed: "We could have sold between 300,000 and 400,000 tickets for just this one game." The passion that rose into the dark night skies from those Moss Side terraces soared loud and it was said could be heard over twenty miles away. People across the city described it as a "Distant thunder". There was a red storm brewing in the rainy city. The mood although apprehensive was also of a quiet confidence. If United started well they possessed the calibre of players to score three goals, this was never doubted, but would the reds be capable of keeping the Basque out as they roared away on their lightning fast, counter-attacks? At just after 7-20.pm, the waiting ended as Roger Byrne and Jesus Garay led out their respective teams. One can only imagine such a wonderfully, evocative moment as beneath the dreamy, floodlit haze and a flashing barrage of photographer's cameras, the two Captains shook hands in the centre-circle.

The Teams.

Manchester United. Wood, Foulkes, Byrne, Colman, Jones, Edwards, Berry, Whelan, Taylor, Viollet and Pegg.

Athletic Bilbao. Carmelo, Drue, Canito, Mauri, Garay, Maguragui, Arteche, Marcaida, Etura, Merodia and Gainza.

A swirling, ghostly mist drifted high across the Main stand adding to the electricity of the occasion, also a light covering of snow on the pitch. The strong smell of tobacco in the air, the tension unbearable. A pretty, raven-haired senorita dressed in traditional Basque costume presented a blushing Byrne with a huge bouquet of flowers. The prestigious Beswick Prize Band was on hand to perform the two national anthems. As the teams lined up on the touchline a hush fell across Maine Road. The Spaniard's was played first. Then, began *"God save the Queen"* sung with an enormous gusto across the ground. Once finished the band marched off to great applause and the crowd erupted in anticipation for kick-off. With the pleasantries completed both teams took up their positions. The referee Herr Dusch once more blew on his whistle and with 70,000 hearts missing a beat, the game began. Tommy Taylor started the contest by rolling the ball to Billy Whelan and all hell broke loose in Manchester!
The action was played out at a frantic pace and simply never relented all evening. On the side-lines Matt Busby stalked whilst clutching tight on a cigarette. He watched anxiously as his team roared forward in search of their Mancunian miracle. Taylor and Jesus Garay swiftly resumed their personal duel from the port of Bilbao with a blood-curdling relish. This was a clash of giants in heart and stature. On ten minutes, United looked to have grabbed an early breakthrough, only for Dusch to disallow it. A Tommy Taylor

knockdown was latched upon by Dennis Viollet, who slide the ball home. Sadly, the home supporters' cheers got stuck in their throats as the linesman flagged offside. Bilbao broke! Their forwards Gainza and Arteche both terrifyingly swift and deadly. The latter came so close to firing off a shot after a mishit back-pass by Bill Foulkes, only for Ray Wood to come rushing out and save the day. Throughout the first-half United pressed forward, but Bilbao held firm. It was a game being played on the edge. Tempers frayed, niggled, blew and at times exploded as the nervous tension from the Maine Road terraces found itself seeping onto the pitch causing the atmosphere to simmer even more.

Inspired by Duncan Edwards, the home side continued to pound away at the Bilbao defence. Working in unison with the clever, elusive Eddie Colman, he commanded the midfield. Edwards was under instructions from Busby to remain in his own half until told otherwise from the bench, and he followed his manager's orders to the letter. Even to the extent of at one stage when running up towards the half-way line, Duncan simply put the brakes on, his arms wind-milling to prevent himself stepping an inch into Basque territory. What the boss said went! Chances appeared for United, a clever ball inside the Athletic full-back Canito by Eddie Colman, saw Johnny Berry go flying through. Looking up the speeding winger spotted Taylor, as ever guarded by the giant Garay. This option closed, Berry found instead Dennis Viollet, who from six-yards drove the ball past Carmelo to ignite Maine Road! Again, they proved false hopes as to the dismay of the crowd Herr Dusch once more ruled offside! In tandem with his linesman the German referee at that moment was in serious danger of being lynched by irate Mancunians baying for his head. Much as United drove on looking for a breakthrough there was little pattern or fluidity in their play, it remained forced, but still exhilarating. All or nothing football with both teams refusing to give an inch as Busby's words from the touchline to "Settle down boys!" Lost amid the thunderous wall of noise inside the stadium. It was carnage and confusion both on the pitch and off. The pressure unyielding, the passion ferocious, who wanted it more? Finally, the call came from the side-lines and let off the leash by Busby, Duncan Edwards set off on a barnstorming charge into the Basque half. Roared forward by a manic crowd screaming his name.

"Go on Dunc!" On he went shrugging off tackles from Mauri and Etura as if swatting flies. Duncan let go a flashing drive that almost ripped a hole in Jesus Garay's midriff. The Basque defender was by this time almost a one man rearguard as he sweated blood to keep United out. Four-minutes of the first period remained when Edwards ventured once more deep into enemy territory. Now, given freedom to roam he was wreaking mayhem. On receiving the ball Duncan again let fly from the edge of the penalty area. A ferocious low-drive which Carmelo failed to hold and for once lady luck shone on the home side, as ghosting in came the inevitable figure of Dennis Viollet to smash past Canelo, unleashing a Mancunian roar that split the heavens! His home town of nearby Fallowfield only a long goal-kick away from Maine Road, Viollet found himself swamped by ecstatic team-mates for this lifeline. Maine Road rocked, swayed and shuddered. One more goal was required for the reds to level the tie. Tempers were flaring once more as the Basque suddenly realised they were in a fight for their footballing lives. Ferdinand Daucik's pre-match smiley grin of outward confidence had vanished, he appeared a fraught, a worried man. Half-time arrived like the police charging through a pub door to stop a riot in its tracks. As both sets of players headed off the field the red shirts were applauded wildly for their gigantic efforts all the way down the tunnel. Manchester United remained within a goal of a Parisian play-off.

In the relative tranquillity of the dressing room, Matt Busby stressed the importance to remain calm, to try and play their football amid all the mad hysteria that surrounded them. A young Bobby Charlton who was present remembers the boss's words like they were yesterday.

"Boys," he said. "Do not panic. Make your passes, do your running, but above all keep your patience. If you can do that we'll get there." As always, Jimmy Murphy stood by Busby's side praising and urging more. Demanding that his boys, his red apples went for the Basque's throats showing no mercy. For Murphy, these boys had no equals and night's like this was the reason he always drove them so hard as youngsters, some even to tears, tough love, for they had been reared to play the Manchester United way. You attack, you never give up. Never! Across the corridor the Basques sat in stunned, muted shock. Jesus Garay nursed battle wounds caused by Tommy Taylor. Never in his illustrious career had he encountered one such as Taylor. Even the genius's, the ball-playing artists of Real Madrid and Barcelona, Di Stefano, Kubala had never troubled him like the United centre-forward. Daucik implored his men to remain strong, be brave, for such was the immense energy being spent by United they surely had to run out of steam. Then Athletic Bilbao would strike and catch them out. From the re-start disaster erred close for the home team when an anxious Eddie Colman was robbed by Bilbao's Arteche, and he flew away towards Ray Wood. As Maine Road watched on in horror, Arteche rounded a stranded Wood and rolled the ball goal-wards, only from nowhere appeared Roger Byrne to race back and clear off the line! As a collective sigh of relief fell across the terraces the infuriated Byrne sought out Colman handing the apologetic Salfordian a very public berating for which Eddie could only put his hands up and apologise! It was a battle royal in Moss Side. A furious hour passed of this pulsating contest, United were still like a red rash all over Bilbao, but failing to convert opportunities when they arose. Taylor again hit the woodwork with a thumping header, Johnny Berry hit the outside of an upright and suddenly only twenty-minutes remained. Berry had been immense. Watching his dad play for United that evening in the Director's box was Johnny Berry's 7-year-old son Neil. Brought up in Davyhulme, Manchester, after Berry joined United from Birmingham City in 1951, Neil was allowed to go to the match, only when a friend of Matt Busby's, a Catholic Canon/Priest, William Sewell, agreed to take him. Never afraid to call on the almighty when the odds appeared against him, Busby gave many tickets away to Manchester Priests, and it was not unknown for entire rows of them to be sat together at Old Trafford! Against Bilbao, even more filled the Maine Road stands as a miracle was deemed to be called for, and a heavenly helping hand would've been hugely appreciated. As time sped on all favours were being called in both in this world and elsewhere! Those around the priests were trying desperately hard to mind their language, but as the action on the field grew ever more intense ultimately giving up! Athletic goalkeeper Carmelo was performing heroically. He was brave, agile and attracted to the ball like a magnet as it flew endlessly across his area. On went David Pegg tearing away down the left-hand touchline. Turning and twisting, desperate to give himself an inch, Pegg sent a cross into the penalty area where arriving like an express train was the magnificent Tommy Taylor. By this stage of an enthralling contest Taylor had run the legs off Jesus Garay. The pride of the Basque was all but on his knees. Roaring free of his flailing, Bilbao shackles the *Smiling Executioner* took the ball in his stride to flash a splendid shot low past Carmelo into the far corner. Manchester exploded! An evening that had threatened to tug at the heartstrings had become something quite extraordinary. Manchester United had fought, scrapped and clawed their way back into the European Cup. The Basques were bleeding, ripe for the taking. Sensing no need for the Paris play-off United went in search of a killer third. Daucik could barely watch as his beleaguered defence were close to collapse. He bore the look of a man trapped in a blazing inferno! Five-minutes remained, Maine Road had become something almost unworldly. 70,000 people producing a barrage of noise deafening to the ear and chilling to the bone. Playing like a man possessed Taylor powered past the exhausted Athletic full-back Canito. On he charged into the penalty area. With the crowd screaming for their hero to let fly, Taylor instead kept his calm and played the ball to an unmarked Johnny Berry in a better position. At full speed Berry hit a scorching drive that roared into the top corner past Carmelo to surely win the tie, causing pure, unadulterated madness to engulf Maine Road! As one the Athletic players fell to the turf, their resistance broken and shattered. 3-0. Although there was many a red shirted hero on that long, gone evening, it was unreservedly Tommy Taylor's night, and welcome to Manchester, Athletic Bilbao! On the touchline, Busby and Murphy danced a jig of delight. In later years Jimmy Murphy was embarrassed about that celebration. "Damn silly, after all these years in the game! But that was my greatest moment in football."

Amongst spectators there were tears of joy and sheer relief. Voices hoarse beyond all call of duty, for they had given equally as the team. There was to be a last minute scare when Bill Foulkes under-hit a back pass to signal a frantic race between Ray Wood and Gainza, which the United goalkeeper put behind for a corner. This came to nothing and the final chance for the Basques had gone. The shrill blast of Herr Dusch's whistle was nothing more than a mimed signal, and even the radio commentators trying to describe the emotional scenes were drowned out amid a barrage of noise from an ecstatic crowd! A heady Mancunian night laced with drama and emotion came to a close. At their first attempt Manchester United had qualified for the European Cup semi-finals. Following the final-whistle there were wonderful scenes of sportsmanship displayed by the beaten Bilbao players. Great dignity was shown. None more than by Jesus Garay who sought out Tommy Taylor to share a quiet word with him before warmly embracing his tormentor.

 That evening at the post-match banquet in the Midland Hotel, ecstatic crowds gathered at the main door to cheer the players in. Though devastated at losing the opportunity to take Real Madrid's crown further on in the competition the Basques proved generous in defeat. Fine words were spoken by the visitors. Ferdinand Daucik praised not only the United team, but the efforts of the crowd. "In all my years in football, I have never encountered noise like it." Daucik's pre-game comments returning to haunt him in a manner he could surely not have imagined after Athletic had scored that fifth goal in Bilbao. Jesus Garay stood up and insisted he be allowed to say a few words in the after-dinner speeches, regarding Tommy Taylor. Garay toasted the United player before stating: "Tommy Taylor is the finest centre-forward that I have ever played against!"
The following day's newspaper headlines were ecstatic with joy at United's sensational victory. The Daily Herald's George Follows described it as: "The greatest football match I have ever seen. The

greatest crowd I have seen, and the greatest centre-forward display, I have ever seen!"

Henry Rose of the Daily Express went even further. "Manchester Magnifico! My hands are trembling as I write. My heart still pounds. And a few hours have passed since, with 70,000 other lucky people, I saw the greatest victory in soccer history! Ninety-minutes of tremendous thrill and excitement that will live forever in the memory. Salute to the eleven red shirted heroes of Manchester United!"

The Daily Mirror's headline proclaimed: "All Berry and Bright!" Their report by Archie Ledbrooke was a whizz of breathless excitement! "Call this the match of the century? I don't know, I haven't lived that long. But I do know that this was one of those matches I'll never forget, one of the best half dozen I've seen in nearly 2000. The crowd will say this morning that they have never seen anything like it. They are probably right."

A side-note to the contest. Athletic Bilbao had been on a £200 a man win bonus that night. Manchester United were on £3. The Basques went home beaten, but unbowed. As for the reds, Real Madrid awaited in the semi-finals. A story yet to unfold. The date on which this memorable football match occurred, 6th February 1957, would in a tragically short time grow to have a terrible poignancy for all concerned with Manchester United. As twelve months to the day, eight players would perish at the end of that infernal Munich runway. Including Tommy Taylor. This was news that broke the heart of one Jesus Garay.

The following Saturday, Manchester United played at home to Arsenal. Many thought after their epic, exhaustive, midweek battle against Athletic Bilbao, United could well suffer from fatigue. As a 63,000 crowd roared their heroes on an unchanged team from Maine Road won 6-2 with goals from Berry (2), Whelan (2) Edwards, and the wonderful Tommy Taylor! Matt Busby and Jimmy Murphy were delighted. Nothing it appeared could stop their *"Golden Apples"*. The step to greatness on foreign fields was under way. It appeared only a matter of time before the Mancunians conquered Europe, as they had already England. In the great footballing cities of Madrid,

Barcelona, Paris, Turin and Milan, the name of Manchester United was already causing shudders, such being the youthful age of their side. It was feared a period of Old Trafford dominance was just a matter of time. 1958 would be that year many claimed...
1958.

CHAPTER EIGHT
FLAMENCO!

1956. The Odeon cinema, Oxford Road.

On *Pathe* News for a few moments the *Madrilenos* appeared as flashing, magical white figures flitting around on the big screen. A fleeting glimpse of a footballing world that you inhabited, but could never dream to visit. The names up in lights, white knights. A sprinkling of gold dust like those of the great Hollywood movie stars. They moved as if to music, an invisible orchestra. Such grace and artistry. Dancing with the ball, a Spanish Flamenco, Ole! Opponents befuddled and bemused, the strutting Di Stefano, the bewildering Gento, the hitman Kopa. Then, they were gone. Not to be seen again until the next visit to the Odeon.

Well, not in the early spring of 1957, for Real Madrid were coming to Manchester. Now, sit comfortably for the main event is set to begin!

On the night of Wednesday 6th February 1957, the result from Maine Road, Manchester, of Matt Busby's exuberant, young team sensationally knocking out the Spanish champions Athletic Bilbao, to reach the European Cup semi-finals reverberated across all of Europe. Nobody did that to the Basques, it was unthinkable, 5-3 down, then to come back and win 3-0? What was going on in Manchester? The Real Madrid President Don Santiago Bernabeu had always feared Athletic Bilbao as the greatest danger to stopping Real retaining their title. Now, with the Basque turned to dust at the hands of these Mancunian Red Devils, a rethink was required by Bernabeu on how to deal with those that were being lovingly labelled *"Los Chicos"* in all the Spanish newspapers. *"The lads"*. The Busby Babes. The master's against the pupils. A battle royal expected against Manchester United and so it was to prove. A tie that would live forever in the annals of both clubs. Touched by gold dust, immortalised by history...

In the inaugural European Cup competition, seemingly happy to gaze fondly in the mirror at their own reflections and suffering worrying delusions of invincible grandeur, Real Madrid simply sauntered into the quarter-finals stage. It was there they almost came flying off the rails in unforgettable fashion. Paired against the tough and hugely talented Yugoslav champions Partizan Belgrade, the dark, ugly face of post-Cold War politics reared its head. Not daring to even risk the hugely, embarrassing possibility of losing to the Communists, General Franco contacted Bernabeu demanding they withdraw instantly from the European Cup. Real Madrid unfortunately at that time were the flag, the symbol of Franco's Fascist regime. For a while it appeared that the *Madrilenos* first attempt at conquering the continent would end in a sad shambles with them having to pull out. However, Bernabeu still had one magnificent card left to play. A man in his inner circle who could charm birds from the air and fish from the sea. The President sent word and his special aide Raimondo Saporta. A handsome man always dressed dapper in a beautiful, handmade suit with a handkerchief in his top pocket, sleeked black hair, an eye for the beautiful ladies and a smile that could light up a football ground. This was Don Raimondo! The representative and fixer extraordinaire for Real Madrid. Saporta went to work on the *Generalissimo* with his considerable wit and intelligence. He argued that it was in Franco's best interest to let Real Madrid play the Yugoslavs, for were they not a magnificent team? Football was the cheap drug the masses craved, it crossed previously, unmanageable borders, changed minds and shifted attitudes. What price in propaganda terms the pride of Spain humbling Tito's finest? All would reflect well back on Franco, let him bask in the glory of Di Stefano and his wonderful orchestra of footballing artists.

So, it was on Christmas Day, 1955, a sly joke played on Partizan Belgrade by Santiago Bernabeu, to let these communists experience some rare, seasonal spirit, they finally clashed. Just to ensure Franco did not have a change of heart and shoot them all at the airport, the Partizan players were smuggled into Spain through a side-gate, by-passing passport control and customs. Their reward for such secrecy came when Real Madrid took apart their Eastern European opponents 4-0. It was a victory capped on seventy-minutes when Alfredo Di Stefano picked up a pass from his Captain Miguel Munoz, to streak clear before firing low past Partizan goalkeeper Stojanovic completing the rout. Earlier, two from reserve winger Castano and one from the electrifying Francisco Gento left the Yugoslavs wondering just what had hit them. This after Partizan began the game on the attack with two goals from their brilliant centre-forward Bora Milutinovic strangely disallowed. No surprise really and swiftly appearing disgruntled the visitors lost heart surely thinking whatever they did, it was not going, or more likely allowed to be their day. At the time, Di Stefano's fourth goal was considered simply icing on the cake for the *Madrilenos* as a place in the semi-finals appeared already sealed. Not so though as events in Belgrade would leave everyone connected with Real Madrid a little humbler, and never again daring to underestimate a fellow champion.

The plane carrying Real Madrid to Yugoslavia, landed at Tito airport in the midst of a blinding, snowstorm and with temperatures ten degrees below zero. Matters hardly improved when the game began in conditions beyond belief. As a raging blizzard swept across the pitch, Partizan ripped into the Spanish aristocrats. Madrid goalkeeper Alonso recalled standing beneath his crossbar when a snarling drive from Partizan's Milutinovic smashed angrily against it, causing the snow which had settled to fall and cover him head to toe! Eager to avenge their humiliation in the *Bernabeu* the Yugoslavs attacked with a real zest. The terraces packed full of comrade soldiers roaring on their team, the Real players slipping and sliding on the treacherous surface, their bewildering ball skills rendered useless in such harsh conditions On thirteen-minutes they fell behind. Hector Rial was swiftly handed the opportunity to equalise from the penalty spot and put the tie out of reach, but the Argentinian fluffed his lines firing haplessly over the crossbar. Much to the chagrin of Di Stefano who handed his fellow countryman a look of murderous disgust. Spurred on by this let off the home team continued to pin back Madrid, and as their supporters chided the struggling *Madrilenos* with endless hails of snowballs (an unofficial cold war), a second goal arrived from the spot when Milutinović, who unlike Rial, mastered the surface slashing his penalty high past a diving Alonso! Suddenly, bedlam had come to Belgrade! Sensing the Spaniards were ripe for the taking Partizan blazed forward and Milutinović upped the stakes even higher when he crashed home a third for the Slavs to leave the Madrid players arguing amongst themselves, standing on the verge of utter humiliation. 3-4 on aggregate, one more was required. The last kick of the match almost saw Milutinović complete a magnificent hat trick, only to see his close-range effort beat Alonso, but cruelly stick in the slush that had built up on the goal-line. Madrid survived only through huge swathes of good fortune and last ditch defending from their snow-battered defence. Notably Manuel Marquitos, who at times was fending off the Belgrade offensive almost single-handedly, as his *compadres* struggled slipping and sliding. The *Madrilenos* departed the Balkans lucky and bruised both in injuries and egos, but they remained alive in the European Cup and into the semi-finals. It had though been oh, so, close. Even today the dramatic events of Belgrade are etched in the rich tapestry of Real Madrid's European history causing them to shudder. Forever remembered as the "Snow Game". A match they would never forget.

The semi-final saw Real pitched against the classy, ultra-professionals of AC Milan. The Italians had splashed out a world record £72,000 for the awesome, attacking prowess of the exceptional Uruguayan forward Juan Schiaffino, and if any team was equipped to knock out the Spanish it was the *Rossoneri*. The first-leg at the *Bernabeu* saw an enthralling encounter as the Italians twice roared back to equalise. With the score at 2-2, Milan fought furiously and with great skill against the *Madrilenos*. Schiaffino in particular handed out heart attacks to the Madrid crowd, his delicate touch, wonderful finesse and a deadly eye for goal posing a constant threat. However, Real possessed in abundance that rare ability to simply ease through gears whenever necessary. Two late strikes from Rial and inevitably Di Stefano saw the *Bernabeu* rise once more in tribute to their side.

In Milan, Real Madrid played with a rare conservatism on a rock hard *San Siro* pitch to ease themselves past their opponents. An early away goal finished clinically by Madrid winger Jocieto put paid to the Milanese challenge, and despite two late Del Monte penalties in a swiftly, emptying stadium, Real remained composed. Come the final-whistle, the white shirts celebrated after booking a place in the European Cup final.

It was to be fitting that the finale would be held in Paris, for the notion of a European Champions Cup was first mooted by the editor of French sports magazine *L'Equipe*. The Parisian Gabriel Hanot. Through nothing but dogged resilience and sheer, bloody mindedness, Hanot saw his dream of the continent's mightiest teams coming together in a single tournament. Amongst Hanot's most committed allies was of course Santiago Bernabeu, and it was felt only fair that his club should be part of such a grand occasion. That their opponents would be French was more surprising. Rheims had amongst their ranks a player deeply coveted by Bernabeu. The son of an immigrant Polish miner, Raymonde Kopa was a devastating winger, mainly on the right side, but equally capable of causing havoc on the left or through the centre. Already, other elite European clubs were planning to swoop for the dynamic Frenchman, convincing the Real president that they had to act fast. For the mouth-watering prospect of Kopa rampaging down one wing and Gento the other meant that once more, Bernabeu summoned his right-hand man Raimondo Saporta. Armed again with a blank cheque and the romance and glory of the white shirt, Saporta travelled to France. With both teams set to play in the final serious doubts were raised on the timing of such a deal. A serious conflict of interest had arisen, but the irresistible pull of Real Madrid and a mind-boggling transfer fee of fifty-two million francs sealed the unlikely coup for the Spaniards. A three-year contract was signed by Raymonde Kopa, yet another truly, audacious coup by this kingmaker and fixer extraordinaire.

After losing out in the league to the fiercely, combative Athletic Bilbao, the *Madrilenos* were under intense pressure to beat Rheims. The Basques had left Madrid trailing after a storming finish to win the championship, meaning only a victory in Paris would enable Real to qualify for the following, season's European Cup competition. 38,000 packed the *Parc Des Princes*, the vast majority desperate to see Rheims put these strutting Spaniards in their place. The signing of Kopa was being seen in France as a grossly, unfair tactic meant to undermine the French beforehand. His loyalty was questioned also, how could he perform at his maximum and help destroy the hand that now would pay him so well? Pouring more fuel onto the fire, Kopa had even made a guest appearance the previous week for Real in a 4-2 victory against Brazilian club Vasco De Gama at the *Bernabeu*. But any doubts regarding the Frenchman's desire to still perform for Rheims appeared misguided as the initial stages saw Kopa run the Madrid defence ragged! Exploding in front of their own people, the French champions roared forward. The exquisite one-touch passing cutting Real to pieces and in just ten-minutes they had built up a two goal lead. The first through midfielder Michel Leblond, before an awful mistake by Juan Alonso was pounced upon and smashed into the net by forward Jean Templin. The Spanish were reeling, their famous swagger invisible, the composure absent. Disaster loomed. Bernabeu's master plan strangled at birth. Suddenly, the orchestra began to perform! Alfredo Di Stefano had decided enough and puffing out his chest the *Blond Arrow* went to work. Single-handedly he dragged Real kicking and screaming back into the contest. On fourteen-minutes, Di Stefano raced into the Rheims area and lashed a shot goal-wards to half the deficit. Madrid had awaken, as if struck by electricity they erupted back into life. Gento and Rial reacting to their talisman's promptings and devilishly, astute passes. A much, deserved equaliser arrived just before half-time, when Rial met Gento's cross to flash a header past Rheims 'goalkeeper Jacquet at his near post. Yet, just when it seemed normal service had been resumed and the Spaniards were running away with the contest, their valiant opponents regained sufficient poise to hit back. On the hour, a free-kick from Kopa found the head of French attacking, midfielder Michel Hidalgo, to beat a flailing Alonso making the score 3-2, and sending the *Parc Des Prince* into raptures! This was not in the Real Madrid script.

They poured forward in search of yet another equaliser. On sixty-seven minutes, their prayers were answered when salvation arrived from a most, unlikely source. Manuel Marquitos stabbing home from six-yards on one of his rare forays forward. With white shirts now moving like ghostly images amongst the courageous, but badly, toiling French, their passes slick, movement hellish and pace incredulous, it appeared just a matter of time before Rheims were handed a knock-out blow. It came eleven-minutes from time when the *Madrilenos* concocted an opportunity for Hector Rial to slot home from eight-yards, surely winning the European Cup? 4-3! The seconds were counted down and one last almighty scare awaited Real Madrid, for as the referee stood with whistle in mouth ready to blow, a desperate Leblond's shot crashed against the Spaniard's crossbar! But it was to be Madrid's trophy. President Don Santiago Bernabeu watched with tears in his eyes as Captain Miguel Munoz, amid a mad, huddle of blinding flashlights and cameras lifted the European Cup aloft. To show his deep appreciation General Franco handed Santiago Bernabeu the freedom of Madrid. Not that the President needed such a decree! So, began a glorious era for the *Madrilenos*. Across Europe, there appeared none capable of living with this white storm that possessed Di Stefano at the very heart. The walls to the *Bernabeu* appeared impregnable.

The following season.
On the 1st November 1956, Real Madrid began the defence of their newly won crown beating the skilful Austrian champions Rapid Vienna 4-2, in a thrilling contest at the *Bernabeu*. A two goal advantage was thought more than sufficient to take over to Vienna, however, on a night of blazing incident and a rip-roaring crowd baying for Madrid blood. A most, unlikely hat trick from Rapid's veteran defender, 33-year-old Ernst Happel to hand the Austrians a 3-0 half-time lead, stunned the *Madrilenos,* leaving them on the verge of a humiliating elimination. It was a breathless showing by the unfancied home side who caught Madrid unaware and a little too sure of themselves. For the magnificent Happel a personal triumph, his

two free-kicks and a penalty leaving Real on their knees and reeling. For the visitors a total embarrassment, none more than to their red-faced President, who was so disgusted with his team that he stormed down to the dressing room to confront them. What Santiago Bernabeu said that day in Vienna was actually recorded on tape and has entered Real Madrid legend. Bernabeu took out a ridiculously, expensive cigar from his mouth and grinded it into the floor with his heel. As the players stared forlornly at their boots, humbled and a little bit wary of their fuming President, Don Santiago let rip!

"No one is getting away from here this easily! We have not come here on holiday, and I want to see more balls out on that field! I don't know if you understand, but you have got the Real Madrid shield on your shirts. I have seen thousands of Spaniards who have come to support us. People who work their hearts out in the factories to earn a living. You can't let them down like this!"

The second half saw a Real Madrid rally and a lone Di Stefano goal ended the overall tie at 5-5. A little pride, if not victory had been restored. To settle matters a play-off would be required and it is here that once again President Bernabeu worked the black magic. He called once more for Raimondo Saporta and sent him to do business with his Austrian opponents. Rather than a neutral venue where the financial benefit would suit neither club, Saporta argued the case for the game to be played at the *Bernabeu*. The incentive for the Austrians was a fifty-percent cut of a guaranteed sell out. After two monumental encounters against the *Madrilenos*, the Rapid officials felt sufficiently confident to take up Don Raimondo's generous offer. The outcome inevitably saw them go out 2-0. Sadly and shamefully, the Austrians preferred the lure of Spanish pesetas to the opportunity of glory. Saporta proved again his business acumen was equal to anything the white knights ever produced on a football pitch.

Following the harrowing experience of Vienna, lessons had been learned and the quarter-final against French champions Nice caused the *Madrilenos* few problems. A 6-2 aggregate score saw Real Madrid one step away from a second, successive final appearance. Confidence was high. Bernabeu had demanded no more slip ups. He paid the best, demanded the best and with such came the power and the glory. On the French Riviera, Nice, 14th March 1957, Matt Busby, accompanied by the northern England press pack were amongst the crowd who watched in awe as an Alfredo Di Stefano, inspired Real Madrid won 3-2 to stake their semi-final place against Manchester United. What Busby saw on that long, gone evening in Eastern France, on the Mediterranean coast captivated his footballing soul. "He is one of the greatest, if not the greatest footballer, I have ever seen. We have forwards and defenders doing separate jobs, but he does everything! When I saw him down there in France, I said to the press afterwards, "I don't think I've seen a better player." Later, when we played Real ourselves there was a reception and Di Stefano came over and said, "I want to take you on as my publicity agent!" But, I think time has proved what I said after that one glimpse of him was right." When asked later if there had been one player Busby would have liked to have signed for United he picked Alfredo. However, at that time Di Stefano was said to be earning £350 a match for Real, whilst the maximum wage in England was just £15!

The *Blond Arrow*. Blessed With breakneck pace, stunning acceleration off the mark, and a wonderful grace and artistry dripping from every inch of his imperial pores. The strutting Di Stefano was a magnificent footballer. A self-appointed king, a leader amongst Real Madrid's, rich tapestry of superstars. The 29-year-old with a balding pate and eyes that filled with disdain anytime a fellow *Madrileno* failed to attain his highest standards. Considered by many arrogant and aloof. He was short-tempered and the absolute worst of losers, but without doubt one of the, if not the best player in the world at that time. On returning to Manchester, Busby was quoted as saying: "I have just witnessed Alfredo the Great! He is simply unique." Worryingly, for the United coaching staff Busby had never spoken of opposing players in such glowing terms, but such was his admiration of Madrid's *Blond Arrow*, he simply could not help himself!

It was the startling manner of how Manchester United did not just eliminate Athletic Bilbao, but also broke their hearts and spirit whilst doing so. This caused raised eyebrows and worry in Madrid. On boarding the plane home to Bilbao, Basque captain Agustin Gainza, could still not believe what had become of his team and the sheer ferocity, passion and speed displayed by their opponents. "United played with such passion we were simply overwhelmed." Busby's side had laid down such a marker that could not be ignored. Madrid had been warned. Yet, whilst there would be huge respect for United, they were hardly shaking with fear in the Spanish capital. Despite all of the Mancunian's flowering wealth of talent, the English champions did not possess a Di Stefano or a Gento. The United players were full of questions to ask the boss about their semi-final opponents.

"Boss, how good are they?"

"Are they really as strong as they say?"

"Is Gento the quickest thing in football?"

"How will we play Di Stefano?"

"Boss, boss, boss!"

On Real's lighting fast winger, *"La Galerna del Cantabrico!"*

" The Gale of the Cantabrian Sea" Francisco Gento, Busby told the defender who would be handed the awesome task of marking him, Bill Foulkes. "Just play the best you can Bill!" Trying hard to play down what United would be up against he did confide in Bobby Charlton, for who there was great hopes at Old Trafford. Busby let slip in a moment of rare weakness and told the prodigious young Geordie just what he actually witnessed in Nice. 'The boss watched Real play at Nice in the previous round, but could not convey what he saw to the players. He was so enthusiastic about them to me though, it was incredible! I discovered I was building a defensive wall inside myself, for a player wants to see for himself. For instance, the boss said Gento was the fastest man he'd ever seen, but what did that mean to Bill Foulkes who had to mark him? How fast was very fast? As hard as the boss talked, however many adjectives and comparisons he used, Gento remained nothing more than fast!" Charlton never repeated Busby's words to his team mates. He does remember having the worrying notion of whooping, Wild-West Indians approaching fast from the other side of the hill that they could hear, but not yet see. With the *Blond Arrow* leading the charge from the front!

As the European Cup semi-final rapidly approached, Manchester United despatched Birmingham City 2-0 in the FA Cup semi-final at Hillsborough, with goals from Johnny Berry and Bobby Charlton. The reds scored early and the game swiftly turned into a walkover. The Busby Babes were that good they simply kept possession amongst themselves. The editor of the Daily Telegraph, Frank Coles was amongst many who was realising Matt Busby's treasured youngsters were so far out of sight of their nearest rivals, it was becoming a chasm. "The reason for their surge of popularity is quite simple. Under the expert and fatherly guidance of Matt Busby, a happy band of young men have developed a team spirit and comradeship, seldom equalled in any of our sports. They give all they have for the club, and in all circumstances they try to play football. United were indeed superbly served by their three young inside-forwards, Whelan, Viollet and Charlton, not as attackers alone, but by the unsparing, willing way they chased back to help whenever their defence was under pressure." Manchester United would go on to play Aston Villa in the FA Cup Final, but that could wait for all talk in the city was of the forthcoming encounter with Real Madrid. United were riding high at the top of the table, a double looked on, but such was the confidence running throughout the club all anybody had on their minds was Real Madrid! It was a footballing Hollywood! Manchester was alive with excitement. The white shirted figures were stepping down from the *Pathe* news and coming to chance their hands on the banks of the River Irwell. For the first time Old Trafford would host a European Cup match with the floodlights finally installed, but beforehand would be the small matter of the first-leg. The opening game in Madrid.

There was an estimated 250,000 applications for tickets at the *Estadio Bernabeu*, with receipts expected to be around an astonishing £55,000. Only the 1950 World Cup match between Brazil and

Uruguay, seven years previous had come close to such an astronomical sum for one match. This at the *Maracana* stadium. Matt Busby thought long and hard on how to contain Real Madrid in the *Bernabeu*, specifically the threat of one Alfredo Di Stefano, for he knew that with the world watching given an inch on his own theatre stage, and in front of an adoring home crowd, Di Stefano would destroy them. This semi-final was being regarded as the biggest game in the brief history of the European Cup with Manchester United viewed as Real's main rivals for the foreseeable future. The *Bernabeu* was the perfect stage for a man who craved and demanded adulation not just from spectators, but the opposition also. This game against United was an opportunity that Di Stefano's ego would not let pass. Sometimes words don't do Don Alfredo justice, for at times strange forces appeared at work in the *Bernabeu* whenever he took possession. As if sparked, electrified by sudden spurts of lightning, Francisco Gento's boots would ignite to then find the ball landing at his feet from a sumptuous Di Stefano raking pass. Gento would fly away to be joined by equally sleight of foot *compadres.* The newly, acquired French goal machine Raymonde Kopa, the Argentinian striker Hector Rial, and local boy Enrique Mateos, who loved to bait opposing defenders like a matador to a bull. All remained forever on the toes, knowing fully well if they made the correct run Di Stefano's radar with passes so perfect would arrive with their name carved upon them. Alfredo Di Stefano was a man also well aware of his financial worth to Madrid as a player. He understood fully that Bernabeu's dream of creating a footballing dynasty to last a generation needed him at its very heart. This was an expensive fact that President Don Santiago also knew only too well, as he made out ever-rising cheques for his priceless asset.

In attempting to stem the deadly, rapier strikes of Di Stefano, the Manchester United manager came up with an unlikely solution. He detailed his ball playing, highly adaptable 24r-year-old Irish central-defender Jackie Blanchflower and Eddie Colman to keep the great man quiet. Busby briefed Colman not to leave Di Stefano's side. ''Follow that man to the ends of the earth young Colman,'' his words.

It was an unenviable task, but one which the Salford born Colman would endeavour to carry out. For those ninety-minutes in the *Bernabeu*, Eddie intended to follow the boss's order to the last word and live in Di Stefano's shadow. Born at number 9 Archie Street, Salford, the real-life Coronation Street. Eddie Colman was perhaps the most loved of the Babes. He was one of their own, a happy go-lucky, mischievous and charming character with an easy, friendly manner and enough devil to excite the Old Trafford regulars. Eddie had few equals in England as he made fools of First Division defenders. Trusted by Busby to stay disciplined, Eddie Colman's unerring ability to twist and turn at great speed also played a significant part in his manager's thinking. In using Colman who would undoubtedly find himself dragged all over the pitch by Di Stefano, Busby could then keep together his back four as Gento, Kopa, Mateos and Rial fell upon them. A pensive Colman was reassured by his manager that he would not be alone in this awesome task, as once the Argentine crossed the halfway line, Jackie Blanchflower would move also to pick up Di Stefano. Originally coming to United as an inside forward, Jackie had quickly realised with rivals such as Bobby Charlton, Dennis Viollet and Liam Whelan battling for two positions opportunities would be limited. After converting himself into a centre-half, Blanchflower was capped by Northern Ireland and new doors opened in his Old Trafford career. An ability to read the game, intercept rather than tackle and a cute eye for a damning pass saw the Belfast-born youngster flourish. Between this pairing of a Salford lad and a boy from Belfast, Busby hoped to limit the destructive capacities of the irrepressible Alfredo Di Stefano.

The United player most perceived best suited to man-mark Di Stefano was the remarkable Duncan Edwards. Already an English international and surely a future Captain of the national side. Blessed with an unfair abundance of all-round talent, Edwards was powerful, ferocious in the tackle, inspirational, could play off either foot with equal brilliance and towering in the air. It said all that whenever the reds were struggling in a game the United supporters simply began to shout: "Give it to Dunc!" As did the bench at times when all appeared lost. If Alfredo Di Stefano was the most precious of Real Madrid's brightest lights, then Duncan Edwards was the Mancunian's heart and soul. Busby felt that in the boiling-hot atmosphere of the *Estadio Bernabeu*, Edwards' unique prowess would never be needed more, as United prepared to withstand what was certain to be a footballing hurricane descending upon them. The anxious Scot was all too aware that even if by some miracle they managed to keep the lid on Di Stefano, Real Madrid's calibre of players elsewhere could all easily destroy them. United would have to perform like never before to survive a beating in the *Bernabeu*. They could not go in all guns blazing, charging about with typical aplomb to the sound of cannon, for to do so risked obliteration at the hands of these Spanish magicians. Instead, they would tread carefully on foreign soil, for Busby knew Madrid was not just unknown territory, it was another world and one potentially lethal also.

Expectations in Manchester after what had been achieved against the much lauded Athletic Bilbao, had reached fever pitch, but they were wildly far off from any semblance of footballing reality. There was not many United supporters who felt Real Madrid, though grand in name and stature could halt what for them was simply a triumphal procession to a first European Cup success. It felt just so inevitable after the beating of the Basques. All that had been viewed of Real Madrid was sporadic clips on the cinema *Pathe* newsreel footage. Though spectacular, angelic even, these knights in white satin flashing across the screen were balletic, undoubtedly beautiful and left a lasting impression, but surely they would be no match for Matt's boys? This was a team built in Busby's own image playing blistering, open-attacking football. One touch, pass and move. It was early Rock and Roll football! The Babes electrified every ground they played at and now that their beat had crossed over onto the continent. Europe's elite clubs were well aware of these flashing, Mancunian red dervishes and the threat they now posed. United were gunning for Real Madrid's European crown. It was all just a matter of time. Santiago Bernabeu's prophesy of an all-conquering club had come to fruition much sooner than even a man of his vision could have envisaged. The flowering years of the European Cup saw Real blow away all opposition. No side on the continent appeared capable of living with Di Stefano and his orchestra of stars. It had been nothing more than a glorious parade. Until now…

Leading up to the first-leg the Spanish press and public devoured every fact and news story about this remarkable, exciting young English team, who were daring to challenge their mighty *Madrilenos,* and they waited with baited-breath Manchester United's arrival on Madrid soil. Accustomed to other team managers fawning in admiration over the brilliance of Real, beaten before they even took to the field, Matt Busby's supreme confidence shocked them rigid. ''Manchester United are a better team, Real Madrid are going to need at least three goals to take back to Manchester.'' These comments caused many Spanish journalists to become a trite apprehensive of just what exactly was coming their way. While Busby remained bullish in public to keep up his player's confidence, privately he felt that the Spaniards were a monumental, if not an impossible mountain to scale for his richly talented side. The Babes being in European terms raw and somewhat naïve in comparison to the continental cunning of coming through such a difficult two-legged tie. For there was more ways of skinning a cat when it came to playing at this level, street wise, even brutal tactics were required and duly existed within the beating heart of Real Madrid, alongside the wonderful football they played. If required there were players in white shirts who would kick their own grandmothers in the air and as she came down volley her away!

The weekend before Real Madrid warmed up by hammering Los Palmas, 5-1, away. A majestic Alfredo Di Stefano helped himself to four appearing primed and ready to go for the English champions. Making the grim error of taking the lead, Los Palmas swiftly found themselves well and truly buried in an avalanche of *Madrileno* goals. A thousand miles away in Manchester, United were involved in a hard fought 0-0 draw against closest title rivals Tottenham Hotspur at Old Trafford. A point with just six games remaining made United huge favourites to win their league once more. Busby's team were minus two of the star players. The left-winger David Pegg and Duncan Edwards, both away on international duty playing for England in a 2-1 victory over Scotland. Come the final whistle, a relieved Matt Busby was able to report a fully-fit squad to take on Real Madrid the following Thursday. Excitement was building, a double was a unique achievement, but a treble? Beyond belief.

On Tuesday 8th April 1957, the Elizabethan aircraft carrying Manchester United, and piloted by Captain Ken Rayment, soared off the runway at Ringway airport taking them to the biggest game in their history. Leaving behind a murky, Mancunian drizzle they landed in beautiful, blazing sunshine at Madrid airport greeted by hundreds of Real supporters, so eager to see these much talked about *Los Chicos* with their own eyes. A barrage of flashbulbs exploded in the player's path as the players resplendent in MUFC blazers walked down the gangway. Immediately, they were besieged by over-eager autograph hunters. The clamour coming from an equal numbers of lady admirers, as well as male football supporters. Dark haired senoritas' who had seen the photographs and newspaper images of these dashing young footballers from a place called Manchester, England, which left them enchanted. These were rock and roll footballers. The Babes played the fashion game, they cut a wonderful, cool swagger with English flannel and grey trilbies dipped acutely over their eyes to give themselves the look of 1930's Chicago hoodlums. Madrid was in love! Chaos ensued, but it was all remarkably good natured as a mad huddle surrounded the charismatic visitors. Manchester United had come to Madrid. This sophisticated, wealthy European city, a world away from murky, post-war Manchester, but on the football pitch they would start as equals. United's centre-forward Tommy Taylor appeared amongst the most, popular players by far, after his epic collision against the colossus Jesus Garay of Athletic Bilbao in the previous round. He and Taylor had fought an epic, personal duel over the two legs with the Barnsley man finally coming out on top, and Taylor's reputation had soared across Europe as a result. Nowhere more so than in Madrid. However, in Real's ranks there lurked equal devilment with defenders and midfielders of the calibre of Manuel Marquitos, the Captain Miguel Munoz and Jose Maria Zarraga. Whilst all technically sublime they verged on the fanatical in the heat of battle playing with an attitude of no mercy. They had been well briefed on the talents of this particular Englishman and would be ready. There was none more brutal than the dark-haired, steely-eyed 27-year-old Marquitos. Blood-curdling when roused, Marquitos had already made it known that he had no intention of going the same way of the Basque Jesus Garay. Marquitos vowed his studs would make their mark on this European Cup semi-final, and in particular Tommy Taylor. Busby's preparation for battle was exceptional, taking absolutely no chances. United took twenty-two players to Madrid, a reserve for every position. Including Bobby Charlton. "For the first time there were crowds waiting to greet us at the airport and I remember saying to Eddie Colman: "Well, we've got something in common with Real, their fans are as daft as ours!" Charlton expected to be awestruck when he first saw the *Estadio Bernabeu* and was not disappointed. The stadium rose high towards the Madrid skies, truly dramatic on the eye. Especially for someone like he, a native of the north-east, an adopted Mancunian, it must have been truly breath-taking at first sight. The *Bernabeu's* two famous columns rising against the beautiful skyline of the Spanish capital. Busby was also given assurances from the manager of the plush five-star Fenix Hotel in the city's heart where United would reside, that just English style food would be served to his party. He also insisted that only bottled water be drunk thus avoiding the dread of all Brits abroad, the infamous Spanish tummy.

Manchester United's arrival heralded a press frenzy the likes of which Madrid had rarely witnessed. The media scrum seemed more fitting for the arrival of a top Hollywood movie star than a visiting football team. Whenever the players set foot out of the hotel they were immediately mobbed. Ever present around the Fenix were the ticket touts demanding a thousand pesetas for a hundred peseta ticket. The prices were outrageous, but with 250,000 ticket applications already made they did brisk business. The day before the match Real Madrid had allowed United to train on the *Bernabeu* pitch, and fully aware that the Spanish would undoubtedly have spies watching their every move, Busby kept the sessions simple giving nothing away. Jackie Blanchflower and Eddie Colman were primed and ready for their man-marking job on Di Stefano, and the manager wanted it to be a big surprise for Don Alfredo! Come the evening Busby took the team for a night out to watch *Antonio and his Spanish Ballet* and they received a standing ovation on being spotted before taking their seats! The Busby Babes out on the town in Madrid winning hearts and minds, but the genuine business would begin the next day. As a full moon shone bright illuminating in shadows the white walls of the *Bernabeu*, the Spanish capital held a collective breath.

Come match day, Madrid awoke to feelings of nerves and exhilaration. Busby recalled: "There was so much excitement going on there that young David Pegg and Eddie Colman became sick, and I didn't think they would be able to play, but eventually they recovered and we went on to the field with them. It really was quite an occasion for anyone in Madrid that day, let alone young players." Situated in one of the more lavish palatial quarters of Madrid, the Chamartin district, the *Estadio Bern*abeu was a majestic, awe-inspiring sporting cathedral fit for the footballing gods. As the day drew on ticketless thousands gathered outside the stadium attempting to rush the barriers, only to be forced back by mounted police. For a while carnage ensued before order was finally restored, and then in they came. Over 130,000 spectators demanding nothing more than a footballing massacre. Tickets were like Spanish gold dust. One of the English press pack, the Daily Mirror's Frank Taylor discovered for himself on the morning of the game after a memorable telephone conversation. "Ah Mr Taylor, you are the famous Tommy Taylor of Manchester United? This is one of the Flamenco dancers from Mr Antonio's troupe who entertained your club. Is it possible to get me a ticket for the game?"

"Madam, I am not Tommy Taylor," Frank quickly passed the phone over to Tommy stood next to him!"

Under one of the *Bernabeu* stands there was a small chapel where the Real players would go to for their pre-match prayers, A quiet moment at one with the almighty before battle commenced in the madness and hysteria of the footballing arena. For hours before kick-off, the terraces were already packed. Easter drew close in this highly, religious Catholic nation. The traditional beginning of the bullfighting season nearby at the *Monumental* plaza. But the supporters of Real Madrid had only one slaughter on their minds, and that was to gore Manchester United's European hopes. For like a red flag to a bull the Babes had antagonised these self-anointed, white knights of European football beyond all comprehension with their brilliance, cockiness and sheer swagger. The expectations were high that the home team would put these English upstarts back in a rightful place, for they had Di Stefano. The visitors would not be without support in the stadium. Five chartered aircraft full of United supporters had travelled over from Manchester to cheer their boys on. Whether they would be heard in such a vast arena when up against such fanatical backing was debatable.

Shortly before kick-off, Manchester United received a visit from suited Madrid officials carrying photographs of the eleven *Madrilenos* they were soon set to face. After handing them to Matt Busby, they in turn asked for pictures of his players who were set to take the field? A non-plussed United manager politely explained that such a custom was unheard of in England, but they had his word that Manchester United would not be including any ringers in the team! Trying hard not to lose his calm as the visitors insinuated all was not as it should be, Busby finally let fly at this unwanted presence in the sanctuary of the dressing room. He informed them that all the passports were safely locked up in the hotel vault, but, if Real wished he would happily show them to whoever after the match had finished. The sullen Spaniards remained insistent and not wanting to cause an international incident Busby instead decided to leave. He headed off for a quiet chat with Jimmy Murphy to check out the playing surface.

Incredibly, due to the rising tide of hysteria that had engulfed the *Bernabeu*, the only place they could hear each other speak was in the centre-circle. There the two men in the very heart of Real Madrid's great stadium, discussed just how they were going to topple this giant from its imperial perch. Matt and Jimmy were a long way from Manchester.

In the mid-afternoon of Thursday 11th April 1957, Real Madrid and Manchester United stepped out into the Spanish sunshine to do battle. The arrival of the two teams was greeted by a magical shower of white roses thrown from the highest bastions of this magnificent stadium. The United players looked on in astonishment as this cascade of flowers floated down onto the pitch. The Real Captain Miguel Munoz applauded his supporters for their remarkable display. It was a truly epic and moving spectacle.

Flashbulbs glittered across the terrace like a million fireflies as the *Bernabeu* exploded in a glorious, deafening symphony of rockets and cheering. A huge posse of photographers scuttled like ants across the turf as both sides posed for their team photos. It was to be an afternoon they would talk about in Madrid for generations to come. The small party of travelling British Journalists luckily enough to be present could not believe the luxurious comfort of the *Bernabeu* press box. There were waiters dressed in immaculate white jackets that dealt with all their needs. Even the Madrid supporters sat below them were obliging, as they passed up to the disbelieving, hard-bitten hacks, pigskin bladders filled with red wine!

The referee Mr Leo Horn, easily Europe's most famous official had been a war hero who fought with great courage for the Dutch resistance. Tragically, a much crueller fate befell his brother Edgar who was murdered by the Nazis in a concentration camp. At the war's end Horn returned to refereeing, and the fact he was also a black belt in Judo meant his no-nonsense approach on the pitch was respected by players of all sides!

The Teams.

Real Madrid. Alonso, Becceril, Lesmes, Munoz, Marquitos, Zarraga, Kopa, Mateos, Di Stefano, Rial and Gento.

Manchester United. Wood, Foulkes, Byrne, Colman, Blanchflower, Edwards, Berry, Whelan, Taylor, Viollet and Pegg.

It began.

For an hour Manchester United fought tooth and nail to stem an endless array of *Madrileno* attacks. Many times they were simply penned back into their own penalty area unable to break out. However, United held firm and unyielding. On the wings, the left-back Roger Byrne was having considerable success against Raymonde Kopa. Byrne's intelligence and pace curtailing the Frenchman's normally, killing-rampaging assaults down the flank. On the other side a totally different story as the right-back Bill Foulkes was in the midst of a living nightmare against the flying machine, Francisco Gento. Repeatedly, Gento would feint to go one way then change direction, switching instantaneously to over-drive with a blistering turn of speed that left Foulkes gasping for breath in the Spaniard's wake. *El Motorcycle* in a flash would be away! Elsewhere on the pitch with Alfredo Di Stefano's every imperious step shadowed by Eddie Colman, the *Blond Arrow* found his aim for once stunted and usual golden touch unsure. There were glowers of disdain, how dare he? The great man became increasingly rattled as Colman followed his every move, a red shadow etched onto a white knight. Whenever it appeared Alfredo's blistering acceleration would take him clear of his Salford nemesis, Belfast's Jackie Blanchflower moved and intercepted to tighten the noose ever further, upsetting Di Stefano's regal state of mind even more so. Finally, the scowling Di Stefano's patience snapped and he launched a sickening lunge on Blanchflower that scythed him down and should have seen the Argentinian expelled from the pitch. The foul was committed only yards away from the referee. Leo Horn appeared to have no option, he had to go, but how do you send off the leading man in his own personal theatre? Not having the nerve Horn for once failed in his duty and allowed Di Stefano to remain on the field. In short he bottled it! A scandalous decision that infuriated Busby and Murphy on the United bench. This undeserved slice of luck though did not save Di Stefano from the wrath of an outraged Bill Foulkes, who on seeing his friend Blanchflower almost decapitated, grabbed him by the shirt and was threatening to do much worse before being wrestled away by team mates.

Occasionally creaking and at times sliced wide open, the reds by some miracle kept the marauding *Madrilenos* at bay. Matt Busby's tactical ploy to keep Di Stefano on a short leash was holding, just! For there were occasions that even with such close attention, Madrid's number nine found space and time to engineer a pass or an attempt at goal. In the rare moments United managed to venture over the half-way line, their swashbuckling centre-forward Tommy Taylor found himself victim to a succession of murderous tackles and challenges that verged on assault from the Madrid defence. Manuel Marquitos foremost, the ghost of Jose Garay forever in his head. Aware of the dangers posed by Taylor, the villainous Marquitos hacked and slashed both on the ball and off. He was ably abetted by partners in crime Munoz and Zarraga, who thought nothing in kicking poor Tommy up in the air for the mere fun of it. Yet, Taylor, brave beyond all cause of duty refused to be intimidated. Shortly before half-time following a cross by David Pegg, he missed by a hair's breadth with a header when it would have been easier to score. United taking the lead would have been daylight robbery such had been Madrid's dominance, but it shown despite being under severe pressure throughout they still possessed a threat. Nevertheless, the first period ended with the home crowd whistling their frustrations. This was not in the script, the Spaniards came to the *Bernabeu* demanding English blood, and all they had seen so far was a peerless display of grit and determination by the visitors. Ninety-minutes though was an awful, long time to test your mettle against this team of such wizards and magicians. One master stroke from Di Stefano's baton and all hell could yet be let loose upon them. Hard work and discipline were worthy attributes, but there remained much to achieve before returning home with satisfaction to Manchester.

With an hour gone the European champions so relentless in their pursuit of an opening goal finally unlocked the red vault. It was Francisco Gento who went powering through with all guns blazing. Teasing and jinking poor Bill Foulkes to distraction, Gento tore away and without even glancing up delivered a superb cross onto the head of Hector Rial, who powered a fierce, stooping header from close, blank-range past a helpless Ray Wood. The *Bernabeu* erupted! Across the huge terraces that stretched forever upwards thousands of white handkerchiefs waved in delight. Madrid was on fire, the deadlock broken. Now, thought the home supporters it was just a matter of how many? With the crowd baying for blood Real moved in for the kill. After enduring a frustrating match Alfredo Di Stefano finally rid himself of a tiring Eddie Colman. Attached like a limpet throughout, Colman's chains fell away and his prisoner broke free! With fearful speed and purpose, like a man wrongly jailed and now determined to right an injustice, Di Stefano roared past a ragged bevy of bedraggled, red shirts to race dangerously clear into the visitor's half. Leading the chase to catch him was the immaculate Roger Byrne, but Di Stefano was in no mood to be caught and with a heavenly precision he executed a perfect chip over Ray Wood, which landed perfectly under the crossbar to double Real's lead. Two goals down and the roof was caving in on Matt Busby's courageous young team. Bobby Charlton himself was high up in the *Bernabeu*. ''I was right up in the gods way above the pitch, and to be honest I was terribly pleased I wasn't playing! I saw Di Stefano and these others and I thought to myself, these people just aren't human, It's not the sort of game I'd been taught.'' Manchester United now faced the serious prospect of being massacred. The *Madrilenos* roared their approval, this was more like it! The crowd were buoyant, expectant, demanding more. ''Ole's!'' rang out across this grand magnificent arena. More now a bullring than a football pitch. Every Madrid touch was cheered to the rafters. It was fiesta time as they taunted their exhausted opponents with keep ball. Never had Busby's team experienced this level of football played with such infinite precision and touch. Theirs' was a technique unmatched, a mastery bewitching. This was a foreign game for many of the United players. Outclassed and outthought their truly outstanding talents such as Duncan Edwards, David Pegg and Liam Whelan were now realising that they still remained mere pupils compared to the master's from Madrid. The self-belief amongst the reds that had built up over the last years, when they had been all but invincible on home soil appeared to be being slowly eviscerated, as the white shirts caressed the ball and teased the visitors to try and take it off them. From the touchline Busby urged his players on and showing incredible spirit United rallied. Suddenly, from appearing down and out they surged forward, the pass and move, the swift interchanging taught and drilled into them endlessly by Jimmy Murphy in the constant Mancunian drizzle, on mud-spattered pitches came to the fore. Madrid were retreating. On the left-wing David Pegg began tormenting and making life horribly uncomfortable for the defender Jose Becerril. Repeatedly Pegg led Becerril a merry dance. Many who witnessed the game claimed he had never played better in a red shirt than that last twenty-minutes in the *Bernabeu*. United pressed on and with just eight-minutes remaining a bedraggled, bleeding, but still fighting Tommy Taylor escaped the clutches of his hatchet men to head a superb Liam Whelan cross past Alonso into the net. A chilly wind blew across the *Bernabeu* as an unexpected lifeline had been grasped by the reds. Back in Manchester, hope sprung eternal in packed households and workplaces as radios crackled with the glad tidings. It had become as predicted beforehand a battle royal. United had somehow dragged themselves back into a contest that in reality should have seen them dead and buried. As the ball crossed the line a deafening silence fell across the terraces, the cheers of present Mancunians apart. An anxiety not noticeable since the opening stages had returned. Taylor found himself mobbed by team mates Dennis Viollet and Johnny Berry, both leaping on top of the United striker. It was game on.

Whether it was the exuberance of youth instead of settling for a 2-1 deficit, United continued to surge forward in search of an equaliser. They came so close to achieving it when Viollet took aim and smashed a low drive against the Madrid post! Shortly after Johnny Berry was sent sprawling in the area by Marquitos in what appeared a definite penalty, only for Horn to inexplicably ignore it waving play on. Never had Real Madrid experienced such pressure on home soil. Typically brash and cocky, Busby's team opened up and the ball was pinged around as they went on the attack. Meanwhile, on the touchline a proud if nervous manager watched his team play out a footballing version of Russian roulette, fighting like tigers to level the score. As the clock wound down and with time almost up they were to pay a heavy price for such youthful belligerence. A brilliant interchange of passes between Gento and Rial let through Mateos. He took aim to fire in off the post past a diving Wood sealing a 3-1 victory for Real Madrid! Mateos stood to attention. He slowly raised his arms to the heavens remaining in this pose for what felt an eternity to receive the adulation of an adoring crowd. It was a heart-breaking goal to lose for United leaving them with a mountain to climb, when only seconds beforehand the task in hand resembled just a steep hill. Come the final-whistle, the home players and supporters celebrated as if they had already won the European Cup itself. This victory meant that much and it was with no little relief that Di Stefano and his team gathered in the centre-circle to take the acclaim of an ecstatic, *Bernabeu* audience.

In the disappointed Manchester United dressing room their trainer Tom Curry heaped praised on the players. "You all deserve gold medals as big as frying pans!" Busby singled out the exhausted Bill Foulkes telling him: "No other defender in England could have played Gento better."

He also told the press: "Madrid were the better side on the day, it was a big occasion, but I still think we have a chance. Our defensive play was splendid."

Busby's Captain Roger Byrne agreed. "Madrid are a good team, but the bounce of the ball did not go our way. I think we can win the return, as we did against Bilbao. We should have had a penalty when Berry was brought down.''

Amidst the gloomy, exhausted faces matters were hardly helped when somebody mentioned Real Madrid were on £350 a man to win the European Cup, a figure more than half a season's wages at United. All at Madrid knew that although a fine victory had been achieved this semi-final was not yet won. Athletic Bilbao had assumed the work was done after taking a two-goal lead to England, and they received a 3-0 drubbing, crushed in spirit at the manner of their humiliating defeat. The Bilbao players spoke of a crowd roar that resembled a plane taking off. Of a raw passion that resonated down from the terraces onto the pitch causing the United players to lift their game to unparalleled heights. Of a magic in the Mancunian air. Murky and grey, half-hidden by smoke and fog. Rain-sodden maybe, but every so often illuminated by a startling, red dash. One capable of lifting hearts and achieving footballing miracles. Just ask the Basque? It was called Manchester United.

As was their stylish manner Real Madrid served up a sumptuous post-match banquet for the English visitors. This was a club not just teeming with class on the pitch, but also off it. Now battle had ceased for a while it was time to show respect. Every United player and member of the coaching staff was presented with a gold watch in lasting memory of their memorable encounter at the *Bernabeu*. One United footballer really touched with this special memento was Duncan Edwards, and he carried it on him until his very end. All were in high spirits, many toasts were raised in what was a wonderful display of generosity by the Madrid hosts. Even Tommy Taylor who had found himself battered throughout the match by Real defenders, now enjoyed many a drink, a laugh and a joke with his tormentors. His killer line to them: ''Let's see what happens in Manchester,'' causing Marquitos and his *compadres* to smile when translated. Don Santiago Bernabeu made a heartfelt speech pledging the importance of friendship between these two great clubs. Matt Busby was particularly taken by Bernabeu's words. He was also totally overwhelmed by Madrid's impeccable staging of the occasion making himself a promise that Manchester United must emulate what had taken place on that special night. As the evening wore on Busby found himself cornered by two Madrid players. One was alleged to have said to him: "Please come and manage us? With you at our helm we would win every trophy in the world." The United manager, though flattered and wondering if Don Santiago was behind this friendly mugging replied with an honesty and class that left his Spanish inquisitors disappointed, but still smiling. "Listen, my dear friends, if you were to give me Di Stefano, United would win every trophy in the world!"

The following day's headlines in the Daily Herald screamed out… **"Murder In Madrid!"** Their reporter George Follows wrote: "I have never witnessed such crude and violent tackling as that seen in the Madrid display. Real got away with murder in front of a crowd estimated at 130,000 in the *Santiago Bernabeu* stadium today, who had paid a world record £55,000 in receipts. They hacked, slashed, kicked and wrestled their way, with a kick by Di Stefano on Jackie Blanchflower being particularly vicious. Marquitos, the centre-half was the worst culprit though, and the Dutch referee Leo Horn was far too lenient with the Madrid players. There really seemed no need for the Spaniards to use such foul and intimidating methods, however their attitude was a mark of respect for it shown just how much they feared United."

The Daily Mail's Eric Thompson concentrated more on the *Madrilenos* shining lights. "This Madrid forward line is full of world class players. Di Stefano strolling through the game with a master's confidence, could not be curbed by Colman. Gento had a razor-edge of speed that worried Foulkes and Kopa kept flashing into sparkling solos."

The last quarter of the contest had shown the tie was not yet fully over, and Busby knew that an early goal at Old Trafford for his team then all bets would be off. Manchester United had survived to fight another day. With their ground ready to hold a European match under floodlights for the first time and 65,000 Mancunians roaring them on,

the possibility of a footballing miracle still existed. The vast majority of the travelling British press seemed to believe that these Spanish ''Fancy dans'' would crumble and United would run riot against them, as they did Athletic Bilbao. Insular to the point of ignorant many English journalists had still failed to grasp just what Busby's side was up against. With baited-breath Manchester now awaited the arrival of the *Madrilenos*. Although they were still rather uncertain of what was actually coming their way. Special? Yes undoubtedly, but unbeatable? Not against their boys in red. Little did Mancunians understand there was indeed a storm coming.
A white storm...

CHAPTER NINE
WHITE ANGELS WITH DIRTY FACES

A swift, brace of victories swiftly followed events in Madrid.
A 2-0 away win over Luton at Kenilworth Road courtesy of a Tommy Taylor double, and a 3-1 victory against Burnley at Turf Moor, a brilliant Liam Whelan hat-trick meant only two more points were now required to clinch Manchester United the First Division title. On Easter Saturday, 20th April 1956, at Old Trafford, with a 58,725 crowd roaring them on the Busby Babes clinched a second, successive championship beating Sunderland 4-0. Two more goals from Liam Whelan and late strikes from Duncan Edwards and Tommy Taylor fired the reds to glory. All thoughts could now be focused on Real Madrid in just five days' time. In the week leading up to the tie, Granada television bowed to massive public pressure to show the full match live, after initially announcing they were only going to provide highlights. This came after the BBC also shown an interest to screen it. Suddenly, Granada moved into gear! They would use three cameras, one behind each goal and another at the side. The interest for the game was incredible. Everybody wanted to be there, the hottest ticket in England. In preparation United had already done a Floodlights test-run previously on 23rd March, in a midweek game against a Bolton Wanderers side playing in an all-white kit acting out the roles of Real Madrid, whilst United were in the all-red kit, used in the *Bernabeu*. Again to be worn for the second-leg. Over 60,000 filled Old Trafford with a further 15,000 locked outside. Walking to the game from miles around, up Warwick Road or across the swing-bridge from the Dirty Old Town, seeing the ground bathed in the hazy, magical glare of the floodlight pylons. In that period Bolton were one of the very few teams to have Manchester United's number, and it proved so again with them spoiling the party winning 2-0. The same score they had beaten United at Burnden Park earlier on in the season.

With a courtesy so typical of the man Matt Busby stood with pipe and trilby in hand at Ringway airport to welcome the great Real Madrid to Manchester. First to greet him was President Santiago Bernabeu. The two men shared a warm embrace with a smiling Bernabeu telling reporters: "It is wonderful to be in Manchester and to see my great friend Matt Busby again." On spotting the United manager every Real Madrid player made a point of coming over to shake his hand. Despite a stormy first-leg a huge respect had already developed between the two clubs. One that would show itself many times throughout the years. However, despite the blossoming, friendly relationship only one team could progress and come kick-off at Old Trafford, Manchester United and Real Madrid were set to go for each other's throat with a real vengeance to win the tie.

"Real Madrid will face hell at Old Trafford!" claimed Roger Byrne, clearly attempting to light a fire under the second-leg. Whereas no real bad blood existed between the two teams, there were many United supporters bitter over what they saw as bad sporting behaviour in the *Bernabeu*. The treatment of Tommy Taylor, the disallowed penalty regarding Johnny Berry. Back at Ringway Airport there was one more than any other who the hundreds of autograph hunters craved for amongst the Real Madrid party. Alfredo Di Stefano found himself besieged by excited schoolboys and football supporters all equally desperate to add the *Blond Arrow's* to their collections. Hardly known for his patience, Di Stefano wearing a classy Peaky Blinders style cap coolly dressed in a beige jacket, a striped shirt with a white handkerchief in his jacket pocket. He appeared the epitome of class and showing another side to his character, Di Stefano stood smiling to cut a surprisingly, obliging figure signing autographs. Finally, with everyone satisfied, Madrid's finest re-joined his *compadres* as they made their way to a waiting coach.

To escape the rising tension sweeping across Manchester, Matt Busby again took his team away to stay at the Norbreck Hydro hotel in Blackpool for a few days. There once more as against Bilbao, on the wide-open beaches with the wind biting in their faces off the North Sea, they would train and make final preparations for the upcoming, all or nothing showdown against the *Madrilenos*. Manchester United stood on the verge of creating footballing history. With the league title safely wrapped up and a place in the FA Cup final versus Aston Villa assured, a unique footballing treble lay in their sights, if they could overcome Real Madrid's two goal first-leg advantage. There was talk elsewhere of a domestic fixture pile-up threatening the treble, but Matt Busby had a plan! Following a 2-0 victory over Burnley at Old Trafford, on Easter Monday, the reds had by then played four games in eight days. Fortunately, with the title wrapped and despite even more protests from Mr Hardaker, Busby rested nine of his players to ensure their fitness for the Real second-leg. (To the fury of Burnley chairman Bob Lord, but much more later.) The team versus Burnley was Wood, Foulkes, Greaves, Goodwin, Cope, McGuinness, Webster, Doherty, Dawson, Viollet and Scanlon. All good enough to play for any other team in the First Division, and yet they were happy to stay and fight for a place at Old Trafford. This saying everything about the ''All for one and one for all'' atmosphere Busby and Murphy had created at United.

The Spaniards were afoot at shenanigans!

Deeply worried at how David Pegg had ripped apart their full-back Jose Becerril in the final twenty-minutes at the *Bernabeu*, Madrid officials acted swiftly and ''loaned'' from Real Zaragoza, the speedy Brazilian defender Manuel Torres. This was not so much breaking the rules but stretching them beyond their limits, and it showed the level of concern about Pegg's pace and skill. On being informed of this move Matt Busby felt aggrieved at what he considered unfair gamesmanship by the Spaniards. Busby letting it be known privately he was considering asking Preston North End if he could borrow Tom Finney and put him in a red shirt for the evening! Whether Busby was truly serious remains debatable, but the manner in which the visitors had hastily contracted Torres to just a six month loan meant that Real Madrid knew this semi-final remained in the melting pot with serious work still to be done. United had petrified them for that last twenty-minutes at the *Bernabeu,* none more so than David Pegg, and he needed to be dealt with. Speaking years later Torres would say he earned more money during that short spell at Real Madrid than in the entire rest of his playing career!

Come match day, Manchester was awash with excitement. An April morning tinged with Spring, a bright sunshine and a brisk cold wind. It was a good day to be alive especially when Real Madrid were in town. Tickets had gone on sale the previous Easter Sunday and swiftly sold out. A huge sigh of relief was felt by many when Tommy Taylor declared his full fitness. Taylor had fully recovered from a thigh knock and was set to resume his duel against the Spaniards. From Manchester United's line up in the *Bernabeu* there would be only one change. An injury to forward Dennis Viollet had let in yet another Busby Babe, Bobby Charlton to be unleashed upon the *Madrilenos*. After watching with his own eyes from the stand in the first-leg, Charlton would now be given the opportunity to share the same pitch. As for tactics to curtail Real Madrid's explosive wide men, Matt Busby and Jimmy Murphy discussed the possibility of an offside trap. However, they were fully aware that the merest error would leave United susceptible to the fearsome acceleration of Kopa and Gento and thought it best to leave well alone. Besides, to concentrate their player's minds solely on Real's wingers may just edge the door open for the likes of the deadly Hector Rial. Far more worryingly the terrifying Alfredo himself. Instead, in a ploy of sound practice the players were instructed to play their normal game. The aged old rules applied. Pass to a red shirt, keep the ball moving, do not lose possession or concentration, for if so Madrid would punish them severely. Chances would arise for United and have to be taken, but they could ill afford to concede another goal.

Further controversy arose on the morning of the match when the Daily Mirror had pictures showing the Old Trafford sprinklers at full force gushing onto the pitch. Under Matt Busby's orders the groundsman was told to flood the surface in order to make it difficult for Real's fleet-footed artisans. Horrified at such scenes Madrid officials raced to the ground demanding they immediately be switched off, otherwise Real would refuse to play. As pools of water gathered across the grass and with Busby not present, it was left to the United

Club Secretary Walter Crickmer to face the irate Spaniards. On being informed by phone of their threat to go home the United manager agreed to turn off the taps. The *Madrilenos* were rattled, Busby's mind games had worked. Now it was down to his players.

As kick off approached 65,000 made their way to Old Trafford, many expectant, some pensive. Across the swing bridge that bestrode the Ship Canal the red hordes swarmed. They knew well of the quality of this Madrid team, but memories of that unforgettable night against Athletic Bilbao still shone bright. Their team had already put one magnificent Spanish team to the sword, so why not dream of miracles? Yet, there was those Mancunians who truly knew their football, who recognised the enormous task that lay ahead. To overcome a two goal deficit against Real Madrid would prove the Busby Babes greatest test and indeed the manager's since he first arrived twelve years previous. Wearing a trilby and clutching a burnt down cigarette. Not much had changed there!

The Teams.

Manchester United. Wood, Foukes, Byrne, Colman, Jones, Edwards, Berry, Whelan, Taylor, Charlton and Pegg.

Real Madrid. Alonso, Torres, Lesmes, Munoz, Marquitos, Zarraga, Kopa, Mateos, Di Stefano, Rial and Gento.

Wednesday 25th April 1957.

In the late Mancunian sunshine, on a balmy April evening at an Old Trafford soon to be swamped in floodlit dreams, the *Madrileno* Captain Miguel Munoz led out the legendary Real Madrid. Alongside Munoz, strode Manchester United fronted by Roger Byrne. The heavenly white shirts of Real against the devil red of United. An electricity sizzled through the Mancunian Spring air. Though hardly statuesque when compared to the grandiose surroundings of the *Bernabeu*, for atmosphere and noise Old Trafford took some beating. It throbbed and heaved, the packed terraces roaring their support for the home team. Amongst the local masses there stood a small, but raucous band of travelling Madrid fans holding a banner high with the words **HALA MADRID** etched upon it. Whilst on the touchline two Spanish senorita's dressed in traditional flamenco costume walked along, smiling and waving at the crowd, trying hard to ignore the wolf whistling and the many suggestions and invitations being shouted in their direction from an enthusiastic, Mancunian audience! The wonderful sight of a clearly bursting Duncan Edwards jumping up and down, full of nervous energy. Raging once more for the game to start and have another crack at these alleged, invincible Spaniards, only helped to create a sense of hope amongst home supporters. The bitter memory of waging a losing fight against insurmountable waves of blurry, white shadows, ghosts swarming around him in the *Bernabeu* left Edwards frustrated. Now, on home soil it was expected he would be operating further forward. The opportunity to show his true worth guiding United into the final dawned and if such a scenario was to occur Duncan Edwards would have to play the game of his young life. Hard to believe the Dudley boy was still only twenty years old.

As Old Trafford held a collective breath Manchester United kicked off. Seemingly caught up in the occasion and the torrid atmosphere they forgot their manager's instructions to begin with a little caution, and roared straight away onto the attack. Tommy Taylor renewed personal acquaintances with Manuel Marquitos, as the two clashed early, this time Marquitos ending up in a heap. Immediately, the Madrid players surrounded Taylor who pleaded innocence, but it was clear the lad from Barnsley was not about to accept the treatment handed out to him in Madrid. Here on his own patch it would be no holds barred. Tommy was going to war! A furious Marquitos rose off the floor giving Taylor a glance that suggested revenge would not be too long away. The initial stages saw United pressing constantly. From a Liam Whelan cross into the Madrid penalty area, Alonso rushed out to punch the ball off Taylor's head. As the home side pinned back their esteemed visitors placing them under intense pressure, it appeared that Madrid could well go the same way as

Bilbao, but with Marquitos and his *compadres* competing for every ball as if their lives depended on the outcome they held firm. Watching on from the side-lines Matt Busby and Jimmy Murphy appeared hypnotised by what was happening on the pitch. Desperate for a breakthrough, but also with one wary eye always on Madrid counter-attacks. Then, it happened. A loose ball from a United shirt was latched onto by Francisco Gento. His fiendish acceleration saw him hurtle clear into the home half before finally being brought to earth by a last ditch Roger Byrne tackle. This lightning burst by Gento brought a gasp from the crowd. The sheer speed off the mark causing disbelief. Madrid were on the move. Rial's incisive through pass found Di Stefano on the edge of the box, who turned and cracked a fierce drive that Wood was forced to tip over the bar. Real came again and with United retreating, Gento exploded into the penalty area, but when about to pull the trigger found himself caught by a thunderous, Edwards' challenge. Busby now watched on anxiously, his eyes falling with dread on one figure. The *Blond Arrow* had been biding his time and then to the United manager's horror he finally made his move. On twenty-three minutes disaster struck for the Red Devils. Di Stefano swooped onto the ball and swept forward. His swift pass released Raymonde Kopa. He raced clear before shooting low past Wood from seven yards, and handing the Spaniards a three-goal aggregate lead. Old Trafford was stunned, the two Spanish *senoritas* who pre-match had so entertained the whistling, expectant crowds now danced along on the touchline watched by thousands of forlorn faces. Suddenly, it was fiesta time! Madrid turned on the style, not simply passing the ball, but cajoling and caressing it. Their arrogance and worrying ease in doing so suggested a total confidence in being able to put United away whenever the mood required. Di Stefano was at their very heart pulling the strings and conducting the orchestra. The *Madrilenos* were putting on a show for their Mancunian hosts. Letting them know in no uncertain terms that the team who plied their sumptuous talents at the *Estadio Bernabeu*, stood on a pedestal of one. Shortly before half-time it was deservedly 2-0. The electrifying Gento careered down the wing before crossing for Hector Rial to

smash home past Wood, surely booking Real Madrid's second, consecutive European Cup final appearance. In later years records would show that Rial was actually forty-years old that night, not the stated thirty as Madrid officials when they originally signed him had been informed! The realisation that United's dream was over lay etched on Matt Busby's face. His team although still bravely battling away had been outclassed by superior opponents. Sensing blood Real went in search of a killer third to end United's challenge. Di Stefano demanded possession off his defenders and away he soared! A rapier one-two with Rial before a pass inside to Gento. He skipped away from Bill Foulkes before returning the ball back to the grand Argentinian. Alone he stood in the centre-circle momentarily statuesque. As if suggesting: "Here I am. You have watched me on *Pathe* news, read the stories, seen the pictures and been told of the rumours. Now you have seen it with your own eyes!"
Alfredo Di Stefano had come to Manchester.

Half-time arrived like a fire engine at the scene of a raging blaze for Manchester United. There was huge applause from the terraces fully appreciating the efforts of their own team, but also the audacious, bravura display of the rampaging Spaniards. One player more than any other. Don Alfredo! The Mancunians had now seen in the flesh this wonder called Real Madrid. Realising it was something both terrifying and spellbinding. They came expecting something special and Di Stefano, Gento, Kopa and Rial had not let them down.
In the home dressing room Busby praised his players for their determination, insisting they were still in the tie. He told them: "Keep playing, keep passing the ball and you will get your rewards." Now four down on aggregate he wished only for them to save the match, and in doing so give the *Madrilenos* a reminder that come the following season Manchester United would again be the team to beat. Determined not to be humiliated on home turf United re-appeared in the second-half inspired. Suddenly, Madrid found themselves on the back foot, as Eddie Colman, Liam Whelan and their first-leg tormentor David Pegg began to attack from wide positions. White

shirts lashed out to stem the all red tide, now it was the Spaniards who were rattled, boots flew high! Marquitos, Munoz and Zarraga took no prisoners though even such a mean and combative trio of hatchet men found themselves unable to combat the colossus that was Duncan Edwards, as he wrestled control almost single-handedly back off what appeared only a brief time before, the impregnable *Madrilenos*. Repeatedly Edwards powered across the halfway line leaving in his wake tumbling bodies. With the crowd reaching fever pitch the roof almost came off Old Trafford on sixty-one minutes when the home side pulled a goal back. A flying David Pegg who was treating the Madrid ringer Torres with the same contempt and ease in which he fired past Becerril in the first-leg raced forward. From a Pegg cross, Tommy Taylor raced between two defenders and under huge pressure bundled a shot onto the Madrid post. As groans engulfed the stadium the ball fell loose but good fortune shone on Irishman Liam Whelan, who from three yards couldn't miss. 1-2! Three down on aggregate and still thirty-minutes left to play. Echoes of Bilbao came flooding back into the minds of the home faithful. Manchester rocked, surely their boys could not do it again? Real were frantic! The first-half poise and beauty had vanished to be replaced by a grim determination and when necessary, an utter ruthlessness to survive this Manchester onslaught. As the crowd bayed for an equaliser white shirts began falling to the turf with alarming regularity. Zarraga, though immense throughout blotted his copybook when he collapsed in a heap after an alleged foul from Tommy Taylor, who looked on in disgust at the Spaniard's play-acting. An outraged home support screamed in derision. All good feelings towards the foreigners had now disappeared as a *Madrileno* huddle surrounded the referee demanding Taylor's expulsion. Tempers ran high. With the final to be played in the *Estadio Bernabeu*, the stakes for the Real Players were huge. Their desire not to succumb meant they felt all foul means were justified, but it hardly dignified their reputation. Howls continued from the terraces as the Spaniards lashed out at anything in red that dared to go by them. The clock for United seemed to be on fast forward, for Madrid, time froze. The battle raged on! From fully twenty-five yards Edwards thundered in a shot, only to see Alonso save magnificently with a flying leap. Tempers flared once more when on a rare foray forward Rial attempted to stop Ray Wood taking a quick kick, and was barged to the floor for his troubles by an angry United goalkeeper. Five-minutes remained when Real Madrid cracked again. It was the young lad so taken by Di Stefano in the first-leg, Bobby Charlton, who levelled with a close range effort setting up a torrid climax to what had been a remarkable evening. Intent on just surviving the remaining moments Real attempted to play keep-ball, but now thirsting for a monumental winner, United, inspired by the still, rampaging Edwards repeatedly won the ball back to continue attacking. Though requiring two more goals the reds refused to give up, and when the Madrid players attempted to time waste tempers flared on both sides. Again, it was Pegg cutting in with the ball clashing with Torres, who then in Oscar winning style collapsed as if shot by a sniper from the stand! Players crowded around the apparently, unconscious defender. The Spaniards were intent on keeping him lying on the ground, whilst the United players tried to push Torres off the pitch so they could carry on with the game. Knowing time was short home Captain Roger Byrne was in no mood for such antics and took it upon himself to drag Torres back to his feet. However, he swiftly found himself confronted by irate Madrid players who lifted their fallen *compadre* away to lay him back on the pitch! White angels with dirty faces! Enter Duncan Edwards. Angered by the cheating tactics of his opponents, he simply stormed through a host of *Madrilenos* and picked up Torres before placing him back over the touchline! A melee followed before calm was finally restored and the final seconds were played out with United still going for more goals at the final whistle. Honours ended even but the battle had been won overall by an exhausted Real Madrid.

A saddened, but proud Matt Busby spoke in glowing terms of his team in the bitter aftermath of their European Cup exit. "Real Madrid beat Manchester United because a great experienced side will always triumph over a great inexperienced side. Their average age is twenty-eight whilst ours is just twenty-one. I still believe my boys possess the potential to beat Real Madrid in a short time. If not next year, then, the one after. Manchester United are coming, make no mistake about that.'' Francisco Gento was later glowing in his appraisal of their opponents. ''For us, the semi-final against Manchester United was the final. They were a powerful and difficult team, and we were very impressed with Tommy Taylor. And like all British teams they played right until the end of the match. All United needed was more experience.''

Donny Davies of the Manchester Guardian gave a lovely, summing up. ''Real Madrid made themselves the toast of two hemispheres and Manchester United, the toast of all English speaking people when they drew 2-2 at Old Trafford tonight, in the semi-finals of the European Cup. After this bedlam Real Madrid will hold no terrors for United.'' A sad note to an unforgettable occasion occurred when United supporters, still irate at the time-wasting antics of the Spaniards in the desperate last twenty-minutes hurled objects at the visitor's coach as it departed Old Trafford. Frustrations overflowed on a night when emotions and anger came to the fore.

As in Madrid, a wonderful banquet was held afterwards in which both teams put aside all animosity to enjoy a fine evening of toasts and goodwill speeches. Away from the dignitaries opposing players mixed happily. Again, Matt Busby was good-naturedly harassed by Real stars to become their coach, much to the annoyance of the incumbent, an indignant Jose Villalonga! Later in the night when the party was in full swing, Don Santiago Bernabeu approached the United manager saying to him: ''If you come to Spain I will make it heaven on earth for you. You will have untold riches that you can only dream of.'' Busby listened intently and promised the Real President he would write soon with an answer. After speaking the matter over with his family there could be only one reply. Two weeks later, a letter arrived on Bernabeu's desk in Madrid from Matt Busby thanking him for the kind offer. ''But my heaven on earth exists right here in Manchester.'' Don Santiago understood that due to the quality and age of their squad Manchester United would pose the greatest threat to Real's European crown. Future investment in his own team was inevitable, including bids for United players to undermine the progress of what was occurring at Old Trafford. Bobby Charlton and Tommy Taylor just two of those being discussed by the Madrid hierarchy. Whether they could ever be prised away from Busby's paternal grasp remained dubious, but the sheer glamour and mystique of Madrid meant such moves could never be ruled out. For to imagine a United team in just two years' time with the likes of Duncan Edwards, Eddie Colman, Bobby Charlton, Tommy Taylor and Liam Whelan performing in Europe with a maturity that came through experience, as spoken of by Gento, could only leave the Madrid supremo shaking with dread. Sadly, fate would decree otherwise.

In the *Bernabeu* afternoon sunshine, on 30th May 1957, a delirious 130,000 home crowd roared with joy as Real Madrid retained their coveted crown with a convincing 2-0 victory over Fiorentina. The defensively-minded Italians came with little desire to attack and fought a negative rearguard action, which for seventy-minutes frustrated the Madrid attackers. It resembled a street fight with the Italians determined to survive by all means, both legal and not. Finally, a stroke of luck for the Spaniards when referee Leo Horn, (Him again!) to the fury of the Italians, deemed a trip by Fiorentina defender Ardico Magnini on Enrique Mateos a penalty. Even though the linesman had already flagged him offside. Up stepped Alfredo Di Stefano to smash a well-driven shot past Viola goalkeeper Guiliano Sarti. Forced for the first time in the contest to step forward in search of an equaliser, Fiorentina were caught on the break, when a sublime through pass by Raymonde Kopa set Francisco Gento free. Off he soared, *El Motorcycle* to beat Sarti with a delicate chip and win for Real Madrid a second European Cup. A fiesta mood descended on the *Bernabeu*! So, to the presentation where to hand the Captain Miguel Munoz the trophy was one of Real's most fanatical followers. General Franco. An uneasy sight for many in Spain, Franco had attached himself to *Madrileno* success like fleas to a dead dog. For their efforts, an ecstatic Santiago Bernabeu paid each player their huge, cash bonus. His dreams of a Madrid dynasty were already bearing fruit. The future looked white. The future looked Real.

As for the Red Devils?
Speaking on the eve of the 1957 FA Cup against Aston Villa, Matt Busby claimed: "We shall not fail for the want of trying. Now that the strain of this hectic season is almost over, and while victory is our crowning ambition, I will be proud of my team come what may." Sadly, the double turned to dust. The season ended in deep disappointment with United going down 2-1 against the underdogs of Villa. A game now etched in cup folklore for the Irish winger Peter McParland's airborne, ferocious challenge on Ray Wood, which left him flat on the ground with blood trickling down his face. United players accusing the Aston Villa man of having head butting Wood. For a moment it appeared Duncan Edwards was set to lay McParland out for the brutal attack on his keeper, but cooler heads prevailed and team mates swiftly pulled him away. Wood's cheek bone had been fractured causing him to leave the pitch concussed after just six-minutes, and Jackie Blanchflower having to take over in goal. A seething Wilf McGuinness was watching from the stand and later called the challenge: "Diabolical." With almost the entire game left to play United had just the ten men. The Busby Babes playing in a change strip of all white with red trimmings reorganised and come half-time it remained goalless. Wood returned out of position for nuisance value only out wide on the right-wing, but clearly was a passenger. Busby later admitting: "He should never have come out for the second-half at all." Adding insult to injury McParland went on to score twice before a late Tommy Taylor header from a Duncan Edwards corner gave United some scant hope, but in the end Wembley defeat left a sour taste in Mancunian mouths. McParland had got two goals and a goalkeeper to win Villa the cup. Bill Foulkes later admitting: "I went after an opponent that day with the intention of nailing him." No need to guess who he was talking about. Later that evening it was a very sombre, sober occasion at United's

post-Cup Final party at their hotel. Nobody was in the mood to celebrate. The Daily Mirror's Frank Taylor did manage to grab a few words off the normally cheerful Eddie Colman. Even he was down that night but tried to stay positive. ''That's football Frank. Never mind, we are good enough to come to Wembley next year for the cup.'' They would indeed return, sadly, Eddie would not. Yet even though the much talked-up treble had gone up in smoke, Matt Busby and Jimmy Murphy had every reason to feel optimistic for the upcoming 1957-58 season. Their ripe apples would be a year older, more wiser and the future for Manchester United promised, to quote President Santiago Bernabeu's words when attempting to whisk away Matt Busby to Madrid. ''Untold riches.'' When asked by a journalist about how he intended to keep United at the top, Matt Busby remarked: ''With our youth teams talented enough to make a monopoly of the FA Youth Cup for five years on the run, there is no reason why Manchester United should not remain in the forefront of English and European soccer for at least another ten years.''
Busby was also asked around that period by Geoffrey Green of The Times. Just what he felt he had done for football and Manchester United? ''The time to judge me is when I'm at the bottom.'' It was coming. The best made plans helpless against fate's cruel hand. So, once empty, the floodlights were switched off and Old Trafford became bathed in darkness. Little was anyone to know such black shadows would soon engulf Manchester United in a manner few could ever have imagined.

CHAPTER TEN
IN DUBLIN'S FAIR CITY

"In Dublin's fair city" the home of fanatical Manchester United support. "Where the girls are so pretty" Liam 'Billy' Whelan came home. On Wednesday 25th September 1957, the League of Ireland champions Shamrock Rovers welcomed the English champions Manchester United to Dalymount Park, for the first of a two-legged European Cup preliminary round, in front of a sell-out 46,000 crowd. It was a huge occasion, for the famous Busby Babes were only ever seen by most Irish people on the *Pathe News* reels at the cinemas. Now, finally, they could be witnessed by Dubliners and others from afar with their own eyes. In the match programme Shamrock chairman Joseph Cunningham paid tribute to their much heralded opponents. "This evening it is my privilege and pleasure on the behalf of my Co-Directors, to extend Manchester United a sincere and hearty welcome to Dublin. To the men who have helped to put this team on the field-Directors, Manager, Coach, Trainer, Scouts, etc. We owe a debt. In this connection I sincerely suggest that when the Manchester United team make their appearance on the field of play tonight we would like them to know that the welcome is not only a salute to a great team, but also a salute to their backroom boys, who have moulded the team to its present greatness."

Two months previous the draw for the European Cup took place in Paris, and Cunningham represented Shamrock Rovers there. He remembered it well. 'I was sitting next to Matt Busby and we were both wondering what far off places we'd have to visit, for it was an open draw. Then, Sir George Graham of Scotland from UEFA pulled the first name out. "Shamrock Rovers!" That left me gasping and while I was getting my breath back he then read out, "Manchester United!" Well, Matt Busby looked at me and we beamed at each other, for it was just what the doctor ordered for both clubs."

Manchester United stayed at their favourite hotel in the Republic, the International in Bray. The self-acclaimed "Gateway to the Garden of

Ireland''. The United lads getting some much welcome fresh sea air on the coast before travelling to Dublin to take on Shamrock Rovers. Come match day, the capital was bubbling with excitement at the thought of their own boys taking on the legendary Busby Babes from across the Irish Sea in Manchester. People had travelled from every county, and the Rover's ticket office were overwhelmed. They had never known anything like it. Demand was incredulous! Tickets were priced at £1 for a seat in the stand, a crown for the reserved terrace, and a half-crown for the open standing, but as the match grew ever closer they were going for five times their normal value.

Manchester United were taking no chances regarding their Irish hosts. Matt Busby himself flew over beforehand on a scouting mission. This was a competition that meant so much to Busby and he didn't want any nasty surprises. He knew Rovers were not to be taken lightly. Writing in his column for the Evening Chronicle newspaper, he made it clear there was profound respect at Old Trafford for Shamrock Rovers. Busby reminded the Chronicle readers what occurred when the League of England team played their equivalents from Ireland, the previous year. The League of Ireland with seven Shamrock Rovers players in the line-up gave their England counterparts containing four United stars-Roger Byrne, Duncan Edwards, Tommy Taylor and Dennis Viollet, a real fright in a game that ended 3-3. Busby was adamant United could ill afford to underestimate Shamrock Rovers. ''Such an upset could happen again unless we play our very best football.'' This game meant an awful lot to many people, but perhaps more so to the lad who was coming home wearing a red shirt. Liam ''Billy'' Whelan. In 1953, on first arriving in Manchester, the shy young Dubliner was asked his name by fellow Irishman, the former United Captain, the great Johnny Carey. ''Liam Whelan sir,'' replied the 18-year-old, a tall, gangling young man who was an awful long way from home. ''Oh, Liam is it?'' smiled Carey. ''Well, hold on to it lad, because they are sure to try and take it away from you in this city!'' So, it was to most Mancunians, he swiftly became Billy Whelan! ''I called him William after his grandfather, my father,'' said

Liam's mother Elizabeth. "But my husband did not want him to be called William, so we settled for the Irish version of Liam."
Liam Whelan arrived back in Dublin with Manchester United, feeling he had a point to prove. Many of the home grown critics were always far too quick to hammer one of their own, rather than praise a boy who played for Home Farm and was born at number 28n St.Attracta Road, in the shadows of Dalymount Park. There were sceptics in the Irish press who were scathing towards him. His, modest record in the Irish green jersey meant that Whelan was depicted in certain quarters as someone who still had it all to prove. Was he really worthy of all the hype that came from across the water? In their case absence made the heart grow colder, as they only really saw Whelan play when he turned out for the Republic a meagre four times. The reason being the Football Association of Ireland decreed any Irishman picked by his club on the Saturday could not be selected the following day. Back in the fifties this now seemingly, crazy notion was a common occurrence, thus restricting Whelan's appearances in the green shirt of his nation. In all honesty, when he did play Whelan never really did himself justice. Apart from one time. A memorable game that he starred in against England on 19th May 1957. A World Cup qualifier where the English needed just a point to qualify for the 1958 World Cup finals in Sweden the follow year. However, after just three-minutes the Sheffield United winger Alf Ringstead put the Republic ahead. It was only a last minute header equaliser from Bristol City John Atyeo that saved England seeing them through. Alongside two magnificent footballers in Preston's Tom Finney and Fulham's Johnny Haynes, there was also four Manchester United player in the England team that day. Pegg, Taylor, Byrne and Edwards. Liam Whelan's speciality/calling card even, was the nutmeg. A trick that at times could prove painful if performed on the wrong player. Against the English Whelan was outstanding throughout. Even at one stage having the temerity to produce his party piece on his big mate Duncan Edwards. "Do that again chief," snarled Duncan, "And you're in for it!" Not being able to help himself Whelan did so and thirty seconds later Edwards smashed him, thereby incensing the Dublin crowd and

making them intent on a "Big Dunc" lynching! Come full-time all was forgotten and forgiven as the two shared a handshake and a laugh!

The Teams.

Manchester United. Wood, Foulkes, Byrne, Goodwin, Blanchflower, Edwards, Berry, Whelan, Taylor T, Viollet and Pegg.

Shamrock Rovers. Darcy, Burke, Mackey, Nolan, Keogh, Hennessey, Peyton, Ambrose, Hamilton, Coad and Tuohy.

Due to no floodlights at Dalymount Park, it was a late tea time kick-off. So, in the midst of a roaring, howling gale blowing across the ground, Shamrock Rovers and Manchester United began and for the first half-hour the Irish champions held their own. It was only when Tommy Taylor struck shortly before half-time, that come the second period United went goal crazy. At their heart creating mayhem and giving a command performance was inevitably Liam "Billy" Whelan. Scoring twice himself, one a stunning header. "Liam had everything," said Bobby Charlton. "Except an extra bit of pace." The other goals came courtesy of Johnny Berry, David Pegg and Taylor once more, saw the game finish 6-0 for the visitors, although Shamrock Rover, despite being well beaten were by no means disgraced. It simply came down to the superior class and fitness of the English champions. None more so than Whelan who had more than made his point to the doubting Thomas's amongst the Irish newspaper hacks. The Shamrock Rovers defender Gerry Mackey's recollection of the game was sort and succinct. "We ran ourselves into the ground. They scored three of their goals when we just couldn't stand up anymore!" The Rovers forward Tommy Hamilton was a former United youth player, but became so bad with homesickness, Busby released him from his contract and let Hamilton return home. That day in Dublin, he was left in awe by Duncan Edwards. "A great player, Two great feet, a fantastic build. He could play cross-field

passes and he could dribble with the ball too. And remember, he was just twenty, going on twenty-one.'' That same evening at a dinner arranged for both teams at the Gresham Hotel, Manchester United presented all the Shamrock Rovers players with travel clocks. Hamilton and the goalkeeper Eamonn D'arcy treasured these mementos and D'arcy was impressed with just how humble the visitors were that evening. So different to their demeanour when on the pitch in that red shirt. ''The strange thing was when you saw all these guys in suits, they were just one of us. Normal! Everyone on the pitch would say: ''Duncan Edwards, what a huge fella!'' But when you actually see him in his regular clothes it was different. You see, it's that illusion of presence that you have on the park.'' The visiting English press pack were wholesome in praise of Busby's team and particularly Liam Whelan. The News Chronicle's Frank Taylor wrote: ''Bill Whelan, the smiling Irishman born just down the road, led this scientific slaughter of Shamrock Rovers' European hopes.''
The Daily Herald's George Follows called it: ''An act of revenge for Whelan in response to local criticism.'' Whilst the vibrant wordsmith from the Daily Express, Henry Rose, was far more defensive and wrote highly of Shamrock Rovers. ''Sounds like a walk-over doesn't it? Sounds like taking candy from a child doesn't it? Take it from me. It was nothing of the kind. Bravo, Shamrock Rovers. You have nothing to reproach yourself for. Better teams have wilted under this smashing, crashing dreadnought!'' Henry on top form!

CHAPTER ELEVEN
THE MISSING COAT HANGER

The Teams.
Manchester United. Wood, Foulkes, Byrne, Colman, Jones M, McGuinness, Berry, Webster, Taylor T, Viollet and Pegg.

Shamrock Rovers. Darcy, Burke, Mackey, Nolan, Keogh, Coad, McCann, Peyton, Ambrose, Hamilton and Tuohy.

Old Trafford. Wednesday 2nd October 1957. Come the second-leg, Rovers did themselves proud going down only 3-2 in a closely fought match, and received a standing ovation from the 33,754 crowd at the final whistle. It was a memorable night for the visitors both on and off the pitch. The Rover's keeper Eamonn D'arcy again: ''When we went into the away dressing room there were coat-hangers which for us was being treated like royalty, a little simple thing like that. They were telling me afterwards that some team played there once and a fella took his with him. His club got an official letter in the post from Manchester United saying player number seven's coat-hanger was missing and they wanted them to send it back!'' The goalkeeper D'arcy, by far the man of the match. He was caught in an early United blitz saving his team repeatedly. The reds were two up at half-time through Dennis Viollet and David Pegg, but it really could have been double figure such was the domination. Then shortly into the second period Rovers grabbed one back! The goal scored by Jimmy ''Maxi'' McCann, dropped for the first-leg was even applauded by United fans. Five-minutes later Viollet struck again, only for the visitors to show their fighting spirit, when Tommy Hamilton shot past Ray Wood making it 3-2. Amongst the crowd was a huge visiting contingent who were delighted with their lad's performance. It could even have been better for them in the dying moments when Hamilton burst through again looking likely to grab an astonishing equaliser on the night. Sadly for Hamilton and his team, Ray Wood saved brilliantly to save United's blushes. The game ended, it had been a wonderfully, sporting occasion under the Old Trafford floodlights. Returning to Dublin with pride restored after their home mauling, the Shamrock players must have felt there was a real possibility they had been eliminated by a team who could easily go on to become European champions. Having by then played them twice, especially at Dalymount Park, when the Busby Babes exploded to hit their scintillating top form in the second-half. The talk being just a few of the continental teams, the champions Real Madrid, by far the best of them could prevent Manchester United winning the 1958 European Cup.

CHAPTER TWELVE
RIP ZAPOTOCKY

The Teams.
Manchester United. Wood, Foulkes, Byrne, Colman, Blanchflower, Edwards, Berry, Whelan, Taylor T, Webster and Pegg.

Dukla Prague. Pavlis, Jecny, Cadek, Novak, Pluskal, Masopust, Vacenovsky, Dvorak, Borovicka, Safranek and Dobai

Old Trafford. Wednesday 20th November 1957. Next up for Manchester United in the European Cup was the Czech champions (Army team) Dukla Prague, and a first trip behind the ominous *Iron Curtain* for the second-leg. First though the opening tie at home in front of an expectant 62,000 crowd. The original date for the game had to be postponed because of the death of the Czech President, 72-year-old Antonin Zapotocky. The Dukla Prague party ordered to return home at short notice. Finally, they were allowed to return and under floodlights before a full house, a 3-0 result flattered United, for the well-drilled, highly technical Czechs played some great football, but lacked any kind of punch near goal. Dukla defended resolutely and the reds had to be patient before finally on seventy-two minutes, to the huge relief of the home supporters, youngster Colin Webster broke the deadlock, followed shortly after by a Tommy Taylor header. Then in the dying moments David Pegg smashed a third from Liam Whelan's astute pass to seal the win. A victory more earned through higher stamina than skill as the Czechs faded badly towards the end. One highlight of the contest was a glorious midfield duel between Dukla's 27-year-old maestro, a left-half, ball player Josef Masopust, (Later to score the opening goal in the 1962 World Cup final and named by Pele, as one of the greatest players of all-time).

And United's own heartbeat, Duncan Edwards. Theirs' was truly a battle royal that ended on equal terms. Unlike the scoreline.

CHAPTER THIRTEEN
FOG BOUND

For the return in Czechoslovakia, played at the Prague Army Stadium, on Wednesday 4th December 1957, 35,000 mostly khaki-clad figures, a fanatical home crowd, overflowing with Czech soldiers on "Special duty" roared out as one for a footballing miracle.

The Teams.

Dukla Prague. Pavlis, Jecny, Cadek, Novak, Pluskal, Masopust, Safranek, Dvorak, Urban, Borovicka and Vacenovsky.

Manchester United. Wood, Foulkes, Byrne, Colman, Jones M, Edwards, Scanlon, Whelan, Taylor T, Webster and Pegg.

On a thawing pitch that soon resembled a mud patch, Manchester United found themselves scrapping for their European Cup lives as the Czechs went hell for leather to get back in the tie. After a nervous opening twenty-minutes, the visitors fell behind to a goal from the exceptionally talented, Prague midfielder, 24-year-old Milan Dvorak. Suddenly, the 3-0 result from Manchester no longer appeared as mountainous to scale, but far too many opportunities were squandered by the Czechs, and they were to ultimately pay the price. With Duncan Edwards operating magnificently alongside Mark Jones at centre-half, it was nothing short of a siege, but through solid defending and large doses of luck United prevailed. A late breakaway goal from Tommy Taylor, who fought a courageous lone battle all through the match was inexplicably ruled out by the German referee Werner Treichel. Seemingly to the visitors consternation for no good reason whatsoever? At the start of that season Taylor was a transfer target for Internazionale of Milan offering United a massive fee of

£65,000, plus a king's ransom in wages for the player. With the enormous money on the table Taylor's head was turned and he informed his manager that he wished to leave for Milan. Matt Busby was apoplectic with rage informing both Taylor and Inter officials that he was going absolutely nowhere. No deal. The Italians backed off. Back then there was no such thing of a downing of tools or sulking and though massively disappointed, Tommy Taylor simply got on with his day job. Busby said publicly to the newspapers: "Everything must take second place to the well-being of the club, and if that seems hard on the individual it is unfortunate, but necessary." The second-leg finished in a 1-0 defeat and it was a relieved and jubilant Manchester United team who celebrated once more reaching the European Cup quarter-finals. Outplayed, but sheer guts was what saw through in far-away Prague, Czechoslovakia. For the players once simply just a name on a map, but not anymore. This being the sheer beauty of European football as it offered the opportunity to open eyes and to view new horizons. Wonderful experiences, exploring magnificent foreign cities. A sidenote to the game was the trouble travelling English journalists had in sending their copy back home. They were not allowed to use the phones in their hotel room, instead watched by security guards the bemused hacks were forced to use one, specifically in the hallway. No doubt being listened into on the line just in case one was a spy! Oh, there were pitfalls, such as getting home. Again, the worrying problem returned of making it back in time to fulfil a League fixture on Saturday against Birmingham City, at Saint Andrews. The Football League Secretary Alan Hardaker would as ever be so keen to punish United if they failed in their obligations to play the game. When it came to the English champions Hardaker remained a bitter and vindictive figure. Busby's initial decision to defy and take flight in the European Cup still irked him. Hardaker wanted his pound of Mancunian flesh. The problem was all of England lay coveted in a dense, thick December fog and BEA's scheduled flight by Viscount did not take off on the Thursday. Manchester and London airport were fog bound. After some desperate telephone calls United managed to obtain just enough seats on a Dutch Airlines flight to Amsterdam. The nearest point clear of the shocking weather from where they could then travel on to England. Whilst en-route from there to Manchester, they were informed that the aircraft was being diverted to Liverpool and after a seemingly, never-ending journey, the Manchester United party finally arrived home at 11.00.pm on the Friday evening. As for the press pack? They unfortunately had to be left behind and make their own way by air from Prague to Zurich to Birmingham, and then British Railways to London Road Manchester. A sixteen hour trip undertaken on the Friday that would have done Manchester United no good at all. It was this struggle to get home that twisted Walter Crickmer and Matt Busby's hand to order a charter plane for the next hurdle in the competition. Another arduous route, a two thousand mile round trip to play Red Star Belgrade in Yugoslavia. For what happened coming home from Prague could never be allowed to happen again.

Against Birmingham City on the Saturday, after travelling to the Midlands in the morning after just a few hours' sleep, a weary Manchester United fought out a quite stunning 3-3 draw. Two from the returning Dennis Violet and one from Tommy Taylor earned United a point. History dictated this was always going to be a tough encounter because the reds had not won at Saint Andrews since 1929, but in reality the effects of the Prague trip was blatantly obvious to all, and Matt Busby realised they were definitely riding their luck. The exhausting schedule was showing just how difficult it was to aim for the heights of a League, FA and European Cup dream haul treble. To keep going to the end on the European fields, whilst trying to maintain the highest standards at home had already broken United the previous season, as they ended up with just one out of the three trophies they were chasing. Could the Busby Babes possible do it this time around?

CHAPTER FOURTEEN
INTO THE MIST

Old Trafford. Manchester United v Red Star Belgrade.
European Cup quarter final first-leg. Tuesday 14th January 1958.

The Teams.
Manchester United. Gregg, Foulkes, Byrne, Colman, Jones M,
Edwards, Morgan, Charlton, Taylor T, Viollet and Scanlon.

Red Star Belgrade. Beara, Tomic, Zekovic, Mitic, Spajic, Popovic,
Borozan, Sekularac, Toplak, Tasic and Kostic.

With Trafford Park's towering chimneys invisible to the human eye, and the fog rolling in off the Manchester canal, the Gypsy hid amongst it. On a memorable, freezing, rain-swept Old Trafford evening, with ghostly pockets of mist swirling eerily across the pitch, and players vanishing like spirits in the night, only then to reappear into sight, the French referee Monsieur Lequesne, raised the whistle to his mouth calling time on this first-leg of the European Cup quarter-final. A match close to be being called off earlier that day because of the horrendous conditions finally given the go ahead later in the afternoon. The drama then duly unfolded.
Manchester United 2-1 Red Star Belgrade.
A 60,000 crowd applauded loudly the mud splattered teams at the full-time whistle. A game despite played out in wretched circumstances was a fantastic contest between two evenly matched sides. Those present on the Old Trafford terraces were forced to try and watch through a dense, pea-soup Mancunian veil as United and Red Star went all out to win the opening leg. On a rock-hard pitch made worse by the slinging, heavy rain that turned parts of it into a murderous, slip-sliding surface, this was a tough, brutal, but always compelling watch. One that was being shown live on Granada

Television. A true rarity back in the fifties, although for any poor soul watching at home on a black and white set, it must have been a vexed, frustrating experience trying to follow what was actually happening! Walking off towards the tunnel the Red Star players, although beaten appeared quite satisfied with the result. The Yugoslav champions had more than given themselves a decent opportunity of retrieving the close deficit in Belgrade when backed by their own fanatical supporters. A pensive Matt Busby in his trilby clutching still tight on a burnt down cigarette appeared a man with a lot on his mind. It had been a testing and at times, harrowing evening against the brilliant Slavs that would give Busby much to think about before they clashed once more. The magical glare of Old Trafford's newly, erected floodlight pylons may only have caught passing glimpses of Red Star, but it was of sufficient quality for the United manager to realise this tie was far from over. Inspired by the prompting of their ball-playing genius, the little inside-forward, 21-year-old Dragoslav Sekularac, playing hide and seek with United defenders in the fog, the first-half especially saw Red Star turn it on with some stunning football to put United on the back foot. Going by the nickname of ''Seki'' he tormented the home side with his beguiling touch and guile causing gasps of astonishment to drift down from the Old Trafford terraces, as this magician from the Balkans raised amongst Romany travellers, cast a bewitching spell over the Manchester crowd. Indeed, such was the impression made by Sekularac, Bobby Charlton was forced to ask in the dressing room afterwards: ''How come I haven't heard of him before?''

The previous season had seen Red Star, like United reach the semi-finals, only to be eliminated by the Italians of Fiorentina 1-0 over two legs. They were streetwise, meeting fire with fire, fiercely determined, but exceptionally skilled and every outfield player blessed with wonderful technique. Ten of the side were Yugoslav internationals. These were tough, troubling opponents for Manchester United. On thirty-five minutes after an opening, fascinating encounter with the visitors looking by far the better side, it came as little surprise that the small, if stocky Sekularac proved instrumental in giving Red Star a much-deserved lead. His pass to the brilliant, Belgrade born midfielder, 27-year-old Lazar Tasic was controlled in a flash and then showing incredulous vision, Tasic lobbed Harry Gregg from fully thirty-yards. Caught out by the swirling fog, a furious Gregg watched on helplessly as the ball soared high, bounced off the underside of the crossbar and into an empty goal to horrify Old Trafford! At least those that could see it. The Daily Mirror's Archie Ledbrooke was one of so many taken aback by the Eastern European's sublime football. ''Suddenly, Red Star had begun to sparkle. For the next ten-minutes United found it difficult to hold out against the accurate short passing of the Yugoslav team.'' It had been a glorious finish by Tasic that rocked Old Trafford. Red star Belgrade were a team packed with talent. Sekularac and Tasic apart, there was others such as their fans favourite 28-year-old Bora Kostic. A stick of dynamite masquerading as an explosive left-winger, blessed with blazing skill and pace. Alongside Kostic was the hugely respected, 36-year-old veteran forward Rajko Mitic. The long-time Captain of Red Star Belgrade and Yugoslavia. It was evident even amid the Mancunian mist and blinding fog, a truly formidable outfit had come from the Balkans intent on beating the famous Busby Babes.

That United came back to grab a vital 2-1 victory in the second-half, after an opening period when they were outclassed, was ultimately down to the sheer will to win of Duncan Edwards. He just kept going playing the visitors on his own. Come the interval Jimmy Murphy had a quiet word with Duncan on taking care of the gypsy. The 21-year-old Edwards was at his marauding best on that bitterly, freezing half-hidden Mancunian evening. Three times in the first-half, he forced magnificent saves from the formidable, 30-year-old Vladimir Beara. A former ballet dancer, known as the *Black Panther* due to his all-black kit and ability to stop shots with an incredible agility. Beara was a formidable presence between the posts. In 1963, five years later, the legendary Russian stopper Lev Yashin himself admitted: ''Vladimir Beara is the finest keeper of all time.'' A huge compliment from the Soviet great.'' As for Edwards, with Jimmy

Murphy's ferocious Welsh brogue still ringing loud in his ears, the second period saw him up the ante even more and he went back to work! With United still behind but finally mastering the surface, Duncan at times appeared unplayable, bouncing off Red Star players and roaring forward. For one so young he was already resembling the finished article, hard to believe how this footballing beast of a young man could become any better. An established England international, Manchester United's beating heart and soul and seemingly determined to drag his club back into the game against Red Star single-handedly. An on fire Sekularac was misguided enough to nick the ball off Duncan's toes with a well-timed interception, only then as he turned to race away find himself being clattered by a fuming Edwards charging in like a steam train! The next thing *Seki* knew he was airborne, finally coming to earth with an almighty bump! This close encounter saw the tricky Serb fade away and suddenly it was all United. On sixty-five minutes a quick-thinking Charlton finished off a wonderful Albert Scanlon cross, and five-minutes from the end Eddie Colman latched onto a Dennis Viollet pass after he had dribbled past three Red Star defenders, to side-foot with lovely aplomb past the diving Beara. The *Black Panther* kicking the turf as the red shirts celebrated. Only Colman's second goal for the senior team. The kid from Ordsall across the river. Born in Old Trafford's shadow with a smile that could illuminate an entire Salford street had given his team a priceless lead. But would it be enough? Come the final-whistle the handsome, smiling, greying Red Star Belgrade manager Milorad Pavic shook hands with Matt Busby and Jimmy Murphy. He appeared satisfied enough with the narrow loss. The affable Pavic spoke good English due to during World War Two, being in captivity in a prisoner-of-war camp with British soldiers. His boys had done him proud.

The Daily Mail's Eric Thompson wrote of the scoreline: ''The margin may just be enough to see them through, but it is perilously slender against a team like Red Star. United did not snatch victory in this pulsating match because of any notable improvement on their

disappointing first-half play, but because they seemed to chase and press and tackle like men with glowing coals in their boots.''
It was only half-time in this European Cup quarter-final. Red Star would return home content they were still well in this tie. This proud club formed in 1945 by anti-fascists only thirteen years previous, as the official team of Belgrade university stood ready to give their much vaunted opponents the game of their young lives when they travelled East behind the *Iron Curtain*, for the return match the coming year in the first week of February. Scheduled for the fifth.

CHAPTER FIFTEEN
EPITAPH TO A BROKEN DREAM

Come 1958, and closing in on the peak of their young, beautiful powers, it is hard to imagine life could have been any better for the team known throughout every household across Great Britain as the pride of that norther outpost. Manchester. The Busby Babes. United had unknowingly crossed the invisible boundary from being a mere First Division football team into superstars off it. Nobody performed like the Mancunian Red Devils in those far off days of the lethal, soaked, leather footballs! Smashed at ferocious speeds by the likes of Taylor, Edwards, Viollet and Charlton into the roof of the net, with such power the opposing goalkeeper unless thinking he was Superman, simply never had a chance. Alas, the world would in such a fleeting time mourn them for the hellish concoction of fire, blood, snow, ice and Munich dawned.

At that time Manchester United belonged not just to Manchester, but to the entire nation. With there being hardly any football on the television tiny screens back in 1958. Just the FA Cup final, England internationals and the rarity of the odd game such as the Athletic Bilbao and Real Madrid European ties in previous seasons, they were mostly viewed and enjoyed on the scattered black and white snatches of *Pathe* newsreels. But the actual sheer excitement that the Busby Babes generated when playing at opposing ground had become off the scale. Imagine the Big Top Circus coming to town, a Hollywood movie having its opening Premier at your local Odeon and all the top stars attending. The Babes promised hope for the future, they put smiles on people's faces in true challenging times. A new way forward. There was something, breathtakingly and completely unorthodox about how the reds set about beating teams. United played not off the cuff, there was always a tactical plan. Every player knew and understood their job. It all came down to working harder than your opponent, so that talent would prevail. Then you could express yourself, and then you won! All this hailed from Jimmy Murphy, alongside Bert Whalley, Tom Curry and Bill Inglis on the Cliff training ground. Armed with a plethora of swear words, an arm around the shoulder if required, but even more curses if a player ever dared to let himself, his family the club and Mr Busby down. Bobby Charlton remembers Jimmy Murphy as a preacher with a fearful bite and a snarl, but also having the most gigantic Welsh heart.

"Jimmy was ever present on the training field in his track suit top and shorts, his pot belly showing with the evidence of how much he liked a pint! He was on me all the time, standing close to me as a practice match unfolded, chiding me, irritating me. I suppose he was testing my patience when things were not going right, as when he stepped into my path and tripped me when I was in full flight. It was two years before he told me that he had completed the first part of his job, which had been, quite simply to turn me from an amateur into a professional."

So, many countless hours was spent by Murphy with Bobby Charlton on the Cliff training ground alone. But Jimmy knew it would be worthwhile because he possessed a footballing sixth sense about what made a Manchester United footballer, and he saw real greatness in the quietly, spoken shy kid from the north-east. Jimmy knew just how to dig deep finding the love needed, the bullying also to bring forth the never-say-die fighting spirit. Any game no matter the odds was not allowed to be lost even in its last dying embers. Above all though it was about the belief for that would allow the magic to shine and Bobby Charlton to flower into a true talent of rare delight. This was the reality that went into creating from birth a Busby Babe to the finished article, and nowhere more so was it on display than a brisk, cold, southern winter's day in London on Saturday 1st February 1958.

The "*Big Smoke*" was the place to be!
The glamour and the glitz, the showbusiness centre of the world! West Side Story was playing to sell-out audiences at Her Majesty's Theatre, Haymarket. Maurice Chevalier was crooning *Thank Heaven for Little Girls* in Gigi at the Odeon, Leicester Square, and arriving in

London by train from the freezing, grim miserable north came Manchester's finest. The Busby Babes!

Matt Busby's Manchester United were unbeaten for eight League and Cup matches, in fourth position and six points behind the leaders Wolverhampton Wanderers, who they were due to play the following Saturday. Two weeks previous United's bogey team Bolton Wanderers travelled the short distance to Old Trafford looking to add more fuel to the fire that a third, successive League title was simply beyond the reigning champions. Already, Bolton had turned them over 4-0 back in September and their supporters with no love for United, the feeling mutual, could not wait to rub further salt in the Mancunian's so-far, less than satisfactory season. Ninety-minutes later such doubts carried a lot less substance after the reds ran riot against the Wanderers 7-2 in front of a 41,360 jubilant crowd! 4-1 up at half-time, all just clicked once more for the Busby Babes! With a strong wind blowing across the stadium throughout an on-fire Bobby Charlton scored a glorious hat-trick, Dennis Viollet, two, Albert Scanlon, one and finally on eighty-seven minutes, a Duncan Edwards penalty blasted so hard past England goalkeeper Eddie Hopkinson, he almost broke the net! On picking the ball up out of the goal Hopkinson was confronted by his defender Tommy Banks, a well-known hard man who would rather eat a winger than let him go past! Banks was shaking his head in disgust. "You can open your eyes and move now Eddie, it's all over!" If there was one shining star of the Babes, despite Busby and Murphy denying publicly such a thing existed it was undoubtedly Duncan Edwards. He simply could not help but stand out even amongst such esteemed company. It was inevitable advertisers would take advantage. A typical example of this would be to see Duncan wearing a Manchester United kit with a ball at his feet in a full-colour page advert of the *Charles Buchan Football Monthly magazine.* A smiling Big Dunc revealing: "Playing in top gear until the final whistle can really take it out of you. That's why I find Dextrosol Glucose Tablets so handy. They're a natural source of energy that you can rely on, anytime, anywhere!"

The public persona written of so widely in print by the newspapers and cleverly engineered by Matt Busby himself, as some fatherly figure to his players was correct to a point, but when required Busby could be equally ruthless as any manager around, if not more so, when dealing with under-performing footballers. Whoever they were, no matter how famous the name or lower down the pecking order at United, be it a reserve or a youth player, the manager acted only ever in the best interests of Manchester United. With an average age of just twenty-two, this United team still had their best years to come and were being tipped to dominate the forthcoming Sixties, both at home and in Europe. With this in mind and such being the wealth of talent on a seemingly, never-ending Old Trafford conveyor-belt, it was hardly surprising Matt Busby turned down European champions Real Madrid, twice, Athletic Bilbao and the Italian nation team invitation to go and manage them. Blessed already with such riches who could blame him for staying put in his adopted Manchester? Besides, he was well paid already by a United board who when asked to dance by Busby, usually only asked how high?

So, it was following a 1-0 home defeat by a late goal to Chelsea, Mr Manchester United acted ruthlessly and axed those misfiring. Firstly, the wingers Johnny Berry and David Pegg and in came the lightning, fast 19-year-old Welshman Kenny Morgans and the Mancunian, 18-year-old Albert Scanlon. The more experienced Berry wasn't happy and he demanded a transfer that Busby instantly turned down. The 32-year-old Johnny Berry was obviously worried his time at United, eight seasons was done, but his manager thought too highly of the winger, and he was not letting him go anywhere. Despite the age gap Berry mixed well with the others, he loved a beer and a smoke, but could never understand the younger one's fascination with playing golf! As for the 23-year-old Doncaster lad David Pegg? He was simply driven and vowed to do better. "I'll just have to play harder and get my place back," said Pegg. Elsewhere, the latest babe on the block Bobby Charlton's nine goals in ten games had done for the under-performing Liam Whelan, and saw him becoming a regular starter. Whelan though was much too good to be on the side-lines for long and Charlton would have to keep performing at his very peak. Nobody understood this more than Bobby. Suddenly, Manchester United injected with such renewed speed, skill and firepower finally looked like their old self again. As ever, Busby's obsession with the European Cup after losing out to Real Madrid in the previous year at the semi-final stage remained all-consuming. Come the new year of The 1957-58 season, United had advance again to the quarter-finals. After beating Red Star Belgrade 2-1 at Old Trafford, the second-leg was set to take place just four days after the Highbury match, the following Wednesday in Yugoslavia. However, despite his deep fascination with the European Cup, Busby also stressed his desire to win the League again. "We would like to win the European Cup, of course. But, above all I would like to win the English League Championship for the third year in succession. Herbert Chapman achieved this with Huddersfield and Arsenal, and it is the ultimate peak for any manager."

On the Saturday morning of the Arsenal game tragedy struck the Old Trafford club, when Manchester businessman and United's oldest director, 82-year-old George E Whittaker, was found dead of a heart attack in his bedroom at the Lancaster Gate Hotel in central London. For twenty-two years Whittaker had been on the Old Trafford board. One of three directors operating under the chairmanship of Harold Hardman. He passed away in his sleep during the night. Manchester United players and staff were awoken from their early morning slumber becoming curious onlookers to this morbid scene, as two policemen arrived to escort Whittaker's body from the building. George Whittaker was well known for his dislike of Matt Busby's friend Louis Edwards, who owned the butchers Louis C. Edwards and sons, with his brother Douglas. He bitterly opposed any recommendation of him becoming a director and earning a place on the United board. Now Whittaker had passed the road was clear for Edwards to make his move. It was decided as a mark of respect players from both teams Manchester United and Arsenal would wear black armbands for the game, and a minute's silence be observed before kick-off. The sad demise of a fellow director meant the others would now not be able to travel on the Belgrade flight in order to attend Whittaker's funeral. With such a hand of fortune the almighty clicked his fingers and fate pointed towards somebody else. In his place instead went another well-known, wealthy Manchester businessman who had made his fortune in the cotton industry. Willie Satinoff. A United fanatic and like Edwards, a good friend of Matt Busby's.

Whilst Manchester United had hit great form, the Arsenal came into the game on the crest of a slump. Struggling in mid-table and a recent humiliating 3-1 defeat at Division Three South, Northampton Town in the FA Cup third round left them and their supporters reeling. A Northampton team lying a lowly nineteenth in their league when they sensationally didn't just knock out the Gunners but outplayed them. A once great club was struggling to rekindle a glorious past. Come 1958 and Manchester United's visit, Arsenal's decline from their former, magnificent, all-conquering side had become a sorry tale for their supporters. During the 1930's, most that glittered in English football was red and white as firstly under the legendary Herbert Chapman, the Gunners won a remarkable five league trophies and two FA Cups. Fantastic players such as Alex James, Cliff Bastin, Eddie Hapgood and David James thrilled and entertained the Highbury masses, as the trophy haul ever increased. Tragically, in the midst of the 1933-34 season, Chapman died from pneumonia aged just 55-years old. His mantle was picked up by assistant Joe Shaw who became caretaker manager along with George Allison, later to take the role full-time with further great successes. Come the outbreak of World War Two, the Football League was suspended for seven years. When football restarted Arsenal won a third FA Cup in 1950, and three years later yet another League title, a record breaking seventh championship. But behind the scenes huge financial problems were bubbling over. The war had taken a serious toll on the Gunners. No other club had more players killed. A horrendous nine of the forty professionals on their books in 1939 were lost.
  The following.

Sidney Pugh.
Harry Cook.
William Parr.
Leslie Lack.
Bobby Daniel.
Hugh Glass.
Cyril Tooze.
Herbie Roberts.
Bill Dean.

Arsenal also found themselves badly in debt paying for their heavily, bombed North Bank Stand that had to be totally reconstructed. No longer were they the reputed *Bank of England* club of pre-war England. These were different, worrying times. Yet, this being English football the constant calls from supporters to keep the trophies coming caused massive stress within the club, and the 60-year-old Arsenal manager Tom Whittaker, who led Arsenal to their early post-war successes died of a heart attack in 1956 whilst still in the job. The pressure to halt the club's decline into mid-table mediocrity proving tragically fatal for the poor Whittaker. By the time of United's visit Tom Whittaker's successor was a former Arsenal player Jack Crayston. He too was also feeling the heat with his job being heavily rumoured in the newspapers to be on the line. One away win since October earned the previous week at Leicester City eased the pressure a little, but the last thing Crayston really needed was the champions, the-all singing and dancing Busby Babes rocking up in the capital looking to put on a display! United were only going one way, the opposite to Arsenal. They had secured two successive League titles and only a highly, controversial FA Cup final defeat to Aston Villa the previous year prevented them from winning an extremely, elusive League and FA Cup double.

Whenever Manchester United played in London, there always appeared an extra stride in their step! A willingness to produce something special for the capitol's vast crowds that flocked to see them. Matt Busby always sensed such on the train south. "They're up for putting on a show again Jimmy!" he would say to Jimmy Murphy.

"God help those cockneys!" United had become so much more than a mere football club they were pure show business. A footballing version of Sunday night at the Palladium. The press hacks treated the footballer like movies stars, dressing and playing up to the part with a beautiful zest for life. After all they were just young lads who craved the latest fashions. In the music charts Buddy Holly's *That'll Be The Day*, Jerry Lee Lewis *Great Balls of Fire*, and Elvis Presley's *Jailhouse Rock*, were riding high and the players adored this vibe! The trendy haircuts, the long raincoats, the trilbies and the suede shoes. The kings of the Manchester dance halls! The princes of the Plazas. The lads about town making the girls hearts flutter, whilst on the football pitch when it was time for work, igniting and illuminating whatever ground they played at. The United players had been taught and learnt well how to control and change the pace of a game at will. They were now capable to up a gear when least expected and blow opponents away. This being the mark of a truly, great team. There was a time not so long ago when a team from Manchester coming to the *Big Smoke,* the mention of flat caps, ferrets, pigeons and billowing chimneys spewing black smoke were certain to feature high and glib in any match report. A lazy habit hard to break, but not anymore for come 1958, Manchester United were not only champions and fighting at the top of the table for another League title, the Busby Babes were sheer rock and roll! There was even a song released about them called *The Manchester United Calypso!* So much for the miserable, northern outpost christened *Cottonopolis.* The rainy city where nobody ever smiled and everything was grey and drab. No sunshine on the darkened, dreary faces. Only thirteen years since the end of the war Manchester was still wrecked from the German Luftwaffe bombing, mounds of rubble everywhere you looked. Flattened warehouses turned into huge car parks. A city still smouldering, burning, visible wounds. Still only four-years on from the finishing of rationing. But also in the mid to late fifties it had become home to the finest, young football team the country had ever witnessed, and those same faces now beamed with pride. Home bred, raised from the crèche. Taught the basics by the preacher man Jimmy Murphy. Pass to a red shirt, keep moving, play hard, play fair and attack! A dash of red angel dust amid the smog coveted the Mancunian sky. No more did Matt Busby play down his boys to outsiders. "My wee lads" or "My boys" were off the leash! There became no need to protect them anymore, for the magic was out of the bottle becoming clear to all who were lucky enough to witness Manchester United perform. For a footballing miracle had occurred in the north of England. The epic European clashes against Athletic Bilbao and Real Madrid saw the Babes become men. The title itself of the Busby Babes was one abhorred by Busby because he felt it did not do his players justice. But the truth being it simply caught the mood of the era. In time the sight of those red shirts running out onto any pitch in the country caused hearts to melt and the excitement level to soar towards the skies. Although many cockneys would never admit it Londoners adored United. They were everything the miserable north was not supposed to be! Bright, brash and bolshie! No doffing the cap with this lot, they were the boys! Ebullient, cocksure, dazzling in red. When Manchester United rolled into their ground it was a carnival of sorts! So much more than a simple football match. The trumpets blazed out and cue the drum roll for the Busby Babes! Truly an occasion to tell your children about.

The Teams.

Arsenal. Kelsey, Charlton, Evans, Ward, Fotheringham, Bowen, Groves, Tapscott, Herd, Bloomfield and Nutt.

Manchester United. Gregg, Foulkes, Byrne, Colman, Jones, Edwards, Morgans, Charlton, Taylor, Viollet and Scanlon.

There was a relaxed if business-like atmosphere in the Manchester United dressing room. Busby passed around the black armbands to honour George Whittaker as his players got changed. Duncan Edwards was fired and ready to explode! "Come on lads, we haven't come all this way for nothing!" The Captain Roger Byrne went from player to player quietly reminding them of their instructions. Byrne at 28, was the oldest player in the team that day. His own man and at times Matt Busby's worst nightmare for he stood the corner of his teammates and in the fifties, this was all but revolution and a red flag flying. One time there was an incident at the Cliff training ground between the two with Byrne telling his manager to "Eff off!" By the afternoon he was on the transfer list, but ultimately Byrne apologised and Busby forgave him. Luckily, there also existed great respect between the men and a common cause which always overcame any hurdle in their United road. At that time Roger Byrne had a sponsorship deal with Raleigh bicycles although he drove a Morris Minor, not always too successfully with a succession of crashes! He also wrote a column for the Manchester Evening News. Byrne was undoubtedly the real leader on the pitch for Manchester United. What he said went. Elsewhere in the dressing room Tommy Taylor and Mark Jones with their broad Yorkshire accent were chatting away as if they were having a couple of pints in a pub vault. Nearby, a smiling Kenny Morgans and Bobby Charlton would be listening in as they tied up their boot laces. The goalkeeper Harry Gregg, however, always kept himself to himself. He needed his own space to prepare for what lay ahead and few were allowed in it! Every player had a ritual as the clock moved ever closer for the time to go and line up in the Highbury tunnel.

Manchester United would play in their away strip of all white with a red dash on their shirts, shorts and socks. The same kit worn in the ill-fated FA Cup final against Aston Villa the previous season As kick-off drew near there was an electricity in Highbury that crackled. A full house of 63,578 supporters who had paid two shillings a ticket. Not a needle thread could be darned between them. It was easily Arsenal's best home crowd of the season and would not be too hard to guess that more than a fair number had come to see the opposition. Imagine the moments before Laurence Olivier walked onto a performance of Macbeth at London's Memorial theatre. Or Frank Sinatra entering onto a New York Broadway stage with a cigarette in hand, clutching a glass of Jack Daniels, as the Count Basie band with

Quincy Jones the arranger started up. This was London town. Highbury. Saturday 1st February 1958.

Out appeared the teams from the tunnel to a thunderous reception from the excited crowd. Immediately, once on the pitch a gaggle of young boys chanced their hand for autographs as they raced from the stands. One of the main targets was Duncan Edwards and there still exist a wonderful photograph of him signing for a little rascal who is gazing up towards the towering United player in complete awe. Behind Edwards the famous Arsenal clock nearly touching three. One of the most poignant images in regards to what was set to occur shortly in Manchester United's history, for they were fast running out of time. Over the Highbury tannoy came an announcement to the crowd. "There will now be a minute's silence in memory of the sad passing of Manchester United Director George E Whittaker." A shrill of the referee Mr Pullen's whistle blew to signal its start. The players of both teams all wearing black armbands standing deathly still. Across the terraces total silence, just the gentle rattle of London town in the distance. The capital city like Manchester devastated by Hitler's bombs, but slowly and surely was coming back to life. Mr Pullen blew once more to end the silence and a huge roar from the Highbury crowd erupted! It was time for the main event.

The Captain's Roger Byrne and the Arsenal and Welsh international skipper Dave Bowen shook hands in the centre-circle, as the furore and noise around the ground rose ever more. Finally, with pleasantries completed the game kicked off and for the next ninety-minutes all hell broke loose in London town! As Matt Busby and Jimmy Murphy took their place on the United bench a voice screamed out from the Arsenal fans behind them. "Hey, Busby! Where's this Duncan Edwards then? Where's Superman?" An angry Murphy stood up, looked around angrily and even caught the supporter's eye, yet as ever the calming influence of Busby restrained Jimmy from giving him a mouthful back! Instead, both sat down nervously chain smoking. The United players always used to joke it looked like smoke signals coming from the bench. Secret messages! In the opening moments, the Liverpool born 28-year-old Arsenal full back Dennis Evans brought United winger Kenny Morgans crashing to earth, as the speeding Welshman threatened to hurtle past him. Evans was an ever-present in the Gunner's line-up and infamous for scoring one of the great own goals of the fifties period. Back on 17th December 1955, Arsenal were playing Stanley Matthews' wonderful orange-shirted Blackpool and winning at a canter 4-0. Towards the end of the match Evans heard the referee's whistle and mistook it for full-time thus feeling free to smash the ball into his own goal past the keeper Con Sullivan! Only, to his horror suddenly realising the whistle was for a free kick! Happily, the Gunners still won comfortably 4-1, but Dennis Evans was never allowed to forget his moment of madness! The resulting Manchester United free-kick came to nothing, but Morgans very quickly was back troubling the home team when he went through with just fellow Welshman, international keeper Jack Kelsey, a former blacksmith from Swansea, to beat, only to scoop a shot over the bar. In a frantic opening Arsenal hit back and United's newly signed Irishman, 26-year-old goalkeeper Harry Gregg from Doncaster Rovers for £23,000, (A then world record fee for a goalkeeper.) was barged over his goal-line by inside forward and local boy from Stepney, Vic Groves. A real grafter in midfield for the Arsenal, the battling, scuffling Groves wasn't always pleasant on the eye. Often finding himself a scapegoat for some of the vicious tongues that stood at the Clock End, who were hardly enjoying their team's headlong journey into decline. Unfairly picked on Grooves was constantly booed and sent abusive letters. His nephew Perry would decades later suffer similar. Arsenal could be a grim place to ply your trade in the mid, bleak winter of 1958. The quick-tempered Gregg swiftly let Vic Groves know what he thought of the challenge handing him a mouthful of ferocious, Gaelic verbal, luckily, hardly recognisable this side of the Irish sea!

It was no coincidence that United's return to form coincided with Gregg's arrival at Old Trafford. An abrasive character, never one to suffer fools, the young man from Londonderry would feel nothing about taking out one of his own defenders if the ball was within what he deemed his space. Gregg though swiftly became hugely respected and admired by his team mates, who in time learned that the big man's bark was far worse than his bite! Although there was one time when touring Holland and sharing a hotel room on the seventh floor with the never, boring Albert Scanlon! Harry had warned Albert not to smoke in the bedroom. Typically, taking no notice he lit up anyway, only for his goalkeeper to walk in unexpectedly, then proceeding to dangle a poor, screaming Albert by his feet from the high-rise hotel window! The former keeper Ray Wood was known as a steadying influence, a man lost in shadows at times, whereas Harry Gregg was a daunting character on the pitch. Bobby Charlton recalled his arrival. "Harry seemed huge and enormously strong. His handling was better than anything I had ever seen, and he gave us all a feeling that nothing could get by him." The Mancunians roared straight back when Tommy Taylor fired in a shot at Kelsey who blocked, but only for the ball to fall to Bobby Charlton. Steadying to shoot he was all but mugged by Arsenal defenders crowding him out. Busby's team had begun on fire looking to hit the Gunners early and hard. On ten-minutes, Dennis Viollet released the Swansea born Morgans who flew past Arsenal's experienced, 29-year-old right-back Stan Charlton, (no relative), before crossing perfectly for an on-rushing Duncan Edwards taking the ball in his stride, and from the edge of the penalty box letting fly a crashing strike that proved too hard for Kelsey to stop. The ball ripping through his hands into the top of the goal! As the United players celebrated with Edwards, on their bench Jimmy Murphy was on his feet searching out the earlier supporter who had slagged off his boy from Dudley. Jimmy spotted him. "That's Duncan!" he shouted. "The big fellow, Superman! That's our Duncan Edwards!" It swiftly turned into a master class as these white-shirted footballers with a dash of red from the smog-filled north passed the ball around on a mud-patch of a pitch, with an alarming speed and accuracy that caused both consternation and no shortage of admiration on the Highbury terraces. A second goal appeared a certainty as United's little known lesser lights, the wingers Morgans and Scanlon ripped incessantly past their markers with an alarming

regularity and worrying ease for the Arsenal supporters. Scanlon's
nickname off the other players was *Joe Friday*, after the detective
hero of a 1950's TV Series called *Dragnet*. (A nephew of the former
Manchester United maverick Charlie Mitten.) He was into everything!
Albert was a huge lover of the movies and spent a lot of time keeping
up with them at the local Manchester flicks, never missing
Hollywood's latest. His team mates always joked if you ever needed
Albert, he was never too hard to find! Indeed, the day before he and
Eddie Colman were allowed to go and see Frank Sinatra's *My Pal
Joey* at the nearby London cinema. Off they strolled out of the
Lancaster Gate Hotel, both wearing their trilbies like their hero
Sinatra! Dennis Viollet said of Albert Scanlon when in full flow:
"He's like a bloody greyhound at Belle Vue!" That very same week
Jack Cranston had phoned Matt Busby to see if there was a possibility
of signing him, but the United manager simply refused to do business.
One memorable incident at Old Trafford typified Albert. It was during
a First Division game. The United players were coming off the pitch
for half-time when he announced the winner to his team mates of the
3-30 at Wincanton. They asked him how could he possible know?
Albert replied, "I was chatting with fans near the touchline!"
On thirty-four minutes the visitors finally doubled their lead and it
was a glorious goal. A devastating turn of pace from Scanlon racing
seventy-yards before finding Bobby Charlton, who let fly a rasping
drive past a diving Kelsey. "What a fantastic run Albert made,"
remembered Charlton. "Its easy Bobby lad!" he said to me when I
gave him a hug! The speed and power of Albert was unbelievable. We
were all trying to keep up with him, then he unleashed a magical pass
for me to score." On a pitch that was soggy, greasy and in many parts
no more than muddy bumps the Red Devils were cutting an
impressive swathe. It was a thunderous goal that would in time
become Charlton's forte. He was playing out of his skin for Bobby
knew well that just one bad game or even training session, such was
the ferocious competition at Old Trafford, you could so easily lose
your place, then god knows when you would get it back? Earlier that
week when Busby named the team and it was either him or a fully-fit

Liam Whelan, Charlton again got the nod accompanied by his
manager's words: "You have achieved another rites of passage Bobby
lad. Keep it up." Whelan remained out in the cold along with such
marvellous players as David Pegg, Johnny Berry and Jackie
Blanchflower. All desperate to grab back a first-team shirt. The
Guardian wrote of the precocious Charlton at that time. "He has
grown from a limited, left-side player of little pace into a brilliant
inside-forward." For that moment Bobby had the shirt but woe betide
his standards ever dropped. Four-minutes before the interval Arsenal
thought they had pulled one back, but their Welsh international, the
inside-right Derek Tapscott was deemed to have been offside by Mr
Pullen. The former apprentice bricklayer Tapscott then watched on in
horror as United swept up field and in an eyeblink Bobby Charlton
was clear through on Kelsey! His shot beat the keeper only for Evans
on the goal-line to block with a concoction of arms and chest clearing
for a corner. Appeals from white shirts for a penalty were dismissed
by the referee, it had been a close shave for the Gunners. Another
chance for the visitors when Dennis Viollet's header was saved
superbly by a besieged Kelsey. It couldn't last though for such
pressure had to pay and on the very stroke of half-time, Manchester
United went 3-0 up. The centre-forward Tommy Taylor finishing off a
stunning move involving once more the brilliantly, incisive duo of
Kenny Morgans and Albert Scanlon. Albert hit a forty-yard cross-field
ball to his fellow tormentor Morgans on the left-hand side, who
crossed first time for Taylor to arrive in perfect time, sweeping his
shot past a helpless Jack Kelsey from six-yards. The United forward's
first goal in seven matches and he cut a much-relieved figure. A
majestic move that summed up overall United's opening forty-five
minutes display. Highbury watched on stunned. Playing in midfield
for the first time in four-years that day was 22-year-old Londoner
Gerry Ward. A lot of the missed time was due to him doing National
Service. Ward was demobbed in 1957, and had finally forcing his way
into the reckoning once more, but he must have cursed his manager
Cranston for picking this of all games to bring him back in!
Incidentally, Gerry Ward was once the Arsenal's youngest ever player.

Ward would later lose his place following the United appearance to a certain Scottish right-half bought from Preston North End by the name of Tommy Docherty. Usually, such a mauling would have had the home fans angry and scowling with discontent, but this time around the mood was simply one of utter amazement at watching these magical boys from the north, these dervishes. Matt Busby's Manchester United had just offered up one of their greatest exhibitions of attacking football under his leadership. The new safe hands of Harry Gregg. The team's heartbeat that existed in the power and skill of Duncan Edwards and Eddie Colman. The bewildering speed of Kenny Morgans and St. Wilfrid's catholic school finest, Albert Scanlon, down both wings, and fronted by the goal-thirsty venomous trio of Bobby Charlton, Dennis Viollet and Tommy Taylor. They were simply irresistible. An irascible performance. Champagne and caviar football by the Busby Babes, who simply adored this London town. A bow and an wink to the Arsenal terraces. Their ego's stroked and caressed by the huge press and media scrums that accompanied their trips south. Admired both on the field and off. "Top of the Bill!" A first-half performance showing once more nobody did it better, even the Arsenal's die-hards in the raucous Clock End handed them grudging respect as smatterings of applause rang out from all corners of the ground at the interval. Manchester United appeared in the job of winning hearts and minds also, not just football matches as they captivated this capital audience. None had strode higher and was more impressive than Duncan Edwards, who appeared on a one-man mission to dominate the match. Duncan's passing against Arsenal both long and short, precise and a delight to watch. His tackling fair, mostly! A fierce will to win frightening and a remarkable ability to suddenly spring forward with deadly results, A footballer such a joy to behold. Edwards' sheer presence caused sometimes opponents into an on pitch surrender and just to give up, thinking what was the point? The Daily Telegraph description of the first-half proceedings. "The Babes played like infants in paradise. The ball, it seemed, had been placed in the arena for their own amusement. With the utmost abandon and cherubic cheerfulness, the Manchester

United marvels kicked, headed and dribbled among themselves. When on rare occasions an Arsenal player knocked them sliding in the mud, or momentarily took their ball away, it was all part of the fun."
The Arsenal centre-forward that day was a 24-year-old Scotsman from Hamilton, Lanarkshire, David Herd. From 1961-68, post Munich, Herd would go on to enjoy a successful seven-year career at Old Trafford. He recalled United's opening forty-five minute masterclass. "Just stunning. I had never seen an English side do the things they did. We were all attacking teams in those days, raiding wingers, two potential strikers and a midfield that tended to pour forward. But United did it all at a different pace. In a way, I was almost enjoying it!" However, Arsenal, despite being horribly outclassed in that opening period had in their midst some characters of their own who would never lie down in a dogfight. As Manchester United were soon set to discover.

All at Highbury that day after witnessing United's blistering first-half showing could only have expected the second to continue in the same vein, but whatever unfolded in the Arsenal dressing room during the break had a truly, dramatic effect. The previous season the Gunners had been like lambs to the slaughter in a 6-2 mauling at Old Trafford. Goals from Whelan (two), Berry (two), Edwards and Taylor sent them back to London humiliated. A more recent thrashing had been back in September. A 4-2 defeat when Whelan, (two) again! Pegg and Taylor did the damage. As the Arsenal dressing room fumed the call went out from amongst their embarrassed players: "Not again! Let's have a real go!" Also, present at Highbury was a delegation of officials from Red Star Belgrade. Red Star had taken Manchester United to the very last whistle in the first-leg of their European Cup quarter-final at Old Trafford. This United team though vastly different in personnel still played with the same scintillating, attacking rhythm and movement. The return game in Belgrade promised to be sensational for Red Star, like the reds only knew one way to play the game. Attack! From the referee's first whistle in the second-half, the Gunners immediately roared on the attack, and thirteen-minutes in

Herd calmly collected a long ball from his Captain Dave Bowen. With Gregg racing towards him, Herd shown lovely composure to calmly slot home past the United keeper. Suddenly, there was renewed hope on the Highbury terraces. Arsenal continued to pour forward. Spurred on by a revitalised Clock End, Vic Groves' low shot beat Harry Gregg only to flash narrowly wide of the post! For the first time in the contest United appeared rattled and sixty-seconds later the home side scored again. Their left-winger Gordon Nutt crossed for Vic Groves again to flick on and the inside-forward Jimmy Bloomfield, a London lad from Notting Hill, his predatory instincts did the rest lashing a shot past Gregg! Highbury went wild! A game only a short while deemed over was now back in the melting pot.

Arsenal 2 Manchester United 3!

The Gunners were on fire and raced back for the restart. Roger Byrne urged his team to concentrate, Duncan Edwards clenched his fist demanding more effort, but Arsenal sensed blood and with their crowd behind them kept going. Again, it was Nutt flying forward. He tore clear of Bill Foulkes and crossed for Bloomfield to burst through a rocking, United rearguard before smashing a ferocious drive past Gregg off the post and into the net! 3-3! It was utter bedlam as north London went mad and Highbury went in raptures! An early example of hooliganism occurred following the equalising goal when fighting broke out on the terraces of the Main Stand between mixed rival fans. Emotions and tempers boiling over causing stewards and police having to wade in and break it up. Chaos engulfed the stadium, both on the field and off. United were reeling from shock and Busby appeared livid on the bench. Jimmy Murphy also. The most important points that both stressed to their players was always play for the shirt, do your job proper and help out your mate. What they were witnessing from the United bench was a collapse of these values. A three-goal lead thrown away did not bode well for events in Belgrade the following Wednesday. The visitor were clearly rattled. Many years later Arsenal's Dennis Evans spoke with great regret about an incident that occurred after United had blown their 3-0 lead. "I saw a frustrated Duncan Edwards leave Gerry Ward sprawling on the running off track, before shouting at him in his broad Black Country accent: "Oh, effin get up!" Danny was too slight to really look after himself, so, I went across and told Duncan to cut it out. A few minutes later a pent-up Duncan got the ball and came charging at us. I was the nearest defender. As he knocked it just too far ahead of him, it flashed through my mind that I really could get revenge for Danny. Big Duncan was already a legend in the game and instinct took over. I simply slid the ball away from him and out of play. Had I gone through with the tackle I know I could have hurt him. Perhaps then he wouldn't have been fit for Belgrade and he wouldn't have been on the plane to Munich?" Another tale of that same incident had Dave Bowen siding up to Edwards who was going round tearing into Arsenal players like a tank out of control. Bowden saying: "Stop taking liberties big fella or we'll gang up and make sure you finish the game on a bloody stretcher!" The incident with Ward clearly did little to halt Edwards resolve to drag the game back into United's hands, according to Albert Scanlon. "Even when Arsenal pulled us back to 3-3 we were not worried. Big Duncan was shouting at us to get stuck in, Mark Jones clenched his fist and shouted out advice, and Roger was cool as a cucumber as he steadied us down and kept telling us to keep our passing game going. This was one of those matches you could never, ever forget. All the team played exceptionally well and we were up and down the pitch non-stop, looking to score goals. These were the kind of games the fans loved and so did the players!"

As the London skies darkened the Highbury floodlights were switched on only adding wonderfully to the electric, riotous atmosphere igniting across the grand old stadium. The elation though would prove a snatched moment of joy, for as if their pride had been somehow challenged, egos pricked, United suddenly found another gear and Arsenal's near-miraculous recovery was brought crashing down to earth four-minutes later. Scanlon again tore off down the left-wing past poor Stan Charlton, leaving him behind as if he was a lamppost, before delivering a wonderful cross from which Dennis Viollet beat Tommy Taylor to before meeting it full on with a wonderful header past a floundering Jack Kelsey! Viollet recalled: "That was some game! I scored with a rare header, Scanny centred the ball for Tommy who liked it delivered fast, high and hard, something Albert could supply with perfection. I somehow got to it before Tommy and glanced the ball into the net. The power of the cross nearly took my head off my shoulders! After that goal Tommy went up even further in my estimation, because he would head those type of crosses umpteen times in a game." The visitors led again and you could almost feel the air seeping out of the Arsenal terraces like a deflating balloon. The home players stood around sick, their fantastic effort had been seemingly now for nothing. Seven-minutes later Kenny Morgans fed an electric Tommy Taylor, who burst between two Arsenal defenders from the right-hand touchline, roared into the penalty area and smashed an unsuspecting shot that beat Kelsey at his near post, surely winning the game for Manchester United. Taylor's 131'st goal for the Red Devils. His last. Now 3-5 with just sixteen-minutes remaining and the Arsenal crowd resigned to defeat. Yet, their team simply refused to lie down and when Groves' defence splitting pass found David Herd, he rounded Gregg before squaring for Tapscott to make it 5-4! Again, there was hope. Pure box office! Arsenal had thirteen-minutes remaining to salvage a draw or even still win the match! Chances still came. In the dying moments Roger Byrne broke out on an overlap and with white shirts racing up in support he crossed for Viollet, who got caught in a tangle with Kelsey and the ball ran loose for a corner. Finally, Mr Pullen brought the credits down and ended proceedings. Both sides dropped to their knees in near exhaustion and the final whistle saw an equally shattered, breathless crowd rise to salute what had been a truly, magnificent occasion. Players left the pitch arm in arm knowing they had taken part in an epic contest. It had been essential United won for elsewhere Wolves had hammered Leicester City 5-1, leaving the gap between the two still six points, but with a huge game coming up between them the following Saturday at Old Trafford. There, Matt Busby's remarkable young team could cut the gap down to just a manageable four points with still half a season to play.

On leaving the bench to shake hands with their Arsenal counterparts, Jimmy Murphy heard a familiar cockney voice shouting his name from the terraces. "Hey Jimmy!" He turned around. The same supporter from previous stood smiling wide. "I take it back Jimmy," he said. "He's not bad is that Edwards! We've scored four goals today. What have we got to do to beat your lot?"

"Just keep praying son," shouted back Murphy!

Busby was asked by a reporter: "Aren't you worried about the four goal you conceded?"

"No, not at all," he replied. "Because we got five! More important, you saw how those sixty odd thousand people enjoyed the game. This is the kind of football the spectators pay to watch." Little did anyone know as those white-shirted lads caked in mud and sweat vanished from sight down the tunnel five of them would never be seen again. It was a score-line that defied belief. Arsenal 4 Manchester United 5. There was no need for words to embellish the match itself. One glorious epitaph. Saturday 1st February 1958. Londoners would never forget the day when the Busby Babes came south for the final time and rocked their city. Dennis Evans again: "Everyone was cheering. Not because of Arsenal, not because of United, but because of the game itself. No one left until five-minutes after the game. They just stood there cheering."

Geoffrey Green of The Times was ecstatic at what he witnessed.

"The thermometer was doing a war-dance. There was no breath left in anyone. The players came off arm in arm. They knew they had finally fashioned something of which to be proud."

Returning home, the United first team was an incredibly, happy bunch of young footballers on the train to Manchester. Busby sat with Jimmy Murphy, his former Captain Johnny Carey, Willie Satinoff and the Evening Chronicle's Alf Clarke, discussing the match and football in general over a few drinks. Elsewhere, the United lads were planning their night out on arriving back at London Road! A celebration in places such as the Plaza Ballroom on Oxford Road, the Locarno Ballroom in Sale, where managers at both venues happily gave their celebrity guests free admission. Or, even for the real night town owls amongst them, way after the last bus had gone, the Cromford club off Market Street. Manchester's most distinguished club. A rich clientele, famed singers, actors, politicians and gangsters. Everyone in Manchester who was anyone would end up in Paddy McGrath's classy joint. Rogues and rabbis, priests and police. Himself, a close pal of Matt Busby's. "I supported United before those kids were born," said McGrath. "I'd watched them since the 1920's, and they never had a side before Matt came to a bomb-site, and took over a team of lads with talent and moulded them by switching one player here, another there and so on."

On stepping off the train Busby gathered his flock around him and gave permission, telling his players to go and enjoy themselves. Within reason! Officially off the leash several headed straight for the Plaza. Many in there, young girls mostly waiting their arrival! The events of what had occurred at Highbury was well known now across the city and everybody wanted to be close to their heroes. On entering a jam-packed Plaza the disk jockey announced their names and the building erupted in cheers. He even got Mark Jones and Eddie Colman up onto the club stage to do their version of Gene Vincent's *Frankie and Johnny.*

A few lines from the song best to end with.

"Now this is the end of my story.

And this is the end of my song".

CHAPTER SIXTEEN
SPRING WAS CLOSE

Sunday 2nd February 1958.

It was time to count the cost of the previous day's epic encounter in London against Arsenal at Highbury. The Manchester United club physio (also Lancashire County Cricket side physio), Ted Dalton, reported to Matt Busby that the reserve centre-forward Welshman Colin Webster, had a bad dose of flu and would be unable to travel. A devastated Webster was sick at not being able to go. ''I was cursing my bloody luck at missing out. We always had good fun on those away trips and it made me feel part of the whole set up at the club. However, it wasn't to be and I remained behind.'' More important, the Captain Roger Byrne was a major doubt after pulling a thigh muscle. Busby could not take the risk and another specialised full-back would be accompanying them. The understudy, himself a brilliant defender, 25-year-old Salford born (Irlam-o'-th'-Heights) Geoff Bent. A former Captain of Salford Boys, Bent had turned out twelve times for Manchester United's first team, his proudest moment by far came against Preston North End, when he performed brilliantly and a newspaper shown him taking the ball off the great Tom Finney. Bent treasured this photo. There were times when he got frustrated and other clubs came knocking including Manchester United's great rivals back then, Stan Cullis's Wolverhampton Wanderers were in for him, but Busby simply refused to let Bent leave Old Trafford. ''There are no first team players at United,'' the manager told him. ''You are all first team probable's.'' Busby would take Bent to Belgrade in place of another fine reserve player, the 24-year-old centre-half Ronnie Cope, who could also double up as a very decent full-back. A couple of weeks earlier Cope was pulled into Matt Busby's office to be told he would be travelling to Yugoslavia, and to hand his passport over to Club Secretary Walter Crickmer, for the entry visa to be stamped. So, it was on later being told the situation had changed Cope was quietly seething and had decided to ask Busby for a transfer when the team returned from Belgrade. ''Can you imagine how I felt when a few weeks later, I got my passport back and saw the visa giving me permission to enter Belgrade stamped on it?'' recalled Cope afterwards. A telephone call was made to Bent's house where he lived with wife Marion and their newly, born baby daughter Karon. Only, for Geoff to be enjoying a pint in his local thinking he was out of the picture regarding the Red Star match. A message was relayed and Geoff Bent was swiftly back home getting himself organised for the trip! Wilf McGuinness should have been going to Belgrade, but fate stepped in when he was seriously injured with a badly torn cartilage. McGuinness had already been ordered to hand his passport into the club for the trip to Yugoslavia, only then to be told by the physio Ted Dalton, no chance. He was going to be side-lined for the considerable future and needed a cartilage operation. All in Wilf would be out for ten to fourteen weeks. There would be no journey behind the *Iron Curtain* for Wilf McGuinness. No fun and games in the mysterious *Eastern Block* with his team mates. Wilf got his passport back and would miss out also on two stop offs at Munich. He would have to make do with hearing all the mad tales from his best mates big Dunc, Eddie and Bobby on their return.

Monday 3rd February 1958.
Delayed for an hour due to creeping fog, shortly after 8.00.am, on a misty rain-sodden Monday morning, British European Airways charter-flight number, Airspeed Ambassador G-ALZU AS57, soared off the end of a Manchester runway heading south on a two thousand mile round trip over the channel. First deep into southern Germany and Munich to refuel then on to Belgrade. The aircraft was piloted by Captain James Thain and co-pilot Kenneth Rayment, They were good friends. Radio officer George William Rodgers and three cabin staff. William Cable, Margaret Bellis and Rosemary Cheverton. All in there were thirty-eight people on board including the players, club officials and nine of the press pack.
 Alf Clark (Manchester Evening Chronicle).
 Don Davies (Manchester Guardian).
 Tom Jackson (Manchester Evening News).

George Follows (Daily Herald).
Archie Ledbrooke (Daily Mirror).
Henry Rose (Daily Express).
Eric Thompson (Daily Mail).
Frank Swift (News of the World).
Frank Taylor (News Chronicle Dispatch).
Also flying with the team was Willie Satinoff. A rich local
businessman, an enthusiastic racehorse owner and friend of Matt
Busby. Satinoff was being heavily rumoured in the national
newspapers to be the next United director after the unfortunate death
of George E Whittaker, on the morning of the recent Arsenal game.
There was also on board the club's travel agent Mr and Mrs Bela
Miklos. Finally, a Mrs Maria Lukic, the wife of the Yugoslav attaché
in London and her baby daughter. Originally, Paddy McGrath,
Busby's other great pal and owner of the Cromford Club was going to
be asked by the manager, but with McGrath's wife heavily pregnant,
Busby's wife Jean told her husband it was not a good idea.
"All right, I'll not ask him then," Busby replied, thus, Paddy
McGrath wasn't on the flight. A journey that would take in all six
hours to reach Belgrade. Mark Jones had been late and after
apologising to the manager received merciless stick off his team
mates already on board! Although there was a familiar face missing.

Jimmy Murphy had reluctantly been talked out of going to
Yugoslavia by Matt Busby, because of international duty in his
position as Welsh team coach. Under Murphy's astute stewardship
Wales now stood on the verge of qualification for the 1958 World
Cup finals in Sweden. A play-off against Israel looked to have already
been sealed after a 2-0 away win in Tel Aviv. Barring disaster it was
signed and sealed and Murphy argued that it was not essential for him
being in Cardiff for the second-leg. For although a proud Welshman,
Murphy's heart bled United red. However, Busby insisted he go, his
reasoning being that Murphy would never forgive himself if by some
strange quirk of footballing fate Wales crashed out. Busby himself
had recently been appointed Scotland's coach. A huge honour at that

time for Manchester United having two international managers So, it
was that Monday morning as United flew high over the channel,
Jimmy stepped onto a train at London Road station taking him to
Cardiff, whilst Bert Whalley sat in the aircraft seat that would
certainly have been his next to Matt Busby.
The airplane landed at Munich for refuelling. Just a short stop. Hot
drinks were served in the terminal building, and Busby was grilled by
the press pack eager for scraps of news on the fitness of Roger Byrne.
He assured them all was good and Byrne appeared likely to play
against Red Star meaning the reds were back at full strength. Soon,
the aircraft was off again heading ever further east across the *Iron
Curtain*. An invisible wall, not so much made out of bricks or stone,
more a Communist state of mind. Onwards for the second-leg to
Belgrade. Back on board the passengers passed the time playing cards
and sleeping. In the background, the constant drone of the
Elizabethan's huge engines hummed away.

Belgrade. Marshall Tito airport.
Finally, after a tiresome if uneventful flight, Captain Thain negotiated
a gentle touch down of the Elizabethan aircraft on the airport's snow-
white runway, glistening in a strange, eerie gleaming sun. Thain
addressed the passengers over the cabin intercom. ''To everybody on
board, may I welcome you to Belgrade. Please can you remain seated
until we are ready to disembark. Once inside the airport building at
customs, be aware they have very little sense of humour here, so I
advise you to just let them see them search your luggage, and answer
any questions they may have. And, to the Manchester United team, all
the best for the football match!'' On ending, a huge cheer went up
from the footballers! Everyone was up standing ready to disembark,
grabbing their suitcases and bags from the overhead compartments.
Players, staff and journalists so looking forward to stretching their
legs and seeing what awaited them in Belgrade. After a long and
weary trawl through customs for this was the height of the Cold War,
hard-eyed suspicions meant every one of the passengers were being

deemed a possible spy! Busby had warned his players: "No wisecracks," whilst the checks were made. "For Siberia was not in the European Cup!" The suitcases of all the passengers were thoroughly checked by Yugoslav airport officials, who themselves were watched over by armed soldiers and they had equally shadowy figures in suits watching them. The *UDBA* (Yugoslav Intelligence Services), President Tito's eyes and ears. Satisfied Manchester United had not come to Belgrade to kick-start a revolution, the travelling party were finally allowed onto their bus to escape the freezing Belgrade cold. It was a short, if eye-opening journey for all on board watching through their windows. Scenes so surreal they could have been from a different world. Huge banners of President Tito hung from the endless, grey dreary tall flats and buildings. Female soldiers were shovelling the paths clear of snow. Army tanks were parked along the roadside. Their occupants sat abreast, smoking and watching. Menacing. People dressed in nothing but rags, queues outside shops with empty windows that stretched forever out of sight around corners. Armed soldiers everywhere. Sheer Paranoia. Dennis Viollet recalled what he witnessed. "We were still suffering in Manchester from the aftermath of the war and rationing had only just finished. But that place was really bad. We felt so sorry for the people especially the older ones and the children. We were amazed to see people walking around without shoes, despite the bad weather, some had used old tyres as makeshift footwear. If this was what Communism was like then they could keep it."

Only two years previous had been the Hungarian Revolution that caused the streets of Budapest to run red with the blood of their citizens trying to fight off Soviet tanks. This was not something President Tito desired to see in Yugoslavia. Tito was no fan of the Russians, indeed himself and Josef Stalin were sworn enemies after once being close. Tito had very cleverly dragged his nation clear of Soviet control, though was always wise enough not to pull the tail of the Russian bear too hard whilst doing so. The atmosphere between the two men remained murderous. Stalin tried many times to assassinate Tito but constantly failed. To the extent a message was delivered back to the Kremlin stating: "Stop sending people to kill me. We've already captured five of them, one of them with a bomb and another with a rifle. If you don't stop sending killers, I'll send one to Moscow, and I won't have to send a second." The massacre in Hungary was clearly a message sent by Moscow and caused serious tremors across the Eastern Block. Mother Russia was watching and so Josip Tito would play the great waiting game.

On arriving at the Hotel Majestic that sat grandly on the banks of the Blue Danube, the Mancunians when heading to allocated rooms found soldiers patrolling on every floor! Leading 2-1, Manchester United had come to Belgrade! A syndicated bulletin hit the newspaper offices across England. "A crowd of autograph hunters stormed the customs hall at Belgrade airport. The reason for the commotion was that Manchester United had just landed. They were 53 minutes late delayed by fog. The audience was undeterred and the players were engulfed." It appeared the excitement of the Busby Babes "Playing in your town" had reached far across the *Iron Curtain* to include the football supporters of the Yugoslav capital!

The day before saw the visitors do some light training on the pitch. The game was to take place at the home of Partizan Belgrade. The *JNA*. Red Star's stadium deemed not up to hosting such a prestigious occasion. The reasons beings it was decidedly smaller and did not have enough lighting. Wild rumours were sweeping Belgrade that President Tito himself would be at the game, but these later proved to be false. Out came the smiling United players to test the surface. Roger Byrne, Bobby Charlton, Eddie Colman, Tommy Taylor. The atmosphere was relaxed, the usual laughter amid the hard work on a swamp of a pitch. Colman fast with a quip leaving defenders in a befuddled heap. All the time watched not just by the British press pack and their Yugoslav counterparts, but the entire crew of the Elizabethan plane. The home journalists watched enchanted, fascinated by these famous young footballers whom so much had been heard of even behind the *Iron Curtain*. The Busby Babes were like the American Hollywood superstars. Tom Curry confirmed to

Matt Busby that Roger Byrne was looking a certainty to be okay following another fitness test. A thumbs up from Byrne to his manager bringing a huge sigh of relief from a thankful Busby. So important to have his Captain on the field for what would surely be a real battle in a concrete arena filled with 52,000 screaming Yugoslavs! Despite the odd clash off field, there was no finer admirer of Byrne than his manager. In later years he would spoke of him in glowing terms. ''Roger was one of the fastest full-backs of all time, but at the same time controlled his movement beautifully, like Nureyev. He would go up the wing to attack, but always had the speed to get back before the opposition could make anything of it. Great as they were, Stanley Matthews and Tom Finney never played well against Roger.''

If, by chance Red Star managed to level the tie after ninety-minutes, there was to be a third match played in Milan. One Busby needed to avoid at all cost. Games were already piling up. Fixture congestion his worst nightmare. Duncan Edwards was asked by the News Chronicle's, Frank Taylor, about the importance of the forthcoming Wolves game the coming Saturday. ''Let's get this Red Star side out of the European Cup first, and then we'll deal with Wolves. All I'll say is that if the boys play like they did against Arsenal, Stan Cullis's boys will need to go some to beat us.''

In the afternoon, the Manchester United party visited the cinema where as they entered paying customers on the front row of seats were ordered to move elsewhere by the armed soldiers escorting the Mancunians! Later, after dinner, back in the Hotel Majestic restaurant, a smiling Matt Busby stood and his players sat scattered around him at nearby tables. Their eyes all focused upon him. Busby's words are related here through various sources that were present. ''Okay boys, tomorrow we're up against a very good team on their own turf, with their own supporters roaring them on. Here in Belgrade, they love their football just as much as we do, but what they don't have, is what we have. You lot. They're going to expect us tomorrow to go out and defend for our lives. To let them have the ball, but you know, as I do, at United we attack! Let's go for them early and finish this! Do your worse boys, and then we go home. Now Get a good night's sleep and I'll see you all in the morning."

Wednesday 5th February 1958.
As match day dawned, such was the icy Belgrade freezing weather, there were early doubts as to whether the quarter-final would actually go ahead, but these eased as across late morning, the sun appeared to slightly thaw out the mud spattered, snowbound pitch at the *Partizan Stadion*. The game was already a complete sell out. Meanwhile, in the hotel Metropole lobby and lounge it was a melee with locals searching for the United players asking for photographs, autographs and souvenirs. Elsewhere, two thousand miles away in Wales, Cardiff, Jimmy Murphy was wearing another hat, that as manager of his beloved national team. At Ninian Park, the Welsh were up against Israel in the second-leg of their World Cup Qualification match. For Jimmy it was great to meet up with his good friend, the wonderful Juventus player John Charles again. A son of Cwmbrwla, Swansea. A magnificent footballer, six-feet-two and equally masterful as both a centre-half and centre-forward. In Turin, he was adored equally so, if not more than the supporters of his former club Leeds United. They had nickname him *Il Buono Gigante! The Gentle Giant*. In his own inimitable way Murphy had managed to persuade Juve to release Charles for the two matches against the Israelis in the middle of the Italian season. A little known fact being Juve had a half-eye on Jimmy to become their coach the following summer and wanted to keep him sweet. Already 2-0 up after winning in Tel Aviv, it was just a question of Wales keeping their nerve to make it to Sweden. Come the day before the second-leg, Murphy confided in John Charles his worries about Matt Busby. A recent leg operation had left him in agony, typical of Busby he never complained, but Jimmy saw him at close quarters and witnessed how the boss was really suffering.
After training finished on the Tuesday afternoon, an Israeli delegation arrived and a beautiful, exotic lady with dark hair and almond eyes presented Jimmy, to his huge embarrassment a large basket of oranges! Wales remained heavy favourites to advance following the

first-leg, and so it proved as they dominated the return match. It took time, but finally on seventy-six minutes, Allchurch held off two Israeli defenders to race through and fire into the top corner igniting Ninian Park and sending Wales to Sweden! Shortly after Spur's Cliff Jones added a second and the celebrations could truly begin. Once back in the dressing room, amid the happiness, joy and sheer jubilation of his countrymen, Jimmy took a short break to try and find out the Manchester United result in Belgrade. His boys.
His red apples...

Belgrade. *JNA* Partizan Stadium.
In the dressing room shortly before kick-off, Matt Busby dressed in a smart looking raincoat and a sharp fitting trilby, stood facing his seated players. He appeared composed as ever and had a last couple of lines to say before battle re-commenced against Red Star.
 "There are no terrors out there boys. We have beaten them once, now, do it again!"
On a pitch with the last remnants of snow still visible, but melting fast in the afternoon sunshine, spring seemed close. The two teams lined up. The Manchester United Captain Roger Byrne looked down the line of his teammates. Harry, Bill, Eddie, Mark, big Dunc looking set to burst! Kenny, Bobby, Tommy, Dennis and Albert. They were ready.

The Teams.
Red Star Belgrade. Beara, Tomic, Zekovic, Mitic, Spajic, Popovic, Borozan, Selularac, Tasic, Kostic and Gokic.

Manchester United. Gregg, Foulkes, Byrne, Colman, Jones M, Edwards, Morgans, Charlton, Taylor T, Viollet and Scanlon.

As the noise level from the capacity crowd grew incessantly louder with everybody seemingly dressed in long overcoats and woollen hats, the Austrian referee Karl Kainer begin proceedings. With everyone expecting it to be Red Star to start off like a rocket, rapier fast, it was indeed Manchester United who began on the front foot and within ninety-seconds of the opening whistle they went in front! A rampaging Tommy Taylor raced from his own half to set up Dennis Viollet, who shrugged off the chasing Red Star defenders to fire impressively past Vladimir Beara. The Yugoslavs were stunned! Caught stone cold. United were on fire and looking to do what their manager had called for, killing the tie dead early doors. Waves of red shirts poured forward and on fourteen-minutes from an Albert Scanlon corner, Viollet's precise header down was met by Bobby Charlton to finish delightfully, only to Red Star's huge relief, the referee blowing inexplicably blowing for offside? This decision left the visitors bewildered? It would not be the first time Herr Kainer's whistle blew to irritate the United players, as he frequently gave fouls against the visitors for challenges that back in England would have been considered fair game At one point an infuriated Duncan Edwards was warned by Herr Kainer for overzealous complaining and anymore he would be sent off! The Guardian's Donny Davies wrote of him: "The Austrian referee whose performance on the whistle assumed the proportions of a flute obligato!" Yet, still despite such good fortune in their favour the Yugoslavs failed to raise their game and stem the flashing red shirts that were swarming like dervishes amongst them. Tempers frayed as winger Kenny Morgans found himself the victim of a brutal, knee-high tackle from Red Star's sublime, but at times extremely volatile Gypsy rose, Dragoslav Sekularac. With the terraces anxious at their team's so far non-appearance matters turned inexplicably worse for Red Star Belgrade, when the magnificent Charlton robbed the ball back off Kostic, a fully forty-yards out and roared onwards before letting fly a glorious low-drive leaving Beara helpless! This was Bobby Charlton's first European Cup trip abroad. The other players joked and tricked him so much about the awful food in Eastern Europe, Bobby stuffed his suitcase with packets of sweets and biscuits! On discovering how nice it actually was in the Majestic hotel, Bobby ended up leaving everything to the lady who cleaned his room!

Two-minutes later with the Red Star supporters watching on in abject horror and disbelief, Charlton was gifted a second when from a melee after an Edwards free kick, with just a fleeting glimpse of the net, he swooped to beat Beara once more from close range. An astonishing 3-0 to the visitors! 5-1, overall on aggregate. With just thirty-minutes gone Manchester United appeared home and dry, playing like European champions elect! A place in the semi-finals sealed and most likely another showdown with their old friends from the *Estadio Bernabeu*. Real Madrid. Busby's swaggering young colts had so far staged a performance to rank alongside anything they had yet produced in the European Cup. As Kainer's whistle resonated for half-time, the Red Star players appeared demoralised. The opening forty-five minutes was most definitely not in the script. Nobody did this to them on home soil, nobody. Even if not in their own stadium it remained Belgrade. In the United dressing room there were injury worries with Kenny Morgans having had his thigh ripped open, and Edwards picking up an ankle injury. Morgans was having whiskey poured upon his thigh to numb the pain, whilst Edwards had ice placed on his ankle. Both would be patched up and thrown back into the thick of battle, because it was clear Red Star would surely in the second-half play better, for they simply could not be any worse. Whatever was said or threatened in the home changing room at half-time had the desired effect, for they did reappear a team transformed. From looking demoralised, especially their star man Sekularac, who in the first-half appeared to lose both his heart and head as the United goal tally mounted, came roaring out, fired up and determined to make amends. Two-minutes in their centre-forward Bora Kostic chanced his luck with a twenty-yard effort that sneaked past Harry Gregg into the far corner to ignite the stadium and rekindle Red Star hopes. Suddenly, Belgrade was in uproar! To United's dismay and discomfort the Gypsy had returned casting spells. Sekularac, blessed with the ability to create and dazzle after vanishing during the opening half, seemingly more intent on hacking down those in red shirts, had come back out determined to force the comeback. *Seki* caused mayhem as he prompted and probed, an artist painting pictures in his head masterminding an all-out assault on Manchester United's goal. His mesmeric flick set up striker Cokic, who thundered a shot goalwards that screamed inches over Gregg's crossbar! The visitors cause was hardly helped by the constant barrage of snowballs launched by the spectators behind the goal at United defenders and their seething goalkeeper! In the previous game when Manchester United played at Highbury, before kick-off, Gregg handed out sweets to smiling young Arsenal fans behind the goal. Not in Belgrade, as he was met only by stern-faced Yugoslav soldiers and policemen lining the perimeters. As the air filled with the playful, if unwanted missiles, the Red Star crowd picked out their targets in red and a very grumpy Irishman in green! The onslaught continued and even the United forwards were being constantly forced back into defensive positions. The visitor's forays up field had become extremely rare, but still packed enough punches to cause heart attacks on the Belgrade terraces when they did occur. No more so than when Kenny Morgans, fighting the pain barrier, broke away to see his shot beat Beara only then to strike the post. It was breath-taking stuff! With Busby's team repeatedly penned in their first-half exhibition of attacking pass and move football appeared a distant dream, as the game turned into a desperate, rearguard action. It was now mostly down to guts and courage. Such intense pressure had to tell and on fifty-five minutes, Red Star were awarded a ridiculously, soft penalty. Herr Kainer again receiving the freedom of Belgrade for a decision that left all of a United persuasion baffled. Midfielder Lazar Tasic falling theatrically in a heap over Bill Foulkes. As the *JNA* held a collective breath, Tasic showed remarkable calm to thrash a precise spot-kick high past the tips of Gregg's fingers. 2-3! Memories of the Arsenal 4-5 result when United let a three goal lead slip returned. The Yugoslavs needed two more to take the tie into a third match decider in Milan. Suddenly, Manchester United found themselves in big trouble. With an injured Duncan Edwards and Albert Scanlon reduced to mere nuisance value, and Harry Gregg lying hopeless on the turf, Sekularac danced past Bill Foulkes leaving him in a heap before setting up Cokic, who somehow, to the abject horror of the terraces contrived to miss an open goal from five-yards. The crowd went wild! Cokic fell to his knees and punched the floor and behind the net hordes of supporters surged down from the terraces onto the running track, many tumbling and collapsing en-masse. Dazed and staggering they were helped to their feet by the Yugoslav soldiers and policemen, many who they had landed on. Meanwhile, back on the pitch the siege went on. Despite almost on one leg Edwards stood his ground helping out the defence, even at one stage bursting the ball with one clearance! As the clock ticked down Sekularac's unerring talent to pick holes in the Mancunian rearguard was at times uncanny. Only by sheer, dogged determination and willingness to throw their bodies into the line of fire saw United surviving. Roger Byrne had been immense as had his fellow defenders Bill Foulkes and centre-half Mark Jones, but there still remained time for all their excellent work to be undone. His goal under siege Harry Gregg ranted, raved and performed heroics to keep the Belgrade forwards at bay. At one stage he came flying off his line to take the ball from Sekularac's toe on the edge of the penalty area. For a second the Irishman lay deathly still much to the distress of Roger Byrne, who seeing what appeared blood on his goalkeeper's white shorts feared he had been badly injured, only for Gregg to leap back up. The colouring being only the marking on the pitch! The Yugoslavs had painted the lines red instead of standard white because of the snow. Three-minutes remained when Kainer struck again and Red Star were awarded a free-kick on the edge of the penalty box. It was a dubious decision awarded against Harry Gregg, as he dived at the feet of tricky Belgrade left-winger Branko Zebec, only then to slide outside the area on the treacherously, slippery surface and be penalised. Two of the English hacks were far from impressed. "Herr Kainer would have given a free-kick against United if one of the ball boys fell on his backside!" wrote Henry Rose of The Daily Express. While the Daily Herald's George Follows was equally damning. "The Blue Danube flows grey and cold through this city of Belgrade, and for all Manchester United care, the referee Karl Kainer of Vienna can jump in it-whistle and all!"

United called everyone back, they were so close. Kostic took aim and let fly a shot that deflected off Dennis Viollet's head on the end of the defensive wall, before slipping agonisingly through Gregg's grasping fingers and into the United goal, levelling at 3-3! 5-4 on aggregate. Red Star needed just one more, Belgrade had gone mad! A limping, bedraggled, exhausted Manchester United had fought out a furious battle, but were all but done. Across the field and not only where the markings were placed, parts of it was blood red from injuries that had bled out onto the pitch. Morgans especially. From the touchline a desperately anxious Matt Busby urged for one last monumental effort. A final time the Gypsy set off into United's half, the ball tied to his dancing feet like an invisible string. Alluring, deadly, only to be stopped in his stride and dropping to one knee as Herr Kainer blew for full time. An epic clash ended with both sides simply spent of all energy. They shook hands, exchanged hugs and a bad tempered, bruising affair was instantly forgotten. A magnificent ovation broke out across the terraces. Not just for their own boys who had staged a fantastic comeback from three down, but also for the team from another world beyond the *Iron Curtain* called Manchester United. Their shattered expressions, faces and red shirts splattered in mud and rain-caked dirt. The Belgrade crowd, though the snowballs continued to rain down clearly recognised they had lost out to an incredibly, special team. Blessed not just with wonderful skill and finesse as shown in the first half, but bags of courage and determination that was so prevalent in the second. United had matched Red Star Belgrade in every forte of what was a most beautiful and brutal encounter. The manager and players were both proud and relieved. "This was our best performance in the European Cup," said a beaming Matt Busby. His Captain sounded more relieved than triumphant. "I have never wanted to hear the final whistle more than I did today. Red Star were much better than in Manchester, particularly in the second-half. Now, we are in the semi-finals, I hope we get Real Madrid again as this year, I feel we can run them much closer."

The *Black Panther* Beara spoke highly of his opponents. "Manchester United are the better qualified team for the semi-final Good luck to them." Once back in the dressing room the victorious players were met by the rest of the squad and the aircrew, as Tom Curry and Bert Whalley, handed out to them welcoming, celebratory bottled beers from crates. Eddie Colman and Tommy Taylor treated everyone to a Latin American rumba draped only in towels! The air hostesses Miss Bellis and Miss Cheverton swiftly exited in case of any accidents! Elsewhere, the manager was typically in the Red Star dressing room shaking the hands of all their players and staff. On stepping out he saw the ladies stood in the corridor and hearing the voice of Tommy Taylor shouting: "Bring those girls back in!" Taylor was more than surprised when Busby re-entered with a terse look upon his face. Silence filled the room for a moment before the manager smiled and said: "Get changed lads and the girls will come back in!"

The Government controlled Yugoslav newspaper *Politika* was not very impressed with what they had seen of Manchester United, and appeared to have taken the defeat badly! "United were unsportsmanlike and often unscrupulous. In the second-half the British players felled opponents in an impermissible manner. Many times we asked ourselves where the renowned British fair play was? That is only a legend. There was not a professional trick that they did not use to bring themselves out of difficult positions, and were often unscrupulous when they tackled, and pushed and tripped."
 The travelling English press pack could not disagree more with *Politika's* stance. They remained ecstatic with the United performance. The next day's wild and wonderful, flowery match reports acted as wonderful epitaphs to a doomed football team and for themselves. On leaving the stadium the Manchester United contingent with the press pack alongside them headed off to the British Embassy in the centre of Belgrade to continue the party. This before an official Post-match banquet to be held back at their Hotel Majestic later that evening hosted by the British ambassador. It was to be a joyous bunch of Mancunians who celebrate into the early hours laid on wonderfully for themselves and Red Star Belgrade. Model Sputniks surrounded them in the hotel banquet suite, very Soviet, but also overwhelmingly

friendly. Speeches of goodwill heard from both sides, endured mostly by the footballers but applauded loudly by all. Gifts were handed out as each visiting player received a tea pot and a bottle of gin! Hostilities forgotten, bad tackles forgiven and for some, those fortunate few, life-long friendships were struck on both sides. Dragoslav Sekularac got on famously with the United lads. Two worlds apart maybe but football as ever crossing every border. The gypsy bringing the teams together. Dropping a shoulder, raising a drink and leaving in his most beautiful, beguiling wake the foreboding *Iron Curtain*. Vast quantities of Belgrade's finest wine downed, toasts made and songs sung. United's Yorkshire trio of Mark Jones, Tommy Taylor and David Pegg gave a rather drunken, but lively rendition of *"On Ilkley Moor Baht 'At"* and received a standing ovation. In a moving scene the meal ended when waiters entered the dining room carrying trays of sweetmeats lit by candles set in ice. The United party stood to applaud the skills of their Yugoslav chef, and Roger Byrne in a tribute to their hosts led his team mates in a rousing, emotional version of: *"We'll meet again, don't know where, don't know when. But I know we'll meet again some sunny day"*.

Later, when official duties had been performed Byrne passed over a scribbled note to Matt Busby asking permission for the players to be allowed a few hours grace? Aware he could trust them not to start World War Three, Busby agreed and to hushed cheers they made their plans. Others such as Harry Gregg, Mark Jones and David Pegg chose instead to remain in the hotel and play cards. Fuelled by the local beverages, mostly the lethal Slivovitz, (An extremely, potent Serbian fruit brandy!) And suitcases stashed with essentials such as corned beef, biscuits and hard boiled eggs, they laughed at being able to play for astronomical stakes using the vastly over-inflated Yugoslav currency. Calls of: "I'll bet you four thousand dinar!"

"I'll raise you six thousand!"

"I'll raise you ten thousand!" This causing much laughter amongst young footballers oblivious to their true worth in far much contrasting times. As for the lads who wanted to see the mystical, dark lights of Belgrade? They ended up in a notorious nightclub called The Crystal.

Here they enjoyed the delights of Eastern European cabaret, Belgrade style! Jugglers, dancers and more exotic cabaret! Away from the manager's prying eyes they could properly let their hair down and celebrate reaching a second, successive European Cup semi-final. One Yugoslav English speaking journalist working for *Politika*, Miro Radojcic, was also in the Crystal that evening and found himself introduced to Duncan Edwards and Tommy Taylor. Incidentally, Dragoslav Sekularac was also present. The little man spellbinding on the pitch was equally enchanting off it ensuring they had a memorable evening. Him and Tommy partying away! At least the United lads could get near him that night! Miro, after chatting and drinking with Edwards and Taylor of whom he thought were delightful company had an idea. On finally returning to his apartment Miro was left alone with his thoughts and decided on the spur of the moment to fly back to Manchester with the team and write a story about the famous Busby Babes. A view of England's top team seen through the eyes of a much, respected Yugoslav journalists. Warmed by the wine and comforted that he still had a few hours to catch some sleep Miro was determined to see this idea through. He sat up throughout most of the night. *Politika* was not a sporting publication, in fact Miro was a political writer, but he had a great love for football, and the flair and glamour of Manchester United's young side attracted him like no other. Finally Miro drifted off. It was daylight once more when he awoke, jumped out of bed and started to pack a suitcase.

Outside the Belgrade sky was thick with snow falling like huge confetti onto the city.

The date. Thursday 6th February 1958.

Soon for Manchester United, it would be time to go home and Miro Radojcic was going with them. On reaching the airport a horrified Miro realised he had forgotten his passport. Miro pleaded with the airport authorities to hold the aircraft for as long as possible, whilst he took a taxi trip back home to retrieve it. By the time Miro returned, the twin-engine Elizabethan had taken off. Homeward bound for England, via Munich, where it was scheduled to stop for a short time whilst re-fuelling. He watched as it disappeared from sight in the Belgrade sky and sighed. Unknown to him at that very moment this was the luckiest day of Miro Radojcic's life.

CHAPTER SEVENTEEN
MUNICH

BBC Radio Newsflash.
…"We interrupt this broadcast of Mrs Dale's diary for a news flash. Reuters reports that a British European Airways Elizabethan aircraft carrying the Manchester United football team has crashed on take-off at Munich airport. Some casualties are feared. We will interrupt programmes with more details as soon as possible"…

"I said cheerio to those lads in the gymnasium. I told them I would see them back in the gymnasium on the Friday. Only when they came back to Old Trafford, they were in their coffins."
   Jimmy Murphy

Manchester.
Jimmy looked at his watch, it was twenty-five minutes to four in the afternoon. He had just arrived back at London Road railway station still clutching the box of oranges presented to him by the Israelis. It was bitterly cold with mountains of snow in the dark, bleak Mancunian heavens. He walked across smiling and whistling to the taxi rank, had a quiet word to the driver and stepped into the back of his cab. Jimmy was Old Trafford bound and in a wonderful mood. Wales in the World Cup finals and Manchester United in the European Cup semi-finals. His two footballing loves. All was well in Jimmy's world. He stared out the windows and the streets were filled with people heading home from work. The traffic was thick, bumper to bumper. Jimmy noticed crowds stood around the newspaper vendors. A lady crying on the pavement. Another man caught his eyes as they passed him. He had a look of incredulity. All, very strange. High above the skies had turned a foreboding dark, almost hellish colour in its gloom. Like a black veil over the city. Small snowflakes were still falling. Jimmy's mind was already racing ahead to Wolverhampton Wanderers on Saturday. Six points behind it was a

game United could not afford to lose. Nothing was more certain that Stan Cullis would have his team revved up for Old Trafford in front of a capacity crowd. United would need to be at their absolute best to beat them. From the little he had heard from Belgrade they were kicked from pillar to post and the situation regarding injuries was worrying. Duncan's ankle and Kenny Morgan's thigh were the main worries. He was already bursting to see the lads and Matt again. Also, Bert and Tom, both salt of the earth types. His pals. Good old boys. Tomorrow, Jimmy would grab them and over a cuppa get the full story of what went on. Who played well, who is tired. Who needs a kick up the backside or an arm around their shoulder. Let the boss get on with the paperwork. The press hacks and the contracts. Jimmy would tell him what he needed to know. The final word always lay with Matt, but these three United men supplied the main ingredients in the cake whilst Busby placed the iced toppings. It may have been the Busby Babes to the supporters and outsiders, but those lads were Jimmy's, Bert's and Tom's. They knew what made the players tick, both on the pitch and off. Who was not getting on with the wife, the girlfriend or mother-in-law. Who was hitting the bottle? Who was enjoying himself too much with the ladies? Dancing with the devil at the bookies. Who needed a kind word or a good old fashioned rollicking? Matt Busby was the politician, the public face of Manchester United. Undoubtedly the boss, but they made the lads ready for that time on match day when he entered the dressing room, and those in red shirts would by then be ready to run through brick walls for him and the club.

Finally, Jimmy's black cab entered onto the Old Trafford forecourt. He paid the driver and stepped out into the icy cold once more. So much to do, still clutching tight on the box of the sweet, smelling oranges. Jimmy made his way inside desperate to see Busby's secretary Alma George for a catch up from Belgrade. What time the plane was due to land and any gossip flying around. Alma was highly thought of by everybody at Old Trafford. Without Alma it was said they would all be whistling in the wind. The woman was incredible. No matter how busy she coped, always smiling and forever in good humour. She also knew when to ignore the language that you could imagine in a football club was at times coarse. Jimmy entered through a staff door and up the stairs to the offices. Nobody appeared to be around when suddenly Alma appeared from an adjoining room with tears falling down her face. It was clear she had been sobbing, holding tight onto a handkerchief. It was then Alma told Jimmy that the aircraft had crashed at Munich, and they did not know who was alive…Or who was dead?

Belgrade.
It was a sorry, looking, hungover group of players, officials and reporters that gathered once more at the airport to board the plane taking them home to Manchester, via refuelling at Munich. Bleary eyed but relieved they had got through. There was a last minute drama on leaving Belgrade when Johnny Berry's passport could not be found. Jokes of being sent to Siberia were aired before it finally appeared and he was allowed through customs, and not placed one way on the Trans-Siberian Express! At around 180 miles per hour, the Elizabethan flight G-ALZU A857 made its wary path over the snow clad Alps towards Germany. The players relaxed, sat scattered around the aircraft. In the middle section Johnny Berry, Roger Byrne and Jackie Blanchflower were playing cards. Harry Gregg, who normally would have been sat with them decided to have a snooze instead nearer the front, as the others refused to play for Yugoslav dinars! Nearby him was the News Chronicle's Frank Taylor. He would usually have been with his press correspondents at the rear, but Taylor had an upset stomach and decided it would be better away from the rocking of the tail. Also, in the middle of the plane was Matt Busby alongside Bert Whalley. Both men now with only one thing on their minds. Back in Belgrade airport, Busby had ushered the players at a brisk pace through customs towards the aircraft! For Wolves were all now consuming, his every thought focused on the coming Saturday at Old Trafford. Even now he knew the Football League Secretary Alan Hardaker would be staring at his watch and the skies. The embittered Hardaker would be so desperate to dock United the two points if they

failed to arrive home on time to fulfil their League commitments. Dukla Prague was close, not again. Never again. If this Elizabethan aircraft had been deemed good enough for Queen Elizabeth 2, who once flew on her then the United manager thought why not his boys?

Around two o'clock the airplane began the descent through dense clouds to land once more at Riem Airport, Munich to refuel. It was scheduled for just a thirty-minutes stay. Cold and desolate, a sight more fitting to an Ice Station Zebra in the North Pole. A dark, lonely silhouette in the snow with tractors and small trucks clustered around static, abandoned, aircraft. The runway edges had been cleared, leaving white straight rivers for the pilots to navigate. A ferocious blizzard was sweeping all in its wake across the airport as they landed with a screech before coming to a halt. As seat belts were taken off there was an announcement for the passengers to depart for a short break in the departure lounge whilst the aircraft was refuelled. Across the runway the players, pressmen and others trundled like lost refugees huddled, rushing through an almighty barrage of snowflakes biting in their faces. As a lovely respite from the bitter cold, hot drinks were passed around by Mrs Miklos playing mum to all the footballers. ''The German coffee tastes like sawdust!'' moaned the Daily Herald's George Follows, as some of his fellow journalist phoned their newspaper offices. Everyone was clearly anxious to get back home, the journalists especially to make a press ball that same evening in Manchester. To pass a little time some of the players went looking for presents. Sweethearts or families. In Johnny Berry's case, he was enjoying himself at a small toy counter, happily keeping the lady there busy by winding up the small toys so he could choose which ones to buy for his kids. After twenty-minutes or so the announcement was made. ''Will all passengers with the Manchester United party please board now''. There was much laughter and joking around as the party made their way back across what was a sea of slushy white on the runway. Meanwhile, the two pilots had remained outside busy checking the wings for ice and both were satisfied all appeared well. At 2-30.pm, the Elizabethan aircraft set off again, but had to swiftly pull up and stall because of an uneven engine noise and return back down the runway. Slowly, gathering speed and with the engines at full power they tried again only for forty-seconds later coming to an ominous, shuddering halt. This time scaring all on board. Permission was sought from the air traffic control tower to try once more, yet something wasn't right and halfway down the runway the take-off was aborted. Captain Rayment assured everybody from over the tannoy that it was just a mere technical hitch and would be sorted, but that they would need to disembark again whilst the fault was checked. Thain had noticed a fluctuation in the boost pressure of one of the engines and had been forced to apply the brakes. It was a worrying, freezing band of travelling Mancunians who made their way back across the tarmac and into the building.

Harry Gregg recalled watching through the windows of the airport lounge. "The snow continued to fall and the aircraft slowly vanished before my eyes." One way or another Manchester United had to get home. Otherwise, they would be forced to forfeit the Wolves game and lose points. Duncan Edwards sent a telegram to his landlady. *"All flights cancelled – stop – flying tomorrow – stop – Duncan."*

Finally, word came through to embark for a third time. The clock touching 4.00.pm, German time. On boarding Gregg loosened his shirt and unfastened his belt to get himself comfortable. The goalkeeper found himself sweating buckets amid a raging blizzard. A last second drama occurred when after a headcount from an air stewardess they realised there was one passenger short.

"It's not one of mine!" quipped Tom Curry. Suddenly, the doors opened to reveal a breathless, red-faced Manchester Evening Chronicle's Alf Clarke, who had just raced across the tarmac. He was greeted by a hail of friendly abuse! Clarke had been in the airport lounge phoning through copy to the Chronicle's office updating them with progress on getting home. The paper was subbing the last pages of their Saturday Pink when Alf's original call came through. He told them United's flight had been delayed by snow. Alf then rang shortly after saying that there had been two aborted take offs, but they were set to try again a third time. This the call that caused the delay. Alf also asked the press guys to pass a message on to his wife that he would see her soon. As all the players happily sang his nickname of "Scoop!" for a few moments the tensions eased as Clarke took his seat and buckled in. Gregg remembers looking around and witnessing nothing but worried expressions. "Roger Byrne was sat opposite me. He looked terrified." The engines started up again. Nervous coughs, mutterings, bad jokes to cover the fear, but Johnny Berry wasn't laughing. "I don't know what you're all laughing at. We're all going to get killed here!" Billy Whelan said if it happened he was prepared to die. "If it's my time I am ready." People began to move seats. At the back of the aircraft was where most of the press pack placed themselves. Many were World War Two veterans and always told it was the safest place to be in case of a crash. Other also began to move around the plane. Bobby Charlton and David Pegg joined the hacks. By this time, the aircraft was motoring on the runway and huge mounds of slush flew past the portholes as it increased in power. They went past places that in the previous two aborted take offs had not even been reached. The wheels lifted off the runway and then the world turned upside.

It was utter carnage. A shuddering, crashing sound and debris began falling and flying. It was light, then darkness, then light again. As if turning a switch on, off, on, off. Bombarded by falling suitcase. A terrible-ripping sound of metal breaking up. A screeching, soaring, deafening noise. Passengers thrown round and round like a nightmarish carousel you could never get off. Yet, through that awful mayhem there was no screaming, no voices. Just sparks and small fires all around. Harry Gregg felt blood in his mouth. "I'd been cracked on the top of my skull and felt scared to touch it in case part of my head had been sliced off."

...Fifty four seconds earlier...

For the third time at 4-03.pm, (German time). Flight G-ALZU A857 rolled at first and then accelerated into the late, afternoon darkness of the Munich runway. At reaching a speed of 117 mph, Captain James Thain noticed a surge in the boost control. The air indicator dropped dramatically and as the runway's end drew ever closer, panic filled

the cockpit. The slush and the sleet from the wheels was hurled up against the portholes as the aircraft sped towards it's tragic end. Rayment at the controls shouted: ''We won't make it!'' Back amongst the passengers many had their eyes shut. Fear was etched on faces as the reality that something had gone dreadfully wrong took hold. Frantically, Thain tried to retract the undercarriage to get them airborne, but the fuselage refused to lift. From that moment on they were out of control. Sparks all around, it was a hellish rollercoaster. The aircraft crashed into a nearby house slashing off its roof, then skidded into an empty army barracks. Forty-yards away sat a fuel dump and part of the wing careered into it causing huge plumes of flames to shoot into the sky. Spinning round and round in ever, maddening, circles, the hulking Elizabethan finally came to a sickening halt, quite literally ripped in two. A ghastly, twisted mess that any time threatened to explode. Carnage had ensued, dazed, confused and disbelieving survivors staggered out and around the wreckage. Bodies lay scattered, some burnt beyond recognition. A shocking silence was broken only by a hissing noise emanating from the downed fuselage. Like a death knell.
Munich's black skies still filled with snow.

Just before the airplane came to a fearsome halt, Harry Gregg was glued to his window porthole watching the huge mounds of slush flying into the air, as they went ever faster. ''I saw the wheels actually lift up off the runway and then?''…When coming around Harry felt the salty taste of blood in his mouth after being cracked on the top of the head. ''I felt sick and dizzy. I remember thinking, although it sounds crazy now, that I couldn't speak German? Then, came the frightening fear that I'd never see my family again.''
After noticing a shaft of light in front of him Harry unfastened his seat belt and crawled towards it. On looking out scenes of carnage greeted him. He saw Bert Whalley lying in the snow motionless. His eyes wide open, not a mark on him but clearly dead. Harry then kicked in the hole bigger managing to squeeze through and jump down onto the ground. All was ghostly quiet apart from a hissing

noise coming from the bulk. A Dante's inferno. The actual snow was burning, there was small fires crackling all around. One of the wings had broken off. Then, from the cockpit Captain Thain appeared with a fire extinguisher in his hands. He spotted Harry and shouted towards him, ''Run it's going to explode!' As Thain ran Harry heard a small cry back inside the airplane. He suddenly remembered a baby with the mother sat just behind him. As Harry climbed back up he noticed four or five figures racing clear of the plane. 'Come back you bastards!'' he screamed! ''There are people still alive in here!'' Ignoring his calls for help, Harry went back inside alone. He crawled to where the cries were coming from finding the baby lying under a pile of suitcase and broken iron. By some miracle she had suffered only a bad cut above one eye. Once back outside one of those who originally ran off had returned. It was the radio operator George Rogers. Harry passed him over the baby called Vesna, and went back in looking for more survivors. He found Vesna's mother. A Yugoslav lady in a terrible state, but he managed also to drag her to safety. But these few apart that were saved and survived, there was many more dead and dying on the end of that Munich runway. Harry spotted the corpses of Roger Byrne, Eddie Colman and Tommy Taylor, scattered around. So much blood in the snow. Now, in the open it became clear to him what had actually occurred. There was a house about sixty-yards away with half its roof torn off. Next to that a compound containing a fuel dump. That now alight. The airplane must have careered off the runway, broken up with part resting at the house, whilst the rest slid onwards. Hans Birnbaum was a Munich fuel merchant and one of only a handful of witnesses to the last moments of the aircraft. "The visibility was poor so not many people saw what happened. I was only 200 metres away when the plane crashed and the force of the explosion of the petrol was so powerful that I was knocked down by it. When I got up I saw flames and smoke pouring out of two houses and debris flying through the air. I ran to the plane and saw the plane had broken in pieces."
As Harry watched on explosions lit up the black sky. Huge plumes of flames leaping high, shooting upwards. The heat melting the snow

turning it into slush and water. Water and blood. He found Ray Wood but could not move him because he was trapped under too much fuselage. As was Albert Scanlon, whose injuries were so bad they made Harry vomit. He desperately needed help, but there was nobody around? No police, no ambulances, no fire engines, nothing. Harry next stumbled upon Bobby Charlton and Denis Viollet, both in shock just stood staring at the airplane. The crash had thrown them over twenty-yards clear whilst still strapped in their seats, and apart from a few bloodied scratches they appeared relatively unscathed. After telling them to go and help the more badly injured survivors, Harry then came across his manager propped up between the aircraft wreckage and remnants of a burning building. At first Harry thought Busby was not too badly injured. Just a small trickle of blood behind an ear, but he was also rubbing his chest and groaning about his legs. After making his boss comfortable as possible Harry moved on to others appearing more seriously hurt. By this time, a few Germans had arrived to help, but still no ambulances or fire engines. He found his best pal Jackie Blanchflower in an awful state. Jackie cried out that his back was broken, and the lower part of an arm looked to Harry as if it had been severed. He tried desperately to make a tourniquet with his tie, but snapped it. Whilst looking to find something else to use, a stewardess appeared from nowhere. Together, they found a rag and stayed with Jackie trying to keep him calm. When Matt Busby was firstly contemplating signing Harry Gregg, he asked Jackie Blanchflower about him. ''He's the best goalkeeper in the word boss,'' answered Jackie.

''No, I'm not talking about his ability,'' replied Busby. ''We'll take care of that. I'm asking about his character.'' The Manchester United was receiving his answer in buckets of courage on that Munich afternoon.

More people were by now on the scene, but it remained nothing resembling organised. There was screams coming from all around, explosions, melting ice and slush, pools of reddish water, yet still the lashing snow fell from the sky, thick enough to blind your eyes. This was no horror story, it was reality. This was Munich. A German with a hypodermic needle in his hand came running towards Harry, only for an explosion to send him flying into the air. Happily, he landed on his backside with the needle still in his hand pointing upwards. A local man turned up in a Volkswagen and Harry and Bill Foulkes loaded Busby and Blanchflower inside. Two others placed another body in the back wearing the tattered, ripped remnants of a United blazer. Neither Harry nor Bill failed to recognise him because he was so severely burned. It later turned out to be Johnny Berry. Both men then jumped in also, stopping only to pick up the Yugoslav girl Maria Mikla and her baby Vesna, whom Harry had pulled out of the airplane previous. A farmer called Hans Wieser owned the land which bordered the runway where the airplane came to its catastrophic end. "The weather was awful. There was so much snow and such low visibility. I was in the stables working when I heard a woman screaming. I came out and saw that a plane had crashed into her house and ripped it from its foundations. She'd been in the cellar ironing and was unhurt. Then I saw the wreckage of the plane smouldering in the field. And the dead bodies."

On arrival at the *Rechts Der Isar* hospital, doctors wanted to keep Harry and Bill in overnight for checks but when hearing the announcement of "Herr Swift Kaput" over the tannoy, they simply could not face it and went back to the hotel. Frank Swift had died as he was being carried into the hospital. Tragically Swift's main aorta artery had been severed by his seat belt.

...BBC Television Newsflash. Five O'clock...

Richard Baker cutting into Children's Hour.

..."And the reason you've come over to the news studio is that we have to report a serious air crash at Munich Airport. We haven't full details yet, but the aircraft that has crashed is an Elizabethan. It was on charter from British European Airways and travelling from Belgrade to Manchester. The crash was at Munich Airport. On board was the Manchester United football team returning from their match in Yugoslavia. With them were sports writers of Fleet Street newspapers and, as far as we know, team officials. Twenty five of the passengers and crew are believed to have died.''…

The next day both Harry Gregg and Bill Foulkes returned to the scene of the disaster. The end of the runway packed with fire engines and ambulances. A case of after the Lord Mayor's show. The airplane fuselage remained smouldering and smoke still visibly rising from the fuel dumps. All that was missing was the bodies of those who had been killed. A German official confronted Harry and Bill and when finding out who they were actually asked them: ''What happened?'' ''You tell me?'' answered a shock Harry.
Both men walked amongst the wreckage. Bill climbed back into the part of the plane where he had been sat. Jammed against the roof in the rack above the seat he found his case totally undamaged. Bill opened it and remarkably inside was a bottle of gin not smashed. They swiftly made short work of it. Harry then found a cap with COLMAN written upon it. The players used to go in the Continental club back in Manchester, where the owner as a gimmick had these made to hand out. Eddie always used to wear his. Harry also found Eddie's red and white scarf and Bill spotted a paper bag containing an apple, orange, some tea and sugar. Eddie's mum had packed them for him. That upset Bill, so they finally came away. On leaving Harry spotted a policeman checking out a briefcase. On asking who it belong to he was told Walter Crickmer's. It contained traveller cheques and Walter's silver hip flask. To both Harry and Bill it appeared and felt like the German authorities were tidying up. Rushing to return back to some kind of normality. Huge diggers clearing the slush and melting ice off the runway. On the afternoon of Thursday 6th February 1958, fifteen flights took off all without problems. Something just did not sit right with Harry Gregg on what he witnessed the day after. Also Harry took great offence with the official story on what supposedly occurred in the immediate aftermath of the crash. ''Don't let anyone ever tell you that it was all hands on when we crashed, because it wasn't. We were on our own for what

felt an eternity, and until the day I die, I will stand by these words.
Until the day I die…''

The six o'clock news (BBC Home Service)
On the radiogram.
…''Here is the news. A British European Airways charter plane
carrying the Manchester United team crashed after taking off from
Munich Airport, at about three o'clock this afternoon. The weather
was said to be poor at the time. BEA stated about half an hour ago
that the plane was carrying a crew of six, and thirty-eight passengers-
including a baby. They say they believe there are about sixteen
survivors, including some of the crew. A Reuters report from Munich
says that survivors include the Manchester United players, Gregg,
Foulkes and Charlton. Reuters says that two other survivors are Mr
Peter Howard, a Daily Mail photographer and his assistant Mr
Ellyard, both from Manchester…''

CHAPTER EIGHTEEN
POISON ARROW

"Everybody lost something at the end of that runway."
  Matt Busby

The year of 1878, saw the birth of the "Galveston Giant" Jack Johnson, the first black heavyweight champion. It was also witness to British soldiers embroiled in bloody battle against a ferocious enemy in the mountains of Afghanistan. A white flash of inspiration enabled inventor Thomas Edison to begin work on the light bulb. Whilst in the American Wild-West, the murderous Lincoln County War began and introduced to a fascinated American audience a certain William H Bonney. Better known as "Billy the kid". Meanwhile, faraway in mid-Victorian Manchester, England, a place called Newton Heath, the age of the Industrial Revolution was at hand. Tall, grimy chimneys poked their miserable noses into permanently murky skies. This the terminus for the Manchester to Leeds railway and against a deafening backdrop of thunderous, rattling, freight trains, in the depot yard on a break, a group of young men with blackened, coal soot faces were happily enjoying kicking a football about. These were employees of the Lancashire and Yorkshire Railway company, and had recently been granted permission to form a works team by the grand gentlemen of the Dining Room Committee and wagon works. Such being the enthusiasm for this new venture the railwaymen happily agreed to pay a subscription for the right to play, but still they required a pitch. Luckily, in a rare show of generosity, the Dining Committee also provided them with a plot of company wasteland and goalposts in nearby North Road for matches. Sat alongside a railway line, the surface cut a pitiable sight resembling a stone strewn, clay scarred pit. A jagged, rock hard death trap in summer, and a mud, splattered swamp during winter. Adding further insult was the constant irritant of thick, swirling mists of steam that enveloped all every time a train passed! But it was a home and here amid such splendour, Newton Heath *LYR* football team were born. Match day preparations started half a mile away at the Three Crowns pub on Oldham Road. Courtesy of a good-hearted landlord, they were allowed to change and then a ten-minute dash to North Road for kick off. Playing in vivid colours of green and gold shirts, *LYR* challenged fellow inter-departmentals and excelled against all of them. Rail yard teams further along the line from Middleton, Earlestown and Oldham came to North Road and were handed a beating. However, there was one side that due to local pride and Newton Heath bragging rights never lay down. Contests versus the neighbouring Company's Motive Power Division or Newton Heath Loco were never for the faint hearted. Loco played home matches just a stone's throw away from North Bank at Ceylon Street. With their team made up from engine drivers and maintenance men, weekday quarrels and fall outs were settled, sometimes brutally on a Saturday afternoon, as the two local rivals flew at each other with a passion! But Loco apart, there was a serious lack of opponents good enough within the company to give Newton Heath *LYR* a decent game. With crowds rising weekly and a growing reputation for tough, but good attacking play reaching well beyond their own works, it was time to spread wings. Invitations were sent further afield for others to try their hand against the mighty "Heathens!" Or as they were also becoming known as. The "Coachbuilders". Letters were posted to such potentially exalted opponents as Manchester Arcadians, Hurst Brook Rovers, Dalton Hall and Blackburn Olympic amongst others. At the Three Crowns pub amid the beery laughter, chit-chat and pipe smoke they awaited with anticipation whether their challenges would be accepted. Small acorns…

Manchester. The Imperial Pub. Sunday 27th April 1902.
   A meeting was taking place to resurrect the bankrupt Newton Heath as a new football club. Almost all issues had been dealt with, the only remaining one was what to name this grand new venture. Present at the legendary meeting were five men. The wealthy brewery owner Mr John Henry Davies of Old Trafford who was hosting. Mr James

Taylor, Mr William Deakin, Mr James Brown and Mr Louis Rocca.
Davies asked all present for suggestions?
Taylor offered up Manchester Central? Deakin though claimed it
sounded too much like a railway station. He put forward Manchester
Celtic, a nudge and a wink towards the Catholic church. Davies
though thought this a non-starter because it would immediately
alienate any Protestant and Jewish support.
 "How about Manchester United?" mentioned Rocca.
Immediately around the table there were murmurs of approval and
nodding of heads in agreement. Hands were raised as Davies asked
them to vote on Louis Rocca's suggestion and it was unanimous!
Manchester United they became.
And now…

Fifty six years later.
"The airplane Jimmy, it's crashed at Munich. We don't know who is
dead or alive." Words that broke the heart and so nearly the spirit of
Jimmy Murphy. "The words seemed to ring in my head. Alma left
me and I went into my office. My head was in a state of confusion
and I started to cry." After a few moments to pull himself together,
Jimmy told Alma to contact the British embassy in Germany. For he
knew people, the families most of all would expect them to know
what had occurred. The club's chief scout Joe Armstrong turned up to
help, and Jimmy asked him to grab a taxi and go call on relatives.
Armstrong noticed on heading across the forecourt there were many
fans obviously still oblivious to what had occurred arriving at the
ground to buy tickets to watch the forthcoming FA Cup tie against
Sheffield Wednesday, due to be played at Old Trafford.
Armstrong found that many of the relatives he set off to visit had
already headed off to Ringway Airport to greet returning loved ones
from Belgrade. To congratulate them on a fantastic performance
against Red Star. Amongst the parents, kids, wives and girlfriends
was Matt Busby's wife Jean. A great excitement hung in the air for
their boys had done United proud again. BEA Flight 609 was

scheduled to arrive home at Manchester's Ringway Airport, five o'clock, but around 4.30.pm, a message hailed over the tannoy. "People waiting for BEA Flight 609 should call at the reception desk in the main hall…''

So, it began. Across the city as the night skies ever darkened, newspaper stands with placards proclaiming loud and grand **"UNITED IN THE SEMIS AGAIN!"** were taken down and replaced by **"UNITED DISASTER!"**

Back at Old Trafford, Jimmy Murphy had started to ring around the newspapers, the police, the BBC, but there was huge difficulty getting an outside line because the club's switchboard system had become completely jammed up with masses of incoming calls. Families and supporters simply desperate for news. It was the journalist Bill Fryer from the Daily Express who originally broke the grim tidings of the fatalities to Jimmy after the Express received a list of names from Reuters News Agency confirming those definitely lost. He also had information on the severely injured, the walking wounded and the relatively unscathed. Fryer explained how the airplane was on its third take off. They overran the runway, the pilot lost control and the airplane careered into catastrophe. He firstly gave Jimmy the list of the players definitely killed.

Roger Byrne.

Tommy Taylor.

David Pegg.

Billy Whelan.

Geoff Bent.

Eddie Colman.

Mark Jones.

Each name a poisoned arrow through Jimmy Murphy's heart.

As Jimmy scribbled down the names of the fallen he was shocked as Fryer then informed him there were even more. Many more.

Tom Curry and Bert Whalley, his dear, dear pals were gone also.

The line went off and Jimmy noticed a bottle of whisky on the shelf. To try and clear his head one drink led to another and before he knew it, the bottle was half gone. Jimmy needed fresh air and on stepping outside Old Trafford, there was large groups of people stood milling around all waiting on for scraps of news, rumours, Absolutely anything. The not knowing was unbearable.

"What's happening Jimmy?"

"Any news Jimmy?"

"Are they all dead Jimmy?"

"Is Matt alive Jimmy?"

"Is big Dunc okay Jimmy?"

"Please tell me Eddie isn't dead Jimmy?"

"Why Jimmy, why, why?"

As they surrounded him two policemen arrived to escort Jimmy back inside. Waiting was Alma to inform of more fatalities. The much loved club secretary Walter Crickmer and eight of the newspaper boys had also been killed, with the BBC reporting twenty-one dead in total, but that total likely to rise.

The lost Journalists.

Alf Clarke from The Manchester Chronicle. Alf was said to have been so biased through ted tinted eyes, that the other press lads would joke when a United player got kicked Alf limped!

Don Davies of The Manchester Guardian. Don's byline being the "Old International." A word poet. As were Eric Thompson of The Daily Mail, George Fellows of The Daily Herald. The Manchester Evening News's Tom Jackson. Archie Ledbrooke of The Daily Mirror. Henry Rose of the Daily Express. A supreme showman, outspoken and at times public enemy number one with the United players because of his scathing comments. But this apart a true gentleman and despite the fact Matt Busby and Jimmy Murphy could happily have throttled him at times he was considered a dear friend by both men. Finally, "Big Swifty". The former Manchester City goalkeeper Frank Swift, who once retired had begun to make a good name for himself as a journalist with the News of the World. He also was another huge pal of Jimmy Murphy's. Both had served together during the war. As the night wore on ever darkening, the phone rang bringing mostly grim tidings, but also moment of salvation. Matt Busby's son Sandy called to say his father was alive and had been taken to the *Rechts Der Isar* hospital. At the time Sandy having no idea that Busby still lay gravely ill, and deemed unlikely to live much longer. The time finally came to ring round the player's families of those that had perished. It was to be Jimmy Murphy's longest and most silent night. A devastated Welsh heart breaking into a thousand piece as his shaking fingers dialled.

Roger Byrne's wife Joy. She sounded in shock and spoke almost in sniffling, joking terms, but Jimmy could hear her heart breaking over the phone. Joy told him she had only known him three February's. The first he had crashed their car into a lamp post. The second into Matt Busby's neighbour's garden, and third got himself killed in a plane crash. Joy let slip also they were expecting a baby and Roger didn't know. She was going to tell him on returning.

Tommy Taylor, Barnsley's finest. Jimmy cried with both his mother and father, Viollet and Charlie. They told him how much Tommy had loved him. David Pegg's mother Jessie sobbed and sobbed.

Liam 'Billy' Whelan. A boy who wanted to be a priest, but only the love of a football saw him put on the red shirt of United, not a cassock and a clerical collar. Jimmy had no number but knew the name of the Dublin road, St Attracta, so found out through the operator a neighbour's phone number. He rang them instead and asked if they could possible go and put Liam's mother on the phone.

She told him: "I could feel my Liam's spirit soar. He is with the angels." Mark Jones' pregnant wife June screaming in despair. Geoff Bent's wife Marion weeping till there was no tears left to fall. She told Jimmy they already had one five-month-old baby and another on the way. Eddie Colman's dad Dickie said little, but Jimmy heard his heart breaking across the River Irwell. Eddie was their life, His grandfather Dickie Senior, who all the players adored. Duncan Edwards, Bobby Charlton and Wilf McGuiness in particular. They would gather in Eddie's living room and the old man would enthrall them with tall, terrible and wonderful tales of his past escapades. There would be singsongs and joy and laughter at number 9 Archie Street. Not anymore. After the call from Jimmy, Dickie simply

headed out the front door, and was found hours later in Piccadilly wearing just his pajamas and slippers, crying and in a daze.
As for Duncan Edwards? Duncan had been confirmed as very seriously ill. His injuries at that time unknown. But Jimmy knew where there was life hope remained and in Big Dunc's case, he was bigger than life itself. So, let anyone try to take him before he had conquered the world. A colossus and such a wonderful lad. They all were to Jimmy. Word came through that the head of the Football League Alan Hardaker wished to speak to Jimmy on the phone and offer his condolences. Manchester United had been at war with this man ever since Matt Busby took them into the European cup. Busby had spoken to Hardaker about a possible postponement of the Wolves match, before setting off to Belgrade, but oh no. He instead threatened United with a point's deduction if they failed in his now infamous words that had become drenched in blood. "Failed to fulfil their commitments to the Football League."
…"Mr Murphy."
"Mr Hardaker sir."
'May I on behalf of the Football League offer our deepest sympathies on your loss.'
"Thank you."
'Obviously in light of what's occurred, the crash, erm, terrible loss of life we will certainly be postponing the game against Wolverhampton Wanderers."
"We appreciate that sir."
"Well, if we can help in any other way please let us know Mr Murphy. Good luck."
…. 'Goodnight Mr Hardaker sir.' The line went dead…

Jimmy had fallen asleep but was awoken from his dark slumber by Alma to be told that Bill Foulkes, Harry Gregg and Bobby Charlton had all been confirmed as survivors. Another small chink of light in a black sea of despair. Although Alma then hit Jimmy with the news that Matt Busby and Duncan Edwards were both deemed as critical.

BEA had also rang to confirm they were putting on an airplane the next morning at nine o'clock, taking him and the family members of the injured over to Munich. For Jimmy Murphy, the night had never felt so black and was about to become an awful lot darker.

CHAPTER NINETEEN
KEEP THE FLAG FLYING

"This is a numbing tragedy. It stuns the mind to try to grasp that the flower of English football has fallen. It is a tragedy that will be felt not only by sports lovers but by all the people of Manchester and indeed by many others all over the world."
  Manchester Evening News editorial. 7th February 1958

A 16-year-old Sir Alex Ferguson was studying in a library that afternoon. "My first awareness of the crash came at about half past six when I arrived for training at my local football club. I remember seeing grown men in a terrible state. Training, of course, was cancelled." In Manchester factories shut down early, no one could concentrate, a city all but paralysed by Munich. Just empty warehouse floors, an eerie silence over Trafford Park and beyond. The pubs and cinemas lay empty. The grief that had engulfed Manchester was palpable. On hearing the terrible news the City goalkeeper Bert Trautmann contacted United to offer his services, whether it be interpreting, or simply offering a shoulder to cry on for those left behind. At a concert in Sheffield, the Halle Orchestra of Manchester played Elgar's *Nimrod* as a memorial tribute. The musicians' traditional farewell to past comrades. The audience of a thousand people stood throughout and there was then a minute's silence. It actually was real…

On Thursday 6th February 1958, the plane carrying Manchester United back from Belgrade after a European Cup quarter-final crashed at Munich airport, killing twenty-one passengers, including seven players. Captain Roger Byrne, Mark Jones, Eddie Colman, Tommy Taylor, Liam Whelan, David Pegg and Geoff Bent. Of the survivors left fighting for their lives in a Munich hospital, they included manager Matt Busby and the living, breathing, heart and soul of the now decimated Busby Babes. Duncan Edwards. Manchester was

aghast in sorrow. Black drapes, wreaths and heartfelt, epic poems to
the fallen coveted houses and shop windows. The coffins of the dead
lay in state at the club gymnasium looked over by two policemen,
whose only task appeared to be handing out tissues for the tears of
weeping visitors. A city's heart lay broken. Manchester United
appeared finished but this was not to be for in time-honoured
tradition, despite untold grief at the loss of so many broken hearts and
unhealed wounds, the show went on and just thirteen days after the
catastrophic air crash, United prepared to host Sheffield Wednesday in
an FA Cup fifth round clash. With their flag flying at half-mast over
the ground as a mark of respect for the fallen, those left behind
prepared for a game that would go down in the folklore of Manchester
United football club. But first to tell of the thirteen days previous
since the crash. A grieving period of deep sadness, morbid shock and
immense despair.

The pilot made his announcement that they were preparing to land
and for the passengers to put on their safety belts. Through the
porthole windows, beneath swirling clouds Munich came into view. A
most elegant city. Regaled with magnificent art galleries, fascinating
museums and legendary beer halls. Sadly, a place also associated with
Adolf Hitler and the Nazis. A beautiful city but etched with a sense of
everlasting evil. Now, in 1958, for everyone connected with
Manchester United Football Club, the name of Munich would make
them shudder forever more. Finally, the airplane doors opened and a
cold air jolted all. Snow was still falling but only a light shower.
Greeting the passengers as they walked down the steps could well
have been a Christmas card, but one drenched with so much
Mancunian blood. Munich airport lay covered in a white sprinkling of
snow. As if trying to hide the hideous events of the previous day.
Smoke could still be seen rising from the crash site at the end of the
runway. A coach stood waiting to take the passengers to the Starthus
hotel in the city, baggage staff were already busy loading cases.
 On board was a doctor who sat next to Jimmy filling him in on the
latest conditions of those at the *Rechts Der Isar*. He was told

worryingly Matt Busby's fate was in the hands of a "Higher force."
Busby remained fifty/fifty. As for Duncan Edwards, it was equally
grim news. Duncan's injuries were much worse than first feared.
Severely damaged kidneys, a collapsed lung, broken pelvis and
multiple fractures of the right thigh. Remarkably, from the neck up
Duncan did not have a mark on him.

The other injured?

Johnny Berry. In a deep coma with a fractured skull and other
fractures.

Albert Scanlon. Left leg badly injured and his scalp gashed.

Dennis Viollet. Head injuries and shock.

Bobby Charlton. Head injuries and shock.

Jackie Blanchflower. Fractured arm and pelvis.

Ray Wood. Leg and arm injuries.

Ken Morgans. Head injury and severe shock.

The other two players Harry Gregg and Bill Foulkes had been allowed
to leave the hospital late the previous evening. Lastly, Jimmy was told
by the doctor: "We are all Manchester United at the *Rechts Der Isar*
now."

 On arriving at the hospital they were introduced to the chief surgeon
in charge of the crash operation, Professor Georg Maurer. A small,
balding figure in glasses, clearly full of vigour. Behind him a host of
white coated doctors, nurses and a holy sister. The Professor was a
war hero. The holder of an Iron Cross, but he was no Nazi. Maurer
saved many lives and on both sides. It was at war zones like Dunkirk
and Stalingrad, where his experience of dealing with mass casualties
meant that when word reached the hospital of the crash they were
already drilled to perfection for their emergency procedures. Even to
the point where the Professor had stationed an engineer at the hospital
in case the lifts broke down. He left no stone unturned. Along with the
player's fiancé Molly Leach, Jimmy's first port of call was checking
in on Duncan Edwards. What they witnessed shocked both to the
core. Duncan wired up to a kidney machine that was keeping him
alive. A lad Jimmy thought of as invincible, but the reality being he
was human after all. Just a 21-year-old lad from Dudley that was

broken and whose survival now depended on a beeping piece of machinery. He was a footballer coming home to his girl. They were going to get married. They were pure and innocent. Duncan lived only for football, his family and Molly. She lived only for Duncan. None of it made sense for Jimmy Murphy. Elsewhere, in the hospital, similar scenes of unremitting grief were occurring. An endless stream of tears as people cried and mourned lost ones. Jimmy left a hysterically, sobbing Molly with Duncan and a German nurse Sister Solemnis, whilst he headed off to see Matt Busby. Already there was a heartbroken Busby's wife Jean and children Sheena and Sandy. Jimmy was informed that Busby was ''very poorly'' and had been given a Tracheotomy operation to enable him to breathe for his chest and lungs had been severely affected. Plus massive internal and external damage. A terribly, worrying prognosis, but Jimmy was told that Busby appeared strong. However, such being the concern it was agreed for him to receive the Last Rites later that evening. On Jimmy entering, Busby lay in an oxygen tent and he struggled to recognised him. Matt Busby was just 48, but appeared twenty-years older. Jimmy spoke hoping that from somewhere deep Busby could hear.
Suddenly, he felt a movement in the hand and his eyes flickered, then opened. He noticed Jimmy and a fearfully, pained smile fell across his face. Busby tried to speak but the words simply would not come. Jimmy leaned in closer to try and catch his strained whispers.
''Keep the flag flying Jimmy until I get back.''
The impassioned comments of an ailing Matt Busby still battling for life to his assistant and friend. "Keep the flag flying Jimmy. Keep the flag flying, keep the flag…''
Then, seemingly spent of all energy Busby's eyes closed once more, as he drifted off back into unconsciousness. Jimmy was given permission to see the other injured United players. Jackie Blanchflower, Kenny Morgans, Ray Wood, Johnny Berry, Denis Viollet, Albert Scanlon and finally Bobby Charlton. It was explained to him that by some miracle Charlton only received minor head injuries. He was given a sedative after the crash but after waking up remained in a severe state of shock. Charlton had that same afternoon

discovered the full extent of the tragedy. A patient in the bed next to him was reading out loud the names of those killed. At first Charlton thought these were the survivors, only to be told they had actually died. He was in a terrible state as Jimmy tried to keep him calm. Charlton just kept repeating: "It just doesn't make any sense?" His voice and heart crushed with the loss of so many of his pals. Jimmy told him that he had to forget about football for a while and go home to stay with his family. Dealing with all this, watching young men like Bobby Charlton driven to the edge after witnessing such terrifying scenes from the depths of hell. He remembered tough, battle-hardened Eighth Army soldiers in North Africa, after months of merciless fighting against Rommel's Afrika Korps in the blazing desert, just breaking down in tears on seeing the Mediterranean ocean.

The next morning Jimmy Murphy returned to the hospital along with Harry Gregg and Bill Foulkes. He had already made preparations to take the two United players home by train and boat. No doubt it would be long and draining, but neither could ever be expected to step foot on an airplane so soon after the disaster. Professor Maurer greeted the three men and informed them that Duncan Edwards had regained consciousness. Maurer told them he was extremely restless and had been crying out for his watch. Duncan appeared very upset about it. For them, the penny dropped immediately. It would have been the same gold watch that all the players and back room staff were presented with off Real Madrid President Santiago Bernabeu, after the first-leg of the 1957 European cup semi-final. Professor Maurer was informed that Duncan adored and was so proud of his watch, and would never be seen without it. Constantly polishing and asking if anybody wanted to know the time? Wherever Duncan went, so did that watch. Then the mood changed drastically as Professor Maurer explained just how ill their young friend was. There could be absolutely no guarantees that Duncan was going to survive his terrible injuries, and if by some miracle this occurred then for the rest of his life he would be in a wheelchair. Powerful Words that undoubtedly hit Jimmy, Harry and Bill like a sledgehammer. Thinking it may well have been far too overwhelming for Duncan seeing the three men all at once, Professor Maurer suggested Jimmy go in in first, whilst Harry and Bill went to visit their other team mates. Once inside Jimmy again said hello to Sister Solemnis thanking her for all she was doing. He sat down beside an ashen-faced Duncan who turned to greet Jimmy with a typical smile and greeting.

"Hello chief."

A clearly very distressed Duncan went on to say how much he was missing the watch, absolutely convinced somebody had stolen it. Jimmy told him not to worry and gave Duncan his own watch. This helped to calm him down a little. On asking how he was feeling Duncan replied he was so very tired, but remembered nothing about the crash or anything that had happened afterwards. He asked Jimmy if everybody was all right, but he simply could not answer, instead telling Duncan to just concentrate on himself and get better.

Then Duncan smiled. "What time's kick off Saturday Jimmy?"

'It's three o'clock lad," he answered.

"Get stuck in chief," said Duncan...

This the same lad when England played Wales at Ninian Park, and wreaking absolute havoc as the visitors were hammering the Welsh 4-1. Edwards was unplayable for the three lions. As ever a red-faced Jimmy Murphy was not giving up screaming blue murder at his players. "Come on boys, get stuck into these English bastards!" Suddenly, a smiling Duncan was next to him taking a throw in. "Is there an early train back to Manchester Jimmy? You're wasting your time here chief!" If it had been anyone else Jimmy would have probably exploded, but instead Jimmy glared back. "I'll see you back in training Duncan. Tell you where you're going wrong!" Back in the present Jimmy Murphy realised that the gods had no favourites after all, they gave and took as they pleased. For to take one so special as Duncan Edwards, to destroy everything he and Matt Busby had strove to create would test anyone's faith. A devout catholic, this firebrand Welshman from the Rhondda valley had seen his own life spared by an act of fate that would haunt him forever. Only Matt Busby's insistence on Murphy not travelling to Belgrade saved his life. This meant that Jimmy's normal seat next to the manager on the plane was taken by Bert Whalley, who was killed outright in the crash. With Duncan drifting off asleep, Jimmy said his goodbyes to Sister Solemnis and quietly slipped back out the room. Desperately needing a few moments alone, he headed through a side door, and sat down at the top of a fire escape stairwell. A little time to compose himself before going to visit Matt Busby and the rest of his lads. Suddenly, everything, the pain, the nerves, the tension, the sheer, emotional trauma finally caught up with Jimmy Murphy, and he began to wail and howl and cry. From a trickle to a river. It was a release from the all-consuming grief. The tears flowed. He recalled praying nobody would hear him and walk through the fire door. Nobody came, but little did Jimmy know Harry Gregg did hear Jimmy's heart breaking, but thought it best to leave him be. Outside the hospital, the sound of traffic, the blare of ambulance sirens. Raised voices in German. Only a mere thirteen-years ago Jimmy Murphy was at war with these people and he hated them. Not anymore, the staff of the *Rechts Der Isar* had performed beyond any expectations. So much kindness and love shown to his fallen golden apples. And still they fought on for the lives of Matt Busby and Duncan Edwards. As Jimmy headed off to see Busby, raised voices were heard coming from his room. A nurse arguing with a press photographer who somehow managed to make it up to the fourth floor where all the most serious cases were being cared for, and was busy taking pictures of Matt in the oxygen tent. After charging in Jimmy almost threw the photographer back out the door. "The flashes are hurting my eyes!" groaned Busby, who remained dreadfully ill. Drained of all colour, appearing grey faced. It felt to Jimmy that his friend did not have much time left. Not only had he received the Last Rites once, but twice. After spending some moments chatting where Busby got really upset blaming himself for the crash, the nurse hinted it may have been better for Jimmy to leave and let him rest. The thought he may never see this man again was simply too painful to bare, so Jimmy just slipped quietly away. The only way possible for him to help Matt Busby was by keeping his word. To keep the flag flying. To ensure Manchester United did not go gently into the night. For a man like him so full of rage and grief, he was prepared to do whatever necessary to keep that same flag flying. No number of funerals or tears would stop him. Jimmy Murphy would in doing so stumble, anger, swear, rant and drink to a stupor at times to ease the pain, but ultimately there would be only one winner.

In his intention to send a message of hope back to the people of Manchester, Jimmy spoke to a pressman. Words spoken I believe with more of a hope and a prayer, than any real sense of true reality at that dark, foreboding time for Manchester United Football Club.

"I have seen the boys. Limbs and hearts may be broken, but the spirit remains. Their message is that the club is not dead. Manchester United lives on. My boss and my greatest friend Matt Busby would want me to tell you that the Red Devils will survive this. We have a motto at Old Trafford which means "Word and Wisdom." The work of the country's finest players and the wisdom of the country's finest manager have made us what we are. It is going to be a long, long struggle, but together, we hope to be back there again."

By this time seven of the Babes were at peace. The suffering had become the curse of the living. People like Jimmy Murphy.

CHAPTER TWENTY

THIRTEEN DAYS

Marshall Tito sent a letter to the British Prime Minister Harold Macmillan, passing on his condolences on behalf of the Yugoslavian people. Also, Red Star Belgrade issued a statement.

"The boys from Manchester played so well and they were such a good team that the management of Red Star has decided to propose to the management of the European Cup that Manchester United should be proclaimed the honorary champions this year. It is impossible to believe that such a team of excellent sportsmen have been struck by such a terrible accident. The news will cause deep sorrow to all Red Star players and all sportsmen of our country."

Their star player Dragoslav Sekularac, who led United a merry dance at times, especially in Belgrade, and also got on famously with Tommy Taylor on the night of the banquet was devastated with the news. "I feel unhappy and depressed as never before in my life. When we parted Tommy said to me: "So long until May when we will meet again in the World Cup in Stockholm. This horrible death has broken my heart, but I will always keep in my heart the remembrance of my good and great friend Tommy Taylor."

Dragoslav also spoke about the severely injured Duncan Edwards. "Edwards is very good and so powerful. He will not be beaten, he is maybe the greatest player in the world. I wish he played for us."

In 2003, on the 45th anniversary of the Munich tragedy, Red Star Belgrade gifted Manchester United a golden football. Inscribed upon it was two words. *Friends Forever*

Jimmy Murphy, Harry Gregg and Bill Foulkes took the train home from Munich via the hook of Holland, a ferry over to Dover. The plan was then another train to London and lastly a taxi to Manchester. It was an uncomfortable time as every brake, screech and jolt in the line had Harry and Bill jumping out of their skins. Foulkes recalled just how uncomfortable it was. "Every time the train braked I was in a cold sweat. It was all I could do not to scream, and at every stop I wanted to get off. When we finally arrived at Dover I could hardly face the rest of the journey. I had to insist that Jimmy kept the windows of the train open.'' Jimmy tried desperately to keep their minds occupied on the trip with other subjects, but with little success. He chatted about players they were going to need. Positions to be filled and such when suddenly a Chinese gentleman entered the carriage and sat down. He smiled, politely removed his hat and nodded to them all. ''Hello my old China!'' said Jimmy. ''Can you play inside left?'' He simply glowered at Jimmy, turned and left leaving Harry and Bill staring at him like he had gone mad!

On arriving at Dover port and coming off the ferry Jimmy noticed a large crowd of pressmen and photographers waiting on the jetty. Including a BBC outside broadcast van. He sensed both Harry and Gregg were in no mood for questions about the crash. This enough to ignite his own temper. Jimmy led first down the gantry towards the waiting hacks. Immediately he started shouting abuse at the shocked press crowd. ''Piss off and let us through otherwise someone is going to get a right hook off me. And don't bastard push me because I'm ready to drop all of you I am!'' Told to steady on by one brave hack only infuriated Jimmy more. Cameras started to flash and click as they got ever closer. Jimmy pushed a way through the melee, reporters with their note books and pens in hand fired questions towards them.

''Are United finished Jimmy?''

''How many people did you save Harry?''

''Did you see any of the dead bodies Bill?''

''Could you have done more Harry?''

''Why did you all get back on the plane?''

''Do any of you boys blame Matt Busby for what happened?''

Jimmy snapped again: ''I piss on all you bastards!'' he shouted with such passion at all the press boys, they were shocked into a momentaly silence. This gave them time to reach the waiting taxi and they were gone. Manchester United were surviving on a life support machine and Jimmy Murphy did not have time to mess around. On reaching close to Manchester, the city had what appeared to have an apocalyptic black sky above. As if the desperate mood down below had affected even the heavens. A broken city enveloped by a dark veil sheltering it from all prying eyes. The Mancunian's pain still so raw, the anguish unrelenting. They were not yet ready to open their ripped, apart hearts to good willing but unwanted outsiders.

Jimmy Murphy was met back at Old Trafford by the club secretary Les Olive. The Salford born Olive had been the one left holding the fort whilst Murphy had been in Munich. His boss Water Crickmer now dead, meant he had taken over the duties. These were huge shoes to fill. Crickmer, a gentle, caring man and thirty-two years of loyal service to Manchester United. Les Olive had been at Old Trafford since he was fourteen starting off as a member of the ground staff, and in the early years played twice for the first team as a goalkeeper. Olive bled United and never had his club needed him more. Jimmy knew he desperately needed more help telling Olive to contact the Luton Town chairman Mr Percival Mitchell asking if there was any possibility, former United goalkeeper and now Luton trainer Jack Crompton could be released from his contract to return to Old Trafford? Olive explained to Jimmy how they were coping or in reality, not. He had spent most of his time organising funerals with the help of Stiles Funeral services based in Collyhurst. The owner's son was in the United youth ranks. A kid by the name of Norbert Stiles for who great hopes existed. Nobby's dad himself a huge United supporters had been ferrying family members around for free. Some of the funeral dates had been already set for that week.
Tuesday 11th February 1958. Willie Satinoff and Henry Rose.
Wednesday 12th February 1958. Roger Byrne, Liam Whelan, Frank Swift, Eric Thompson and Archie Ledbrooke.
Thursday 13th February 1958. Tommy Taylor, Geoff Bent, Bert Whalley, Tom Curry and Alf Clark.
Friday 14th February 1958. Eddie Colman, Walter Crickmer and Tom Jackson.

Olive also informed Jimmy of a forthcoming board meeting where he would be required to attend, and also feared the worst with talk of the board wanting to shut down United for a temporary period. This like a red rag to a raging bull for Jimmy, but primarily on his mind, what did they have left to fight with. He told Olive to organise a get together for the next morning of all the reserve and youth team players at the Cliff training ground. Also to ring around the local amateur clubs asking them to send over their best lads for trials. United had already been offered reserve team players from Liverpool, Leeds United and Nottingham Forest, but something far more extraordinary had been taking place. People had been sending money, not just a pound here or there. It had been arriving by the sack load! Thousands of pounds. Such was the amount pouring in Alma had to call in volunteers to help deal with it! Schoolboys were sending their dinner money and weekly spends. Old ladies their life savings. There was wage packets, charity donations, local businesses had collections. Work vans pulling up on the Old Trafford forecourt dropping off bags of cash! The Manchester Lord Mayor had set an appeal up that also proved overwhelming. At the Plaza Ballroom, people never danced, instead threw money onto the dance floor. They even had twelve guineas brought in by a police officer from Strangeways after prisoners had a whip round! It was a start, but Jimmy Murphy knew he would need a forest fire at his back to build up a momentum so to convince the board not to throw in the towel.

Across the city there was heartfelt sympathy from the club in blue. The goalkeeper Bert Trautmann. ''I still find it hard it hard to believe that these men whose hands I'd held in friendship so long won't be here anymore. We all feel that way about it at Maine Road. It has struck us very hard because although we were possibly United's strongest rivals, we were also neighbours, which means friends.''

Riem Airport. With a military salute and a holy blessing on the runway, those that were lost came home. The flag draped coffins were brought along the streets of Munich, later through a guard of honour on the tarmac, formed by the blue-coated Munich city police. The coffins of the twenty-one footballers, sportswriters and others who died in the crash were ever so gently loaded aboard the BEA Viscount. For half an hour beforehand the plane took off for London on its way to Manchester, a solemn procession of government, civic officials and friends walked one after the other to the foot of the black shrouded gangway to hand in wreaths. Following a short service attended by the British consul finally it was time to depart. As the airplane taxied away, the 160 men in the guard of honour raised their white-gloved hands to salute. Before soaring high it passed low over the crashed broken up fuselage on the outskirts of the airport. Now forever infamous as beyond that Munich runway

The Viscount arrived later at Ringway airport around 10.00.pm, via London, where with tender care the coffins of David Pegg and Liam Whelan had been taken off. Pegg's, to his is parent's home in Doncaster, and Whelan's flown back to Dublin. Soon the Viscount was back in the air heading north. On arrival, one by one the coffins were carried from the plane to waiting hearses and in a single line they set off on a final journey to Old Trafford. Along the ten-mile route, hundreds of thousands of broken-hearted people lined the pavements to pay their last respects. Wailing and screaming, others simply red eyed, sniffing, hiding disbelieving faces behind handkerchiefs. Many simply speechless and unable to believe what they were watching. Finally, the realisation kicking in. Surreal, but true, their boys were really dead. The cortege made its way in a slow, respectful single column. A morbid night. Nobody spoke, just a grief stricken silence. Broken only by the sound of sobbing and the gentle hum of the hearses. Flowers were thrown onto their roofs and in the paths. Then, as if he could hold it in no more the almighty wept also and the heavens opened. It was only apt the Mancunian rain came down in torrents and a city wept for its lost sons. On arrival at Old Trafford, the column came to a halt as the thousands of people on the forecourt blocked their path. But then like the parting of a red sea the crowds opened, and the hearses drove up to the south stand where the coffins were to be placed in the club gym. A Temporary chapel of rest. Two policemen would stand guard over them, but their only task appeared to be handing out tissues for the tears of weeping family members.

Some rare, good news shown itself in the return of Jack Crompton to Manchester United as personal assistant trainer in place of the much-lamented Tom Curry. But far more so came an extraordinary offer of help from Real Madrid President Don Santiago Bernabeu. In Madrid, the hearts of all went out to Manchester United in their darkest of hours. The 1957 semi-final clashes established a flowering friendship between the clubs especially between Bernabeu and Matt Busby. In an early act of wonderful support they came up with a special memorial pennant. It was conferred by Real Madrid to commemorate the destroyed English team and entitled "Champions of Honour".

On it read the names of the dead players of which all considerable proceeds were sent on to Old Trafford. A further show of Real's nobility of spirit came later that same summer when they contacted Manchester United offering free holidays in Spain to Munich survivors with all expenses paid. But most fascinating was the offer of one Alfredo Di Stefano being loaned to United for the rest of the season with Real paying half his wages. Word was sent to Old Trafford that the *Blond Arrow* was prepared to swap a white shirt for a red to help out the Mancunian until the summer. This never happened because the Football League refused to allow, claiming it would block the place of a potential British player? Such insular attitudes typical back then of Alan Hardaker's regime. He even mentioned to Jimmy Murphy about Duncan Edwards. How he did okay for them after being swept away from Dudley under the nose of Wolverhampton Wonderers. This incensing Jimmy and making him realise in Hardaker, Manchester United faced a man with a grudge that even existed beyond the graves of so many. Matt Busby's defiance of him taking his club into Europe still a thorn in Hardaker's ego. Too far above their station, not prepared to doff their caps in his direction. Hardaker was one of a loathsome few in the game who privately, but never publicly spoke out that Manchester United should have locked the gates post Munich, after biting off more than they could chew with all their European Cup business. Bitter and twisted not doing Hardaker justice where United were concerned.

With Di Stefano now not an option, Jimmy's eyes turned elsewhere towards the seaside. The Blackpool FC diminutive, five-foot-four playmaker Ernie Taylor. Jimmy knew that Taylor was made of the right stuff and just what United needed at that time. A ball-playing experienced veteran who could put his foot on the ball and calm things down. An international also, Taylor played for England in the legendary 6-3 thrashing by Ferenc Puskas' Hungary. Five years previous at Wembley on 25th November 1953. He had been around. A former Submariner in World War two, Pressure to Ernie was surviving deep under the North Atlantic whilst hunting and being hunted by the German Navy. Anything that could occur on a football field faded swiftly in comparison to this. The Blackpool board wanted £8000 for Taylor. Non-negotiable. Unless they lowered their asking price nothing would happen. Step forward Paddy McGrath! Jimmy thought that nothing short of kidnapping Eddie would get him to Old Trafford, but soon as Paddy got involved things swiftly began to unfold. Not exactly a kidnapping, though not far off!

Paddy McGrath was always much closer to Busby than Jimmy, best pals, but they too had always got on well. A tall, dark looking man. Always immaculately dressed, the sharpest suits with the shiniest shoes and splendid cufflinks. The silver cigarette case, a smile and a wink for all. Paddy resembled one of Chicago's finest! A friendly, kind man but his business's interests was said to mostly exist in that Mancunian shade between what was legal and not! A gangster some dared whisper but never within earshot. McGrath first heard about the crash that same morbid afternoon and helped out enormously with the families, as news first broke of whom had lived and died. He allegedly made his money in Blackpool during the war running a host of clubs and casinos. "His town" they called it! Paddy also owned the Norbreck Hydro hotel where United regularly stayed before big matches. When finding out that Ernie was desperate to sign for United, he acted to ensure the transfer went through. For despite Taylor's initial worries about his directors insistence on the £8000 fee, not a penny less, it turned out that they only owned Blackpool FC Football Club. Paddy McGrath owned Blackpool! Ernie Taylor became a red! A little known fact was that Matt Busby almost signed Taylor shortly before the crash. The Blackpool manager Joe Swift at the same time had offered £12,000 for Colin Webster. They began talk of a straight swap deal, but Busby put it on the back burner, saying they would sort it out after returning from Belgrade. Thinking he had all the time in the world.

With the Wolves game postponed Manchester United would next take to the field on Wednesday 19th February at Old Trafford. An FA Cup fifth round match against Sheffield Wednesday. Jimmy Murphy had three definite starters for that match. The monumental scale of United's dilemma meant Jimmy was left with little option but to ask Harry Gregg and Bill Foulkes, if not to keep the red flag flying, then least at half-mast. With neither having the heart or will to say no, Gregg and Foulkes both promised Jimmy they would turn out against Sheffield Wednesday. And now alongside them Ernie Taylor. The rest of the team lay in the lap of the footballing gods. There were new apples chomping to come off the tree. All rough and ready but nowhere near the quality that had been lost. In normal circumstances, Jimmy Murphy would not have dreamt of telling Busby that most of those he was set to risk were ready, but desperate days called for even more desperate measures. It was 10th February. Jimmy Murphy had nine days, but first there remained the infinitely, larger subject of keeping Manchester United alive till then. A board meeting loomed that was set to decide United's immediate future, and Jimmy Murphy was ready to go to war against any who called for this dying of the light.

On the morning of Tuesday 11th February 1958, as sleet fell heavily across the city, Jimmy attended Matt Busby's good friend Willie Satinoff's funeral. Satinoff was the first of the crash victims to be buried. He had gone to Belgrade as a guest of the club and especially Busby's. The recent death of club director George Whittaker meant a position on the board had become available. Satinoff's and Busby's other great pal Louis Edwards were the major candidates. With there being just one seat left free on the airplane, Matt met with both and said the only fair way would be to toss a coin for it. Satinoff won, but lost. Such is the cruel, cold hearted, twisted hand of fate.

That same afternoon, Jimmy also attended The Daily Express's poor Henry Rose's funeral, he too given a lovely send off. The swashbuckling Henry. Dashing, charismatic, a larger than life character. A thick, portly figure. The brown trilby hat and of course the inevitable cigar. Such was the fondness that existed in Manchester for Henry, all the black cab taxi drivers had volunteered to transfer for free anybody at the Express, or indeed anyone who wished to go to his funeral six miles away at Southern Cemetery in Chorlton. A huge fleet of black cabs stopped off at the Express offices in Great Ancoats street in town. And then they headed off. A long, thin black line of wailing and weeping that broke the hearts of all who witnessed it. Henry was Jewish and so at his graveside the mourners wore headwear. A grieving, silent mass of Homborgs, fedoras, headscarves, bowler hats and berets. Then the last blessing of the Rabbi. A final show of respect for a lovely man and scribe laid to rest under black skies and in the midst of a bitterly, cold Mancunian afternoon. Following this Jimmy Murphy headed off for the board meeting at Old Trafford, for what he intended to ensure was not his third funeral of the day. On arrival he was met by Alma who had updates from Munich. On Matt Busby it was good news at last! Professor Maurer had said he was making a remarkable recovery and being treated as a normal patient. But the update on Duncan Edwards swiftly turned any feeling of joy over Busby to dust. Edwards had taken a turn for the worse. The doctors were alarmed at the unusually, high nitrogen levels in his blood. He had six times more than was normal in a human. Duncan was in serious trouble.

The following is based on a 1959 BBC Radio screenplay taken direct from the meeting's minutes. The screenplay was never aired but still exists.

Jimmy entered and walked slowly across to the long boardroom table where waiting for him were the Chairman Harold Hardman, directors Alan Gibson, William Petherbridge, the newly appointed Louis Edwards and club secretary Les Olive. This was one of Jimmy's least favourite places in the world. He always thanked god Matt dealt with all the business side of the football club. He had never been one to doff his cap to anybody and did not intend starting now.

"Afternoon Jimmy," said Olive. "Take a seat old pal." He did so noticing a half-filled whiskey bottle on the table. There was a nervousness in the air. All were smiling towards him but Jimmy sensed trouble was coming.

"Jimmy," began Hardman. "May I begin by saying how much we all appreciate your huge efforts these last few days."

"Hear, hear!" The others replied in unison.

"Thank you gentlemen, well I've managed to acquire the services of Ernie Taylor from Blackpool for a small fee, as I'm sure you're aware. I'm busy ringing round, plus some of the young lads are looking quite promising in training. I think with a bit of luck and a fair wind we should be able to put out eleven players against Sheffield Wednesday on the 19th. A rag tag bunch but…"

"Hold on a second Jimmy," interrupted Hardman, "It's not that simple. I hear you, but we have to be realistic. You must remember the players killed wasn't insured and there's simply no money in the kitty. Now we've talked about this as an option and feel it is best practical and indeed honourable. I'm sorry but after much discussion and with huge regret, myself and the board feel it is in the best interests of all concerned that for the time being we shut down Manchester United until further notice."

"No, no you can't do that, we're needed more than ever now."

"Jimmy, you're never going to get enough players to pull on a Manchester United shirt in just eight days. It's simply impossible."

"I can do it."

"It can't be done!" snapped back Hardman.

Now Jimmy was close to snapping! "Don't you tell me what can and can't be done! When Matt first brought me here after the war to a bombed-out shell of a ground they told me it couldn't be done. That Manchester United was finished. We'd never be a success. We'd never win the league playing with kids. That we'd never match the best sides in Europe. The Athletic Bilbao's and the Real Madrid's and every bloody time we proved them wrong. So, please. With respect. Don't tell me it can't be done. It can and I'll make sure of it!''

''Jimmy old friend,'' said Alan Gibson. ''You're letting your grief dictate your actions.''

''Aye you're damn right I am Alan, because what else have we got left? No players or money, no hope, grief is our fuel now. It has to be our lifeblood.'

''You're simply not being rational Jimmy,'' jumped in Hardman. I...''

''Bloody rational! Now, I knew those lads that were killed better than anyone. I found and nurtured them, I studied them through dark, miserable, bitter and cold Mancunian mornings. In the pissing, wet through rain. In fogs and gales. On ice and snow. I flogged them on mud patches until they moved like ballerinas and stung like dervishes. Like red devils. They allowed me to mould their lives from the ground up. To make them the best this country has ever seen. And the most loved. And they repaid me with their skill, courage, passion and now at the end of that damned runway with their lives. And you lot think I'm going to turn my back on them Mr Chairman by giving up and lowering the red flag? Never!''

Hardman appeared crestfallen: ''Jimmy, we all want to honour the memory of those who've died.''

''No, no, you don't understand! It's not about their memories. Those boys are going to live forever. It's about those who are left behind showing who we are to the world. We cannot let this be the end. That we, this club cannot afford to be bowed by tragedy. Because how Manchester United are in the future will be founded on the way we behave today. Now I'm putting out a team against Sheffield Wednesday, and you are either with or against me. Am I understood?''

Around the table all heads were down except a smiling Les Olive.

"I have to say gentlemen, I'm with Jimmy!"

All eyes fell upon him. Les just shrugged his shoulders toward them. "Can you blame me?" He pointed in Jimmy's. "Is anyone at this table really going to bet against this man?"

Hardman smiled also: "Quite. Okay then best put it to the vote. All those in favour of carrying on raise your hand."

They all do so. "Well that appeared quite unanimous," quipped Hardman.

Jimmy smiled: "There's one other thing gentlemen. Before I have to get on with things."

"Go on Jimmy," replied Hardman.

"I need to get the boys out of Manchester and away to our normal spot in Blackpool. It's too stifling here. The atmosphere is overwhelming and we need to be able to breathe and to think straight. Especially Harry and Bill. Every time I look at them their eyes are still on that runway. They don't get a moment's peace here. Either from the press or supporters. A little sea air and change of scenery is needed I believe. Get us away from the tears and the grief on every street corner in the city. It's just too much."

"Very well. When do you wish to go?"

"Tomorrow."

Hardman glanced around the table to be met by a host of nods.

"We'll contact the Norbreck. Send me a postcard Jimmy," said Hardman.

Jimmy nodded and stood to leave. "You need to stay strong gentlemen. We are in a battle for our very existence and cannot afford a moment's weakness. Now good day to you all."

That said Jimmy walked out the door, but stayed just behind it to listen back in! "Has he just bollocked us?" asked a startled Louis Edwards.

"I believe so," replied Hardman, "And to be honest, I think we deserved it!"

Just four of the many funerals laying to rest those killed at Munich…

The next day a service was held at Flixton's Saint Michael Parish church for Captain Roger Byrne. A red and white rosette had been hung next to the service board on the outside wall of the church, where hundreds gathered to pay respect, before the huge funeral cortege moved onto Manchester crematorium. There more huge crowds gathered in solemn silence to say goodbye to the Captain of Manchester United.

In Dublin, following a service at Christ the King church, Liam 'Billy' Whelan was laid to rest amid heart-breaking scenes of grief at Glasnevin cemetery close to his family house. When Liam's body was originally brought home the roads from the airport were lined with thousands of people all the way back to Cabra, and home. Lost at just 22-years-old, Liam had been due to marry his fiancé Ruby McCullagh in four months' time.

In Doncaster at David Pegg's funeral his father Bill arranged for the playing of "Abide with Me". Bill was a miner, a banksman, responsible for the safety of fellow miners travelling to and from the coal face in cages. He promised himself not to cry that day when they buried his son. 'I wanted dry eyes,' said Bill. Like his boy would have wanted.

Friday 14th February 1958. It was a grey, grim morning on the day Eddie Colman was laid to rest at Weaste cemetery in Salford. Firstly, a service at Saint Clements where a packed congregation and hundreds outside watched as pall bearers carried Eddie's coffin into the church. On entering, a group of Yugoslav immigrants who came to Salford ten years previous, and whose team were Red Star Belgrade, but also had adopted Manchester United, approached the coffin. A lady in a black shawl placed upon it a wreath inscribed: *From the immigrants of Yugoslavia.* The mass was no celebration of Eddie's short life, despite the Priest's best attempts to make it so. More just a feeling of overwhelming grief. The larcenous nature of death that strikes when least expected had shaken not just the Colman family, but all of Ordsall, Salford and Manchester. People wanted to remember Eddie, there was also an underlying question. Why had this been allowed to happen? Around those parts the Luftwaffe had almost razed it to the ground during the blitz, due to the closeness to the docks. The loss of civilian life was horrific. Everybody suffered, blood ran free on the Ordsall cobbles and now once more they were being forced to mourn the untimely loss of one of their own. Eddie's death was one too many to take. Solemn faces watched as the coffin was brought past them up to the altar. The family following behind. As the organ started to play and the tears fall they gently lay Eddie down. Following, thousands lined the roadsides to Weaste cemetery as the funeral cortege slowly made its way. Schools and factories were shut for nobody's heart and mind anywhere but with Eddie. It appears all of Salford had turned out to say goodbye to their favourite son alongside Regent's Road and Eccles New Road. Many wearing United scarves and hats as Eddie's coffin was driven past them. However, one firm called Boxmakers Manchester Ltd took exception to their workers drifting outside to watch the funeral cortege, and duly sacked twenty-seven of them! This decision after local fury was reaped upon the management's heads was swiftly repealed. On arrival at the cemetery, the crowds stood alongside the paths carrying sheaths of flowers as they entered through the gates. For as far as the eye could see in the cemetery, people stood waiting to pay their last respect. A fitting, but utterly heart-breaking send-off for the boy from Ordsall, blessed not just with unique footballing skills, but maybe more importantly, as they say in these parts. Just a lovely fella. ''Our Eddie.' The Dirty Old Town lay in despair. For a short while Eddie Colman dreamed the dream by the old canal and enchanted, before Munich cast its awful spell to take him from Manchester and Salford's loving arms.

Help did arrive for Manchester United in the manner of players from a most unexpected and delightful source. County Durham in northern England, a town and Britain's most famous and successful amateur football team called Bishop Auckland. A friendship between Matt Busby and their Captain Bob Hardisty that stemmed back to the 1948 Olympics saw reinforcements turn up at Old Trafford. Three players, a wing-half, Hardisty himself, a centre-forward Derek Lewin and a very talented, Hyde born, young outside-right called Warren Bradley. Busby had managed the 48 Great Britain Olympic team with Hardisty his skipper back then. But it was Lewin just after the crash, who in a conversation with Jimmy Murphy discussed the idea. He himself had trained briefly with the United squad just eighteen months previous. Lewin contacted Hardisty and Bradley and they immediately agreed to come. Hardisty's words to Lewin on being asked: "Of course I would be honoured." The plan was use them in the reserve matches at Central League level to stabilise the club and bring on the youngsters. Jimmy had his hands full with just keeping United going. Experienced men with fine character such as 37-year-old Bob Hardisty, (A former Bishop Auckland Captain and England amateur) who came out of retirement to help would be worth their weight in gold behind the scenes. Not forgetting all three were excellent footballers. It was no coincidence that Bishop Auckland had won the FA Amateur Cup for the last three seasons and Lewin had scored in every one of them. With this being one of the few matches shown live every season on television most of their players were household names amongst football fans. For a short period Hardisty and Lewin wore the red shirt with pride, as for the brilliant Warren Bradley, Manchester United signed him up as a part-time professional in November 1958, whilst he took a job as a teacher in Stretford. In 1959, Bradley was picked for his national side to become the only footballer to play for England both at amateur and professional level in the same season. Bishop Auckland was (and still are) a class football club, run by decent football people, and when Manchester United were in desperate need they were the first to answer the call. A fact that should never be forgotten whenever the subject of the Munich air crash is written upon. Jimmy Murphy could not thank them enough. "I have been in soccer a long time now and I have never heard of such a happening, a big professional club approaching a big amateur club for the loan of its stars. And getting them. Auckland have been magnificent. Manchester United will be long indebted to them and to their players for the spontaneous manner in which they agreed to come to Old Trafford and help us out."

CHAPTER TWENTY ONE
WE SEND OUR LOVE FROM TORINO

Superga. Wednesday 4th May 1949.

Il Grande Torino, the finest football team in Italian history were returning home from a friendly match in Portugal. Having departed Lisbon at 9.40.am, their airplane touched down in Barcelona around 13.00.pm. Whilst being refuelled, they had a chance encounter at the airport with the AC Milan team on their way to a game in Madrid. Having a little time to spare the two squads shared some lunch. Come 14.50.pm, they again embarked to begin the last part of the journey home to Turin, expected back around 5.00.pm. local time. Weather conditions were dreadfully poor that late afternoon. Unusually so for the time of year. A late afternoon dark as the night. A Turin on flood alert in May? An unwanted and mysterious, heavy fog. As such, local air traffic controllers warned the pilots of low clouds, and extremely bad visibility levels. Plus strong rain and winds. Just before the expected airplane's arrival, at 16.55.pm, the airport communicated the weather situation to the pilot confirming: "Clouds almost touching the ground, showers, strong southwest wind gusts, and very poor horizontal visibility."

There followed a disturbing four minutes of radio silence, before Captain Pierluigi Meroni eventually responded: "We are two thousand metres above sea level. We'll cut through *Superga.*"

As rain slammed like bullets, thunder crashed and lightning bolts slashed apart the Turin sky, Il Grande Torino were in the dying moments of their young lives. Through his mist-laden cockpit window, the experienced 34-year old Captain Meroni, attempted to navigate the worst storm in living memory. Unable through radio malfunction to confirm his exact position, Meroni flew on a wing and a whispered prayer. Here was a war hero who had won five medals of honour, but he was simply flying blind. Meroni had test flown this airplane from Paris to Milan only the previous week, but even he was helpless when up against such horrific weather conditions. There was increasing panic amongst the passengers as the thick fog and mist simply grew worse, and ferocious winds rocked the aeroplane to and fro. To escape severe turbulence, Captain Meroni was left with no option but to drop lower. Italian Airline Fiat G212CP, *Avio Linee Italiane* (Italian Airlines), now flying way off course and totally in the lap of the gods...

A little after 5.00.pm, the airplane then smashed horrifically into a lower wall at the back of the Basilica *Superga*. The terribly poor visibility would have left the pilots insufficient time to react once the reality of the collision with the Basilica became evident. It was just too late. At 5.05.pm the airport transmitted once more, but received no response. All thirty-one passengers never had a chance as a monstrous fireball ignited the surrounding hillside. Moments later, an intense flash of light illuminated *Superga*. Like some kind of unholy vision. But this was no miracle.

More than half of the plane disintegrated on impact with just part of the tail left visible. The explosion like a thousand bombs loud enough to stir the royal dead entombed deep in the crypts of the Basilica.

A group of monks led by Chaplain Don Ricca Tancredi emerged to be first on the scene of the crash. Don Tancredi had been reading his prayer book on the first floor of the Basilica. He heard only the roar of the approaching plane, but hardly noticed as many passed on that route to the city airport. But it became more and more deafening, then the thud and a huge explosion that rocked the Basilica. Don Ricca recalled the moment realising something awful had just occurred. "A terrible blow, just like an explosion."

It seemed that the massive walls of the eighteenth century Basilica trembled. Then, an awful, muted silence, followed by a lone voice from outside screaming loud: "A Plane has fallen!"

At 5.12.pm, a car screeched to a dramatic halt in a small square close by to *Superga*. In lashing rain a man got out and sprinted into a restaurant, screaming for the use of a phone to request help.

"It is a disaster!" he cried! The airplane had crashed into a wall at the back of the Basilica. Huge column of dense black smoke rose high in front of a chilling spectacle. A four metre breach opened up by the

inferno. Burning tires, a smashed propeller lodged in the muddied ground, but mostly and above all there existed a terribly, deafening silence. No shouting for help. Remnants of bodies, luggage and wreckage were spread across a wide area, and the woods around the church blazed with raging fires. There were no survivors. One of the monks opened a suitcase still miraculously intact to find it full of Torino shirts decorated with the *Scudetto*. ''It's Torino!'' the cry went up. Only then did they realise who had been on the plane. Don Ricca walked amongst the dead making the signs of the cross. A horrific picture of instant, cruel death and utter destruction. Black incinerated bodies lay strewn in ungodly poses among the scattered wreckage of the plane. Early reports read that twenty charred corpses had been pulled out of the airplane wreckage. Shortly after, *Associated Press* announced: *"The death toll is thirty-one passengers''*.
II Grande Torino were no more.

The Death toll at Superga

Players
Valerio Bacigalupo
Aldo Ballarin
Dino Ballarin
Émile Bongiorni
Eusebio Castigliano
Rubens Fadini
Guglielmo Gabetto
Ruggero Grava
Giuseppe Grezar
Ezio Loik
Virgilio Maroso
Danilo Martelli
Valentino Mazzola (Captain)
Romeo Menti

Piero Operto
Franco Ossola
Mario Rigamonti
Július Schubert

Coaching staff

Ottavio Corina: Massage Therapist
Egri Erbstein: Manager
Leslie Lievesley: Coach

Club officials

Arnaldo Agnisetta: General Manager
Andrea Bonaiuti: Travel Organiser
Ippolito Civalleri: Travel Escort

Journalists

Renato Casalbore
Luigi Cavallero
Renato Tosatti

Flight crew

Cesare Biancardi: Co-Pilot
Celestino D'Inca: Engineer
Pierluigi Meroni: Pilot
Antonio Pangrazi: Radio Operator

Nine years later…
Word reached Manchester from Turin, Italy, of their heartfelt sorrow over Munich. The words of Torino club secretary Gino Giusti.
"The hearts of all Italians go out to Manchester United. We know what it means. We went through the torture and hell of a similar catastrophe. We send our love from Torino."

CHAPTER TWENTY TWO
CRYING IN THE RAIN

"Had we lost that match against Sheffield Wednesday I think
Manchester United would have died from a broken heart."
Sir Bobby Charlton

Manchester was a city in mourning.
Numbed with shook, shattered and in despair. In order to escape such
a doom-laden atmosphere the decimated United squad disembarked to
their normal refuge of the Norbreck Hydro hotel. Its huge
glass-fronted windows overlooked the rough waters of the Irish Sea.
There Jimmy Murphy gazed at the far horizon and planned for an
uncertain future. Jimmy had half a mind for a team to contest the
forthcoming FA Cup tie, but it was one by no means set in stone.
Most of the players he was planning to put in were far too raw and
inexperienced and it would be a desperate gamble to play them. Lads
like Alex Dawson, Freddie Goodwin, Shay Brennan, Colin Webster
and Mark Pearson and others would give United a fighting chance
against Sheffield Wednesday. At that time life itself, never mind
football had become nothing more than a game of bluff. Trying to
create an illusion, one that despite being devastated by Munich and on
their knees everything would be okay in the end. Outsiders looking in
from afar that read the newspapers. Those who wrote of bravery and
the courage to go on. A worldwide tidal wave of goodwill to ensure
Manchester United stayed alive at least in name. All this and yet? Plus
the offer of loan players from other clubs, Jimmy sensed overall a
desire to not let United get back in the game. There was one club in
particularly looking to take advantage. Whilst in Blackpool, a
representative from Arsenal approached Jimmy in an attempted to
lure him south to the capital and Highbury. The lure of £10,000 a
year, plus a huge signing on fee when the contract was signed simply
disgusted him, and the man was swiftly sent packing with what can be
described as colourful Welsh dialogue!

There was a sea of sad wreaths.

There was deathly two minute silences a plenty across the land.

There was a million and more generous words spoken in print, but to Jimmy Murphy it all somehow felt like throwing a drowning man a brick. There was one though who Jimmy knew most definitely had Manchester United at heart. His pal John Charles at Juventus inquired with the Turin Hierarchy if it was possible for him to be released and help United out until the end of the season. Charles was turned down flat. On informing Jimmy of the bad tidings he wished him all the best with the words, ''Pob lwc fy ffrind.'' ''Good luck my friend.''

The Norbreck had become Manchester United's second home and the staff like family. Back home it had become hard to breathe since the crash. Their city lay broken with grief and had responded by throwing a protective, if unhealthy, strangling arm around them. Jimmy needed to get his players away from not just the genuine do-gooders, but also the curious and the wanton morbid.

 ''What was Eddie like?''

''What was Roger like?''

'What was Tommy like?''

''What was Mark Jones like…''

And on…

Question such as these were asked of the remaining players whenever they stepped out in public. Then there was the national press, not hacks, more so jackals feeding off the bones of the lads killed and the grieving families. Parked on doorsteps, offering money to fathers, mothers, brothers, sisters and girlfriends for their stories. Shaming their own journalist killed in that plane. A different breed. But there on those Blackpool sand dunes on a cold and bitter February morning away from prying eyes, Jimmy Murphy could live with the fact Manchester United were going to stand or fall by their own efforts. Many times he had scribbled down a team for the Sheffield Wednesday game, only then to rip it up and start again? He had five definite starters. Harry Gregg, Bill Foulkes, Ernie Taylor and the two youngsters Alex Dawson and Mark Pearson. Both tough and streetwise beyond their years and would jump off a mountain if

Jimmy asked them to. But there remained still six spots to fill. Others like Colin Webster, Ian Greaves, Freddie Goodwin and Ron Cope had all played for the first team before, but were never good enough to hold down a place. Once upon a time being able to play in most first division teams meant nothing at Old Trafford, but in the world United now inhabited that would sadly have to be enough. There was also another kid, a young Irish Manchester boy called Shay Brennan. Confident and cocky, but not in a manner to find grating. A laid back character, but Brennan had fire in his eyes. Irish Wythenshawe was some concoction! Jimmy liked him. United were going to have to play with what they had. It would come down to Jimmy Murphy to inspire, to rant, rave and say the right words to make sure those chosen performed like possessed devils against Sheffield Wednesday, in the red shirts of devil's past. As for the two survivors, Harry Gregg and Bill Foulkes, they tended to just keep each other's company. Both men were as quiet as the night sky. Whatever was saw and heard at the end of that Munich runway would undoubtedly stay with them forever. The beautiful game must have felt a long way off in those Blackpool sand dunes. Since Munich, for all concerned with Manchester United, it had become just a game.

Later that same night in the Norbreck, Jimmy received an update from Professor Maurer on Duncan Edwards. For the first time regarding Duncan it felt like more than a slight modicum of hope, bordering on miraculous. Matt Busby had continued to improve dramatically and deemed well enough to even have a glass of beer. As for Duncan? It was a comeback so typical of the boy from Dudley. Prayers were being said in the *Rechts Der Isar* as Duncan's valiant struggle for life appeared to have been over. There was one last thing that could save him. An artificial kidney to help filter the nitrogen out of his bloodstream. Unfortunately, the closest one to Munich was over 210 miles away. Typically, Maurer went to work and arranged an urgent collection. They could only pray Duncan held on. Finally, it arrived and the artificial kidney was rushed to his side. Attached and left running with the hope it took the strain off Duncan's severely damaged ones. This allowed the blood to return to its normal circulating system. So, they waited. Twenty-four hours passed and with Duncan's bed surrounded by doctors and nurses silently praying, he opened his eyes! ''Where am I?'' he said. It was a miracle because Duncan's nitrogen intake was 500, when 45 was the figure for normal people. He should have been dead. The kidney machine had worked, and there were many cheers and tears amongst the *Rechts Der Isar* staff. Maurer had also passed on that he was pleased with Duncan's progress and had even allowed him a little milk. Alongside his bedside constantly was now not just Molly and Sister Solemnis, but Duncan's mother and father. Sarah Anne (Annie) and Gladstone. Though remaining still in a perilous condition, his battle for life far from over, hope remained he could still pull through. A young man with a heart of a lion was not yet ready to go.

Wednesday 19th February 1958.
Come the day of the match, United travelled back to Manchester and stayed at the Midland hotel. Bobby Charlton arrived unexpectedly from his home town of Ashington in the north-east, after being drove up by his uncle. After returning from Germany, Bobby spent two weeks at home thinking he never wanted to kick a ball again. Neither in anger nor joy. But something took hold, his was a duty of sorts and though still not ready to play Bobby told Jimmy Murphy give him another week, and he would be ready for selection. His mind was in turmoil after the crash, but after much soul searching, Bobby realised life and the club he so proudly represented had to go on. Otherwise what meaning would those whose lives were lost have? That night Bobby just needed to be back in amongst it and cheering on his pals. By mid-afternoon, the tension was risible across the city. Jimmy Murphy was still wrestling with the line-up. He had ten players. Gregg, Foulkes, Greaves, Goodwin, Cope, Webster, Taylor, Dawson, Pearson and Brennan. Jimmy only informed Brennan that same day because he did not really want to give him time to worry. The one position that remained a problem was Duncan's. There was one name, but with it being so late in the day? In the previous season's FA Cup

final, Aston Villa's tough tackling, but talented wing-half Stan
Crowther had impressed and supremely irritated both Busby and
Murphy on the bench. Not known for his sensitive side and a nasty
piece of work, but the blond-haired Crowther's decent ability on the
ball added to how he cajoled his Villa team mates and thoroughly got
stuck into their own players left a lasting impression on the United
management. Not so much a Busby type player, but Crowther was
definitely a Murphy prototype! He would anger and annoy opponents,
tapping ankles, at times going over the top, ruthless if required.
Crowther gave everything back on that Wembley afternoon to ensure
the *Villains* defied United to win the cup. Jimmy had contacted the
Villa manager Eric Houghton with who he was friendly asking if
there was any chance of signing Crowther? Happily settled in the
Midlands at first the player himself was not of a mind to go anywhere.
Crowther knew he would be talked up as a Duncan Edwards
replacement and who on earth could live up to that mantle? Luckily,
Houghton convinced Stan into travelling to Manchester to watch the
game and just maybe have a little word with Jimmy!
More drama occurred when Les Olive rang Jimmy from the ground.
They were ready to go to print with the match programme, but needed
the United team line-up. Jimmy told him they were still waiting on
Crowther, so between them it was decided to leave the United side
blank and the supporters could fill it in for themselves when
announced over the tannoy. Little did Crowther know Houghton had
placed his boots in the back of the car because nothing was more
certain to him that once Jimmy Murphy got in his ear, game over! So
it proved. Jimmy calmed Crowther's ''Huge shoes to fill'' worries
about the comparisons 60,000 United supporters were sure to make
about him being Duncan's replacement. Crowther was adamant of
being slaughtered every time he made a bad pass, but Jimmy
convinced him of the complete opposite. That when he put on that red
shirt Stan would be cheered to the heavens. How they would have
deeply appreciated him signing in their darkest hour. It was some
pitch by the Welsh firebrand and worked! Stan Crowther signed for a
fee of £32,000. He later said about that chat: ''I told Jimmy that I'm

signing for Manchester United because I didn't want him as an enemy for life!'' With Crowther having already played for the holders Aston Villa against Stoke City in the FA Cup third round, special dispensation would have to granted by the Football Association and in a rare show of good favour they waived the rule for him to play against Sheffield Wednesday. Jimmy Murphy had his team.

On that same afternoon, another Munich update arrived from Professor Maurer. Whilst Matt Busby's recovery continued to go well. To the extent that The Daily Express were setting up a phone line commentary of the match for him to listen in. Busby also sent a telegram to Old Trafford.

"Good luck and best wishes from the Boss and all his boys".

But Duncan? His position remained frightfully precarious. Professor Maurer explained that he was fighting hard but had now developed severe haemorrhages that reduced the ability of his blood to clot. Immediately, the Professor had arranged for police cars to race round to some Munich blood donors. These were brought to the *Rechts Der Isar* and after several transfusions the bleeding was brought to a halt. Although Duncan remained dangerously ill. He also commented on how fellow doctors and nurses were astonished at his immense will to live. How nurses queued to be by his bedside. He was now conscious all the time but restless and confused. Shouting and screaming. At times even regaining moments of clarity, on one occasion telling the Professor he was scared. Maurer held his hand and still the boy from Dudley was fighting on and on. Duncan's parents and girlfriend Molly remained at his side leaving only to sleep or go pray in the hospital chapel. Praying for a miracle.

Come five-thirty, the gates at Old Trafford were already locked. This meant there would be no full house for such was the chaos outside those with tickets could not get near the entrance turnstiles. Police horses were brought in to deal with the enormous crowds. People got stamped on and the atmosphere turned ugly. Inevitably, tension mounted with the kick-off drawing ever nearer. The official attendance was later given as 59,848, seven thousand below full capacity, and an estimated 30,000 milling around on the forecourt and nearby. Emotions were roused and at times the situation became close to spiralling out of control. Someone would pay and it was mostly the ticket spivs paying painfully for their greed charging ten times the normal price. Many received a good hiding. United supporters not in any mood to have them make rich picking by leaching off those killed at Munich. Like vultures scrapping off the bones of their dead players. Trouble inevitably flared because everyone wanted to be inside and the spivs were swiftly relieved of their tickets. Jimmy, Stan Crowther and Eric Houghton arrived at the ground just forty-minutes before kick-off. With the help of a police escort the taxi dropped them close enough to avoid the frenzied crowds and race inside. With events so hectic Jimmy had not given thought to what he was going to say to the players. He missed his friends Tom Curry and Bert Whalley so much. It was a lonely world for Jimmy Murphy without Tosh and Bert. Matt Busby would later say: ''Everybody lost something at the end of that Munich runway.'' Maybe so but to United supporters they had the beating heart and soul ripped out of their football club. It lay in the falling Munich snow, on puddles of blood and water. Amidst shattered wreckage and a silent, ripped off fuselage that forever more would symbolise Manchester United and Munich. That with Jimmy leading the fightback they had garnered enough strength and indeed bodies to carry the torch onwards was a small miracle. But not for Jimmy, there had been far too much blood. A massacre of all that he had known and loved. Too much heartache and the mere relevance of just being able to put on a football match was hardly worthy of miraculous status. He had kept his promise to Busby of keeping the flag flying. It had come down to a question of tossing a coin calling either salvation or disaster. If United lost that night would they really have possessed the heart to go on?

Manchester United's flag remained at half-mast as a mark of respect. This would be no normal football match. More a funeral without coffins and a burial service. Shortly before kick-off in the dressing room, Jimmy Murphy introduced Stan Crowther to his new team mates, then attempted a speech. But nothing came out, words would not form. Finally, he was cracking. The nerves and emotion of the last thirteen days appeared to have overwhelmed him. Outside, the roar of "UNITED!" blasted through the walls. What Jimmy finally said was short and precise before breaking down. "I've only got a couple of minutes boys so I'll keep it simple. The ball is round to go around. You pass to your mate and he will pass to you. Everybody attacks, everybody defends. Now you play hard for yourselves, for the players who are dead and for the great name of this club you represent. Manchester United!" Jimmy Murphy had lit the spark and filled those blank spaces in the match programme On the front of the United Review blazed out UNITED WILL GO ON! The club chairman Harold Hardman penned a memorable eulogy that would become etched in the rich tapestry of United folklore.

"Although we mourn our dead and grieve for our wounded, we believe that great days are not done for us. The sympathy and encouragement of the football world and particularly of our supporters will justify and inspire us. The road back may be long and hard but with the memory of those who died at Munich, of their stirring achievements and wonderful sportsmanship ever with us. Manchester United will rise again."

The Teams.

Manchester United. Gregg, Foulkes, Greaves, Goodwin, Cope, Crowther, Webster, Taylor E, Dawson, Pearson and Dawson

Sheffield Wednesday. Ryalls, Martin, Curtis, Kay, Swan, O'Donnell, Wilkinson, Quixall, Johnson, Froggatt and Cargill

With no option Harry Gregg and Bill Foulkes played, but the true reality of their situation was that both men were in a state of bewilderment after the crash, and in no mental state to partake in what was sure to be a traumatic occasion. The rest of the side a hotchpotch concoction of promising youth and reserve players, allied together with those who had been brought in to see the club through the eye of the storm. Beyond that infamous Munich runway lay a new red dawn. A fearful place, one certain to be beset with trauma and worry. For those chosen to continue it would sadly be a case of drown or cover yourself in glory. Jimmy Murphy had few options with what he had left. 26-year-old Ian Greaves came in at left-back for United Captain Roger Byrne and his usual deputy Geoff Bent. Both dead. Greaves, now one of the most experienced players left alive at Old Trafford, recalled the horror and sadness of those terrible days for Manchester United. "Having lost so many friends it was hard to take. Those first two or three weeks we were training and going to our friends' funerals, too. Geoff Bent was my best friend. I should have been on that trip myself, but because of an injury situation Geoff went instead. But that was the thing about Munich, we all lost a best friend."

Reserve Freddie Goodwin played at right-half instead of Eddie Colman. Dead. 24-year-old former amateur footballer Ronnie Cope was at centre-half for Mark Jones, also killed, and Jackie Blanchflower, so seriously hurt that his career was over. The highly rated Colin Webster was on the right-wing for Johnny Berry, who like Blanchflower, was soon forced into injury-related retirement. At centre-forward the prodigious, battering ram Alex Dawson led the attack, as he bravely attempted to follow in the footsteps of the late, much-lamented Tommy Taylor. Another talented reservist was Irishman Shay Brennan and potentially the best of the surviving United youngsters, along with Bobby Charlton, was 22-year-old Mark Pearson. He filled in for the severely injured Dennis Viollet and the lost David Pegg. Alongside the home bred players, the two newcomers. Blackpool's inside-forward Ernie Taylor and finally the former Aston Villa wing-half Stan Crowther signed only an hour and sixteen minutes before kick-off. Greaves again on United's late arrival. "We were in the dressing-room and at ten past seven Stan Crowther arrived in a taxi! We didn't know him, we just went out on the pitch and we didn't even know what he could do. We just got on with it. We had to. While you were playing it just went from your mind, you were chasing a ball again and you didn't feel sorry for yourself any more. You were playing a game of football. Against Sheffield Wednesday, you just couldn't allow your mind to go."

As both teams headed up the tunnel a dreadful silence around the stadium greeted the names of the Manchester United team over the loudspeaker. Broken only by sobbing or the screaming out loud of a dead player's name. Cries almost primeval in their grief-stricken state. In a voice shaking with emotion the tannoy announcer conducted his painful task, but first asking for people to write in the names on the program sheet left blank. A poignancy beyond mere words, just eleven empty spaces. Few bothered simply preferring to listen and weep. To honour the dead many supporters went dressed in black overcoats whilst adorning red/white scarves around their wrist or necks. Shops across Manchester had sold out of black ties. Then, to a tumultuous roar Captain Bill Foulkes and Harry Gregg appeared followed by red-shirted strangers in the Mancunian night. The sight of their two lads who had survived the crash brought the atmosphere inside Old Trafford, which was already bordering close to boiling point, beyond the point of no return. Old Trafford erupted with a monumental concoction of hysteria and excitement. The ground shook! A tidal wave of emotion exploded, one that for thirteen days had remained dormant. United were back but everywhere around there were just scenes of utter heartbreak on people's faces. A cheer for every tear. As said previous it was no normal football crowd gathered on those terraces that night, more so a congregation at a wake determined to wake the dead with their noise. Grown men and women openly weeping. A pain still so raw igniting passions beyond the heavens and burning the soul. Beneath the glary haze of the floodlights eleven red shirts waved to the crowd before breaking to warm up. The referee Mr Alf Bond from London, the owner of a newsagents business in Fulham, called the two Captains together. Bill Foulkes and Albert Quixall. Foulkes recalled that moment. "We shook hands and I looked at Albert and he looked at me and neither of us wanted to play. It was like what are we doing here?" There followed a one minute silence in honour of those killed. The atmosphere was unnerving and unnatural, a communal grief. Even hard nose policemen told by superiors to always keep a stiff upper lip had tears rolling down their faces. Old Trafford has witnessed many nights both before and since that have left unforgettable scenes of drama, but none ever came remotely close to matching what occurred on that fateful evening. Earlier in the season Sheffield Wednesday had gone to Old Trafford and given the Busby Babes an almighty fright before going down in a closely fought match 2-1. On paper, given the circumstances, the visitors from across the Pennines had been handed a fantastic opportunity to beat United and earn themselves a place in the FA Cup quarter-finals. Unfortunately for Sheffield Wednesday they were up against not merely eleven players in red, but also a sheer Red sea of human emotion that ultimately overwhelmed them. Some spectators were halfway up the floodlight pylons holding on for dear life with one hand, whilst whirling their red scarves with the other. In a furious opening, Jimmy Murphy's patched up Manchester United tore into the Yorkshiremen. The visitors were a fine side, tough but fair, and in no way deserving the intolerable pressure placed upon them as Manchester let lose all the sadness, anger and despair of the past fortnight upon their heads. A simple cruel twist of fate that left them the bad guys to those who had refused to go gently into the murderous, Munich night. Wednesday had walked into a cacophony of breaking hearts. The deafening, continuous chants of "UNITED!" Thundered out endlessly from the terraces and may have given the impression of this being just another game. But then those who were shouting until their throat were red raw did so with tears streaming down faces for a football club that had been brought to its knees. Sheffield Wednesday's Albert Quixall, who signed for United the following September, would later say: "We were playing more than just eleven players we were playing 60,000 fans as well." With Stan Crowther crashing into tackles and Ernie Taylor the playmaker, constantly encouraging the youngsters around him, United played as if lives were at stake, and in a cruel manner out of their skins. On fifteen-minutes new signing Taylor so nearly became an instant Old Trafford legend when his fierce drive from twenty-yards smashed against the Wednesday post. The noise from the crowd greeting the near miss was unworldly and deafening, what did this club have to do to get a break, had they not suffered enough? Still, the blood red shirts pressed forward. On twenty-seven minutes the heavens cupped their ears as a goal arrived from a most unlikely source. Deputising as a left-winger, it was one of the new boys, 20-year-old Shay Brennan scoring direct from a corner after the goalkeeper Brian Ryalls fumbled the ball on his goal-line. The affable young Irish Mancunian only informed that same morning he would be playing celebrated wildly! Jimmy Murphy too punched the air. God bless the Wythenshawe Irish! Brennan recalled: "I had no idea I was going to play. I can say this now, the night before I went out with a friend of mine. I hadn't even been mentioned in the papers! Anyway, we had a few drinks, so when Jimmy called me to the hotel and said I was playing? I wished I hadn't been out the night before. But at least I didn't have time to get nervous. The first goal was sheer luck. It was from a corner and all I wanted to do was make it look decent. It was a windy night, the goalkeeper made a bad mistake and the wind caught the ball and sent it straight in the net. I certainly wasn't trying to put it in. But it made me a hero." As Old Trafford exploded like never before, Shay Brennan's name became immortalised in Manchester United history. As the game wore on it became blatantly obvious to neutrals that the Sheffield players were clearly not up to spoiling what was a cruel contest. Who would ever wish to cause upset at a wake? Throughout United's football was full of fire and heart, thrilling at times if sometimes lacking the quality their supporters were used to. Murphy's scratch team gave everything but a lack of understanding and class was obvious in certain positions. Yet still they defied all logic by playing well above themselves. Both Taylor and Crowther had been immense throughout showing huge character after being thrown into what was nothing more than a hellish, Mancunian furnace of wrecked emotions and broken dreams. United hammered away endlessly at the Sheffield Wednesday goal, shots rained in, but it was not until twenty-minutes from time that they finally made another count, when once more the unlikely Shay Brennan seized onto a rebound from close-range to flash a shot past Ryalls! Five-minutes from the end it was 3-0 when Alex Dawson, the son of a Grimsby trawlerman, capped an unforgettable night of drama by crashing a third low and hard into a besieged Ryall's net, confirming United's place in the FA Cup quarter-finals. The newspapers later hailed it the "Murphy Miracle" but no one at Old Trafford really believed in miracles any more. It had been a remarkable performance by Jimmy Murphy's boys as they ran and fought like dervishes, the searing pain of Munich slightly easing, only to surface instantly once more in the cold light of the final whistle. At the finish most of the United youngsters were in tears with the overwhelming emotion of the evening taking a heavy toll. Many on their knees through sheer exhaustion and nerves. Back in the sacred surroundings of the dressing room, Jimmy Murphy addressed his team once more telling them how proud the lads who had died would have been of them. Then he broke down again to be consoled by all. Both Harry Gregg and Bill Foulkes simply sat quietly in a corner remembering dead friends, their hearts and minds still languishing amid the snow and ice of that far away German runway. Best left alone. A *Pathè* news crew arrived armed with a bottle of bubbly to present to the players to celebrate a great victory, though when the pictures are viewed there are few smiles to be seen. Nevertheless, it still remains the most important game in the history of Manchester United. This rag tag team of crash survivors, youth players, reserves and a pair of new signings had all combined to ensure that Harold Hardman's evocative words were given real flesh and bone. Most importantly United had proved they were not yet willing to lock the gates any time soon. Priceless, breathing space was earned that night. The veiled curtains that had lay drawn across the city were opened ever so slightly to reveal the merest chink of light A state of grace.

The Manchester Evening News. "Forget the idea that the crippling blow of Munich has put paid to Manchester United. I saw enough last night to convince me that Old Trafford is far from down and out." The above written by a young Manchester Evening News journalist who had taken over from the dearly missed Tom Jackson. He was called David Meek and would report on the reds for forty-seven years before retiring in 1995. And then…Sadly, any modicum of hope grasped vanished only two days later, when the skies once more fell in on Manchester United.

CHAPTER TWENTY THREE
THERE WILL ONLY EVER BE ONE DUNCAN EDWARDS

BBC HOME SERVICE NEWS (8.00am bulletin)
Friday 21st February 1958.
…"In Munich early today, the Manchester United and England player Duncan Edwards died of injuries he received in the air disaster, fifteen days ago. His injuries included severely damaged kidneys, and in the fight to save his life doctors used an artificial kidney which had been specially sent to Munich. A week ago one of the doctors said that only Edwards's tremendous physical strength had kept him going. No ordinary person would have survived so long. Edwards, who was twenty-one, was the Manchester United left-half and had played for England eighteen times in full internationals..."

It was fifteen days on from the disaster that a phone call received from Munich confirmed the news all had been dreading. At 01.12.am, (German time) Duncan Edwards had taken his last breath and was gone. Eight players had now died at Munich. Once announced it became hard for anyone with a United persuasion and others who loved the Babes to breathe. Some German doctors said it was a simple lust for life that kept him alive so long. A distressed Professor Maurer appeared close to tears when interviewed on Duncan's death.
''I do not think anyone other than this young man could have survived so long.'' Later that morning after Duncan's passing, Maurer confirmed the dreadful news to the survivors. Dennis Viollet, Albert Scanlon, Kenny Morgan and Ray Wood. Maurer decided against telling Matt Busby. He remained far from well enough to hear such grim tidings. At that time Busby still had no idea who had lived or died. Edwards' parents Gladstone, Annie and fiancé Molly were taken to see him one last time at the hospital mortuary, but were all so upset

and hysterical they ended up having to be sedated. Their worst nightmare realised.

At the age of just fifteen and eight months, Duncan Edwards made his debut for United against Cardiff on Good Friday, 1953, at Old Trafford. The club's youngest ever player. Two years later he also became England's youngest player at seventeen years and eight months against Scotland at Wembley, the home side winning 7-2.

Nine Schoolboy caps.

Three Youth Championship medals.

Two First Division Championship medals.

One FA Cup losers medal.

Nineteen full England caps.

Duncan Edwards was just 21-years-old on passing.

Though every soul lost at Munich was a jagged spear through the heart the belated loss of Duncan was felt most, for he represented the chance of a miracle. That night tears fell equally in Manchester and Munich. Even today our two cities share a special bond, though one borne out of tragedy. In time, as the years went on Duncan's legend grew beyond all measure. That despite the football programmes stating different he was actually seven-foot-tall, spat thunder and unleashed lightning bolts from both feet. Others, a certain vintage, will tell you such is nonsense. Duncan was even better than that. Matt Busby said of his finest player: ''Just the sight of Duncan blasting his way up the pitch with the ball was enough to scare the bravest goalkeeper to death!'' Of all the great players who have worn the red shirt with distinction over past decades none have inspired more debate or devotion than the boy who cycled to Old Trafford on his bike. Not just in Dudley, the absolute heart of the Black Country, did they weep when Duncan was finally laid to rest, they cried from Manchester to Madrid. From Belgium to Belgrade and Bilbao. They cried across the country and across the world.

Monday 26th February 1958.

Duncan Edward's funeral took place at St Francis' Church which was two miles from his home. Five thousand people gathered outside. Matching the grim, sombre mood of the crowds standing in mournful silence the weather itself was freezing, a bitter cold wind. Even the grieving tears froze on faces. A deep sadness engulfed the skies above. All was black in the Black country like never before. The thought he was never going to be seen again simply too much for many present. This was to be Duncan Edwards last homecoming and the people of Dudley wished to honour their lad with a send-off, one full of grace and respect to help Duncan on to the next life as he had lived his first. On the way to the church the funeral cortege had passed many of his old haunts as a young boy. The rolling fields of Priory Park with the magical heavens gates, those goal posts where he played football under the ever, watchful eye of the foreboding iron work plants that filled the skyline. The factory chimneys dipped in immense, blurred smoke. They got many of the local kids into their grasp to work and toil an uneventful life bereft of childhood dreams, but they never got Duncan. He lived his and short it may have been, for a time it was a beautiful Mancunian red canvas, etched with a swish of England white. The pall bearers were originally supposed to have been his best mate Gordon Clayton and Bobby English, along with Wolves and England Captain Billy Wright, Ray Barlow and Ronnie Clayton. A heavy snowstorm delayed Gordon and Bobby making it from Manchester, so in stepped Peter McParland and Pat Saward. Ironically, McParland the man who injured Ray Wood in the 1957 Cup final and Duncan coming so close taking retribution. Who could ever have conceived in such a short period of time, less than a year, this awful scenario would be being playing out.

Inside Saint Francis' as outside there was hardly room to breathe, never mind move as Duncan's coffin was carried down the aisle. Sniffles and cries. A congregation drowning in despair. Men in their best black suits with ashen grey faces, women in their black shawls with red bloodshot eyes. Gladstone, Annie and Molly sat together holding each other tight in the front pew, daring not to look back in case what was coming their way broke them completely. The very Reverend A.D. Catterall delivered the service to three hundred friends and family. All with their hearts ripped out. ''We are proud that the great Duncan Edwards was one of our sons. He goes to join the immortal company of Steve Bloomer and Alex James. Talent and even genius we shall see again, But there will only ever be one Duncan Edwards.''

Once the service was complete the hearse took Duncan to his final resting place at Queen's Cross cemetery. His grave elaborate. The headstone with an ingrained picture of him in a football kit holding a ball above his head for a throw-in. The inscription.

"A day of Memory, sad to recall,
Without Farewell, He Left Us All.''

In time Duncan's father Gladstone would tend the grave every day. He gave up a full time job as a polisher at the local iron works to go work in the cemetery and be near his son. Many times Manchester United supporters would visit. Some in twos or threes, a dozen, larger even. Fifty or so. They would gently place red and white scarves and fresh flowers on the grave. Maybe say a swift prayer before being on their way. Nobody knew or probably never even noticed who the quiet, little man was standing not far away clutching a shovel, just watching. This monument, this love for his boy. Duncan was extraordinary. Born in Dudley, but a Manchester United vintage. Jimmy Murphy spoke movingly of his big Dunc. "Sports writers use the word great when describing a soccer player far too often. Tom Finney was a great, so was Alex James, so was John Charles, and so was Duncan Edwards. Great players occur perhaps once in a decade. My definition of a great player is one who not only has talent, but who motivates every other member of the team. When you have a truly great player you start with him, and then build the rest of the team around him. That's what made the loss of Duncan such a savage one."

Saturday 8ᵗʰ September 1956. Manchester United were away to Newcastle and both teams were lining up in the tunnel. The noise of 50,000 Geordies resonated loud from the entrance and their hero of the terraces undoubtedly was Jackie Milburn. A spectacular goal scorer, the undoubted king of the north east who walked on water in those parts. He was stood opposite Duncan Edwards, as ever

bouncing on his toes. Bursting to get stuck in. Back in the dressing room Jimmy Murphy had spoken to Duncan telling him Jackie was his man today and to get in his face. Rattle him, have a word in the great man's ear. With a smile and a wink Jimmy had given Duncan his orders! So, it was he tapped Milburn on the shoulder in the tunnel. "Listen up, I don't care about reputations chief. They mean nothing to me. Any bother from you and I'll boot you over the stand!"
He was 19-years-old.

CHAPTER TWENTY FOUR
TEDDY BOYS AND THE BUTCHER!

The Saturday following the news that Duncan Edwards had passed, Manchester United returned to First Division action with a home match against Nottingham Forest. The programme cover was bare, no picture, just emblazoned with Harold Hardman's words once more: "UNITED WILL GO ON"

Beneath this he penned…

"On 6th February 1958, an aircraft returning from Belgrade crashed at Munich Airport. Of the twenty-one passengers who died twelve were players and officials of Manchester United Football Club. Many others still lie injured. It is the sad duty of we who serve United to offer the bereaved our heartfelt sympathy and condolences. Here is a tragedy which will sadden us for years to come, but in this we are not alone. An unprecedented blow to British football has touched the hearts of millions and we express our deep gratitude to the many who have sent us messages of sympathy and floral tributes. Wherever football is played United is mourned, but we rejoice that many of our party have been spared and wish them a speedy and a complete recovery. Words are inadequate to describe our thanks and appreciation of the truly magnificent work of the surgeons and nurses of the *Rechts Der Isar* Hospital at Munich. But for their superb skill and deep compassion our casualties must have been greater. To Professor Georg Maurer, Chief Surgeon, we offer our eternal gratitude. Although we mourn our dead and grieve for our wounded we believe that great days are not done for us. The sympathy and encouragement of the football world and particularly of our supporters will fortify and inspire us. The road back may be long and hard but with the memory of those who died at Munich, of those stirring achievements and wonderful sportsmanship ever with us, Manchester United will rise again."

Snow was falling before kick-off as a short service of remembrance was held on the pitch. Present that day were representatives of Red

Star Belgrade and the Yugoslav ambassador. Following the prayers and a minutes silence it was time to switch minds to football once more. The Old Trafford gates were locked and the biggest crowd since 1920, 66,346 had flooded into Old Trafford. Ultimately, Jimmy Murphy's patched up, new United battled hard to earn a 1-1 draw after being a goal down at half-time. During the interval, the Beswick Prizes Band performed a moving rendition of "Abide With Me". Come the second period with Ernie Taylor again sublime, Alex Dawson equalised from a Mark Pearson corner to ignite the ground on seventy-five minutes. The last fifteen-minutes saw the reds desperate to grab a winner but it was not to be. The fall-off in talent incomparable to what the supporters were used to, like putting a plaster on a broken leg, but it could never be said they would be found lacking in heart and effort. However, all events on the pitch faded into comparison with Edwards death the previous day. Many supporters openly weeping on the terraces.

In the league United struggled terribly winning only one more match after Munich, away against Sunderland 2-1, with both goals from Colin Webster and made by Ernie Taylor. It was in this game Wilf McGuinness made a surprise comeback. So desperate to help United and Jimmy out, who Wilf adored, he had only been side-lined for five weeks. This a worryingly, fast return from a cartilage operation in the fifties. Far too soon than the expected ten to fourteen. It was rash from Wilf, his heart over-ruling his head. Afterwards the knee would be horribly swollen and he would be forced to sit out the next match, then come back, out again, and on. In all Wilf managed four appearances, a remarkable feat still when considering what he was fighting against. Another quiet hero of those dark days. That the reds hit a slump after the crash was hardly a surprise. It was never a question of lack of will and endeavour, Jimmy Murphy always ensured his United fought the good fight in abundance. To the extent that there were some games when Jimmy had wound his players up that much they appeared capable of starting World War Three on the pitch! None more so than when United were away at Turf Moor against Bob Lord's Burnley. Not exactly the red's biggest fan.

The Teams.
Burnley.
McDonald, Smith, Winton, Shannon, Adamson, Miller, Newlands, McIlroy, Shackleton, Cheesebrough and Pilkington.

Manchester United. Gregg, Foulkes, Greaves, Goodwin, Cope, Crowther, Webster, Harrop, Dawson, Pearson and Charlton.

The controversial Chairman, Lord, the *"Burnley Butcher"* never had any love for the Old Trafford club. Indeed his crass, insensitive comments made shortly after the crash left a nasty taste in the mouths of all connected with Manchester United. "United should not expect other clubs to weaken their staffs just to help them out of trouble." These words had not been forgotten or forgiven and that afternoon at Turf Moor saw the hot tempered Mark "Pancho' 'Pearson, with his Teddy boy sideburns and a broken nose after a kicking at Belle Vue, sent off in the first-half. Harry Gregg also seemingly wanted to start a fight with every Burnley player that came near him! Although Gregg's anger was justified after being clobbered several times early doors by the Burnley strikers. Their centre-forward Alan Shackleton the worst by far booting Gregg in the head! His dander up, Harry went on the warpath! Ian Greaves and Stan Crowther also lashing out as their opponents returned it gladly. Trouble also flared on the terraces as the travelling supporters whipped up already by Lord's comments were subjected to some disgusting chants aimed at them about Munich. United held out till half-time, but were well beaten 3-0 by the end, despite going down quite literally fighting. Ernie Taylor had been badly missed with a pulled muscle. The final-whistle was far from the end of hostilities as Bob Lord's mouth went into overdrive post-match with more anti-United comments. "Manchester United played like Teddy boys! If they are allowed to continue like they did this afternoon it means the whole structure of League football will be at stake. They will do the game a great deal of harm, and will lose the

sympathy which the public have for them at the moment. Everybody was grieved by the terrible tragedy at Munich, but now I'm afraid that the public spotlight focused on the new United has meant that some of the players are losing their heads." Not surprisingly on hearing this Jimmy Murphy went mad! During the fifties, the mentioning of a Teddy boy conjured up nasty images of youthful fights and violence. Bill Haley was their hero and if they could not sing like him they could "Rock around the clock" and try damn hard to dress like him! When Haley played at the Odeon in Manchester, almost all of the Oxford Street shops were boarded up! The brylcreem hair slicked high at the front and swept back revealing scowling faces. A youth phenomenon at the time, unruly and more frightening to those in power than anything previously known? The England of the fifties was outraged. A new generation that did not so much doff their caps to the supposed betters and elders, but spat in their faces. The long sideburns, the lengthy draped jackets with velvet collars, the bootlace ties, the drain-pipe trouser and lastly the crepe-soled shoes. The trouble causers, these Teddy Boys wreaking havoc in the dance halls and cinemas. Ripping up the seats and dancing in the aisles like mad men. Hardly an endearing image for a football team. An incensed Jimmy hit back! "Mr Lord's remarks were totally unjustified, and I think this is a shocking thing. It is disgraceful coming from the Chairman of a football club. In defence of my team I must say we object most strongly to the remarks about "Teddy boys."
Lord had his say again the following morning in the Sunday newspapers. "Manchester people are still swayed by what happened at Munich. It isn't good for the game. There is far too much sentiment about Manchester United in Manchester. All the talk since Munich seems to have gone to the heads of the United players. All they have had to withstand in recent weeks seems to have been a bit too much for some of these young men."
It would be many years before there was decent relations between the two clubs again. Far as Manchester United were concerned Bob Lord was a real piece of work. To state it nicely. Lord's despicable comments was thought by some to stem back to the previous March

when a full strength United team turned up at Turf Moor and hammered Burnley 3-1 to all but seal a second consecutive First Division title. Courtesy of some Irish magic, a stunning Liam Whelan hat trick. More so the return game at Old Trafford on Easter Friday, when Matt Busby made nine changes (United reserves!), because of the European Cup semi-final against Real Madrid, the coming Thursday. A seething Bob Lord viewed United's line up as an insult to his club, and told all who would listen he would never forget or forgive it. A last reason was that Lord did not take kindly to Matt Busby's attempt to sign his best player Jimmy McIlroy, also a year earlier. As if United could just ride roughshod and sign anybody they pleased. Whatever the cause the *Burnley Butcher* found himself public enemy number one with the Old Trafford supporters for his toxic words.

It was a mammoth task at that time for any player having to wear the Manchester United shirt. So many youngsters who should have been just learning their trade. A fair few were simply not good enough and others simply blinded by the sheer emotion that engulfed every United game post-Munich. Having to be thrown into absolute turmoil before being truly ready. The reds drew five more matches and lost eight to finish in a ninth position, but in the FA Cup they were an entirely different proposition.

CHAPTER TWENTY FIVE
HELL FOR LEATHER!

After beating Sheffield Wednesday 3-0 in the fifth round on that unforgettable, but strange night at Old Trafford, United were drawn away at the Hawthorns against a very hard, classy and cultured West Bromwich Albion side. One of the best in the League. Featuring players such as Bobby Robson, Don Howe and Ronnie Allen. To reach Wembley and actually win the FA Cup in that of all seasons amid so much grief and sadness would have been a truly remarkable triumph. A magnificent feat in itself. The West Brom manager Vic Buckingham spoke well in an article written for the Daily Herald. Buckingham later donated his fee for the article to The Manchester Lord Mayor's Disaster Fund. "If I were Jimmy Murphy I would go into the West Bromwich Albion dressing room just before next Saturday's game and say, "Look lads, I know you are very sympathetic towards us. I know you want Manchester United to rise again. But I want you to go out there this afternoon and knock the stuffing out of us because that's what we are going to do." I would do that because I am a realist. And as such I am concerned solely with West Bromwich Albion. I sympathise with the sympathisers but the game goes on. Of course I was stunned by the tragic crash. But my immediate reaction was what can we do for the dependants? As much as we possibly can. That over, then on with the game. Finally, again if I were Jimmy Murphy, I would go in to the dressing room after Saturday's game to say, "Thanks for the game lads, that's the best memorial you could ever have paid to players who died at Munich."

Fine words by Buckingham setting the scene for an absolute classic FA Cup encounter! In the days leading up to the match Manchester United stayed at a hotel in Droitwich, Worcestershire. With time to pass one afternoon, all the squad gathered together in the lounge. An old fashioned, but impressive room bedecked with comfy chairs and sofas, a large blazing fire, a wall of books, huge glass windows and pride of place a magnificent grand piano. Not being able to resist and

well known for his tinkering, Jimmy Murphy sat down at it and the shouts went out for him to give them a song! So Jimmy did, many of! He began with a haunting version of Chopin-Prelude 4 and just went on and on. A love of music stretching back to when he first started playing the church organ at fourteen in his home town of Ton Pentre, South Wales. There was so much more than met the eye when it came to Jimmy Murphy. Harry Gregg recalled seeing tears in Jimmy's eyes as he played. No doubts where his thought lay as he became lost in the music. Harry remembered something else that happened later in the day. "That evening I'm heading upstairs to my bedroom when I catch the drift of a conversation taking place on the landing in front of me. A man and a woman. "Did you see that in the lounge earlier? It was so strange. All those young men with tears in their eyes listening to that older gentleman on the piano. Who was it? Do you know?'' ''That was Manchester United my dear,'' replied the man. ''Or what's left of them.''
The band was playing on.

The Teams.
West Bromwich Albion. Macedo, Howe, Williams S, Dudley, Kennedy, Barlow, Whitehouse, Robson, Allen, Kevan and Horobin.

Manchester United. Gregg, Foulkes, Greaves, Goodwin, Cope, Crowther, Webster, Taylor E, Dawson, Pearson and Charlton.

The Hawthorns.
Saturday 1st March 1958.
The huge team news for Manchester United was Bobby Charlton back in the line-up. Technically, Charlton belonged to the Military serving his two years of National Service. He was still "Technically" off sick due to injuries and the traumas sustain in the crash. So, the club had problems to solve, firstly to find out if Charlton was physically fit enough to play, and also seek permission off the Army. After some complications they finally allowed the boy from Ashington to turn out

for United. Bobby had impressed immensely in training and on chatting with him, Jimmy Murphy felt sufficiently confident after the horrors of Munich to put Bobby back in the team. Since doing his article in the Daily Herald and then donating his fee, Vic Buckingham suddenly declared on the very eve of the quarter-final: "We're going to beat Manchester United 6-0!" So, be it. Game on.

A 58, 250 crowd held their breath. Though hugely outnumbered, the Mancunian away supporters easily drowned out their home counterparts, and on the pitch marshalled superbly by Ernie Taylor, and no undoubtedly fired up by Jimmy Murphy beforehand, United tore into West Brom. After only six-minutes they took the lead. The scheming Taylor firing home after the returning Bobby Charlton's shot was initially blocked by Howe. A wonderfully, entertaining contest ensued with Vic Buckingham's side doing exactly as he wanted them to do in his article. Showing no sympathy and giving it their all. It took only six-minutes for West Brom to draw level. The forward Derek Kevan's shot was only parried away by Harry Gregg and in the chaos that ensued, Ronnie Allen smashed home an equaliser! The game continued to ebb and flow. It was fast and furious and no prisoners were being taken by either side. Three minutes before the interval the reds were back in front. Again, Ernie Taylor was instrumental when his twenty-five yard pile driver crashed against the crossbar, only for Alex Dawson to swoop with a fine header and put away the rebound! Come the second period the home team pushed increasingly forward, only to find themselves exposed and hit constantly on the break by Murphy's men. Supporters of both clubs held their breath as the clock ticked down. United had enjoyed some good fortune, adding to Harry Gregg performing absolute heroics in goal, but with just four-minutes left to play their luck finally ran out. Allen took hold of a loose ball and let fly a half volley. Gregg saved but failed to hold and in to take advantage swooped the West Brom forward Roy Horobin. However, as the ball reached the goal-line, Gregg along with his defender Ronnie Cope somehow appeared to scoop it away! Only then for the referee Kevin Howley to immediately call it a goal, 2-2, and the vast majority of the Hawthorns erupted in sheer relief! Manchester United had been robbed at the last. Knowing how close his team had been to a magnificent victory, a furious Gregg threw a glove at Mr Howley, but somehow escaped being sent off! The game ended amid scenes of United players still protesting. They had been so close. Man of the match by far was Ernie Taylor. Jimmy Murphy's simple instruction beforehand: "If chance just give it Ernie!" had proved so close to seeing the reds through. Interviewed post-match Jimmy had no real complaints.

"On the run of the play and abilities of the teams, I think a draw was correct. Every player did his part nobly. That is good enough for me." However when one newspaper hack asked him about the criticism that United were trading on the disaster, and United's opponents were being put under unfair pressure due to their "Hysterical supporters" Jimmy went mad! "I'm not like Matt Busby. Matt can keep quiet when he's really upset. I cannot keep quiet when I see and hear the players and now the supporters made the victims of cheap criticisms. The Manchester United fans have shared our successes. They have been the proudest supporters in the country. Of course they stuck out their chests and boasted that they belonged to Manchester United. We had the good fortune to give them something to boast about. All we ask is to be allowed to play our own way and try to get to Wembley. Our fans are fantastic, shouting us to Wembley!"

Also, when speaking to newspapermen Harry Gregg came clean.

"The ball hit me on the leg and rolled towards goal. Ronnie scooped it clear, but it had been over the line all right! The tension and excitement made me appeal. It was a terrible thing to happen with us so close to winning."

Wednesday 5th March 1958.

Four days later events moved onto Old Trafford for the replay. A fanatical, emotionally wrecked crowd of 60, 523 crowd crammed inside. From 5-15.pm, they started pouring in and by 6.30.pm, an hour before kick-off, the bells rang out around the ground signalling the doors to be locked. To the utter dismay of those left outside. Old Trafford was full. This situation had hardly been helped by United not having time to print tickets since the Saturday, and supporters having to pay at the gate. In pouring rain the queues originally started to form at around midday. As the afternoon unfolded they stretched out towards the swing bridge and down Warwick Road. Such was the desire to witness those now being hailed "Murphy's marvels" by the newspapers, (Jimmy hated that tag.) There were riotous scenes beforehand when an estimated 30,000 were left outside unable to enter the ground. Many tried to gate crash only to be thwarted by the mounted police on horseback forcing them back. Some did manage to smash down one entrance but were dealt with by waiting Policemen with truncheons who swiftly turned them around. The views amongst many journalist was that Manchester United had their chance at the Hawthorn. Now the classy Midlands outfit despite what was sure to be a mad, frenzied atmosphere at Old Trafford, would prove too much for Jimmy Murphy's brave but limited team. The Manchester Evening News Keith Dewhurst was of such opinion. "If the issue is still undecided at about the 70th minute, or if the game goes into extra time. I fear that West Brom will pull out that little bit extra and win." The match programme that night carried a solemn tribute to Duncan Edwards...

..."We who thrilled to his inspiring demonstrations of seeming invincibility, coupled with a joy of living that infected his comrades whenever and wherever the going was tough, will always remember..."

The Teams.

Manchester United. Gregg, Foulkes, Greaves, Goodwin, Cope, Harrop, Webster, Taylor E, Dawson, Pearson and Charlton.

West Bromwich Albion.

Saunders, Howe, Williams S, Dudley, Kennedy, Barlow, Whitehouse, Robson, Allen, Kevan and Horobin.

Problems for United when the influential Stan Crowther was ruled out through a heel injury, and in came yet another youngster for his debut. 22-year-old Manchester born Bobby Harrop. The game began at a hundred miles an hour and never slowed. Similar to their opening encounter it was a breathless affair. Full of nerve wracking suspense and unrelenting drama. West Brom came to Manchester to attack and for large swathes of the game appeared the better team, shooting on sight ensuring Harry Gregg once more was kept busy. A magnificent save from Bobby Robson on just twelve-minutes a sight to behold. United hung on throughout by sheer guts and desire. Ernie Taylor again by far United's best player, followed by the electrifying Bobby Charlton. Never forgetting the uproarious backing of a home crowd whose throats were not so much hoarse, more burnt out. But for those of a red persuasion it was mostly grim and simply a case of keeping their fingers crossed. Slowly United found their feet With Charlton going close just before half-time, only for the keeper Jimmy Sanders, (A former World War two RAF gunner pilot) to push around the post. As the game wore on it appeared extra-time would be called for with West Brom impressing on the attack, and United, like the first game, looking to hit them on the break. Come the last moments the home side were most definitely nailed against the ropes unable to get off, surviving just and running only on pure adrenaline. If it had been a boxing match the *Baggies* would have won easily on points, they just so needed a knockout blow, and in the cup if you did not find one there always remained the chance it could well return to haunt. Jimmy Murphy looked at his watch, one minute remained to play when Bill Foulkes played a long pass out of defence, and United broke out! Sprinting like a gazelle Bobby Charlton pushed the ball past the Albion left-back Stuart Williams on the wing, and just went hell for leather! Old Trafford held a collective breath. Charlton recalled he had to beat Williams to the ball after noticing from the corner of his eye, the referee readying to blow the final whistle. Jimmy Murphy always told him: "Catch the defender on his heels Bobby lad, and by the time he's turned you've gone!" Amid a blur of blue and white shirts Charlton sought out the single red one. His low cross found Colin Webster who reacted first to flash and side-foot a shot past Sanders into the net! Old Trafford went mad both inside and out, as thousands had stayed to follow the match by the crowd noises emanating from inside the ground. Windows in the nearby streets shook! The BBC nine o'clock news had gone live to the match for an update just as the goal went in! United had won it at the last and against all odds made the FA Cup semi-finals, where they would face Second Division Fulham. Colin Webster appeared in a state of shock when being interviewed afterwards. "I've been in a whirl ever since I saw the ball go into the net. Although it was only from a three-yards range, it was a strain at the time. But it all looked so easy on television." Easily West Brom's best player on the night Bobby Robson was devastated with the result. "We got bloody nothing from the referee, we didn't get the bounce of the ball, and then they go and score right at the end." The celebrations on the forecourt went long into the night! Unrestrained relief and joy for the United supporters! A momentarily release from the still, grieving fresh wounds. Whilst over at the *Rechts Der Isar,* the game was followed on a special radio commentary by the Munich survivors. The chairman Harold Hardman ringing them shortly after the final-whistle saying this result was for them and those lost. He also passed on a message from the delighted boss back to Old Trafford. Three words from Matt Busby. "Bang on! Wonderful!" Suddenly, Manchester United were being quoted by local bookies as 7/4 favourites. Jimmy's boys were up for the cup, and for the new United, the dreams of Wembley glory would go on.

The following Saturday the gates were locked once more as West Bromwich Albion returned for a League match, duly thrashing United 4-0. Ronnie Allen grabbed two, Kevan one, the other an own goal by Ian Greaves. A most unwanted sense of reality returned to the packed Old Trafford terraces. Of the 63,479 present very few were not surprised, for the pressure on the team to perform week after week was simply far beyond their capabilities. All hopes and dreams were being piled onto a successful cup run. However, the entire afternoon was put into the shade when before kick-off, Professor Georg Maurer, his wife, deputies and members of staff from the *Rechts Der Isar,* were introduced by club chairman Harold Hardman over the tannoy and appeared into sight. There was not a dry eye in the ground. All had all been invited from Munich by United to be their guests of honour at the game. Every supporter roared out and clapped them to the heavens. Mancunians forever in their debt and hearts for how they had fought to try and keep their boys alive. All but one made it, but Duncan Edwards' injuries were just too severe. Despite their monumental efforts they never had a chance as the angels simply tugged far too hard. Maurer's wife was presented with a large red and white bouquet of flowers by Captain Bill Foulkes, whilst the other survivor present Harry Gregg, did similar to the youngest nurse who had come over. Then came the silence as Old Trafford waited to hear the voice of their manager. A message to be relayed over the tannoy by Matt Busby from his hospital bed in Munich. For a few momenta all you could hear was a spluttered cough, a gentle cry, and the distant rattle of a freight train across the way at Trafford Park. Silent as a church at midnight. Then, a crackling on the line was heard and…

"Ladies and Gentlemen.

I am speaking to you from my bed in the *Rechts Der Isar* hospital, in Germany, where I have been since the tragic accident at Munich, just over a month ago. You will be glad, I am sure, to know, that the remaining players here and myself are now considered out of danger. And this can only be attributed to the wonderful treatment and attention given us by Professor Maurer and his fine staff. I am obliged to Empire News for giving me this opportunity to speak to you. For it is only in this last two or three days that I have been able to be told anything about football. And I am delighted to hear that the club have reached the semi-finals of the FA Cup. And I enclose my best wishes to everyone. And, finally, may I just say.

God bless you all."

CHAPTER TWENTY SIX
STOOD ON A NAIL

In the days leading up to the FA Cup semi-final to be played at Villa Park, against second Division Fulham, "The Preston Plumber" the great Tom Finney spoke of his admiration in how Jimmy Murphy had led Manchester United to this point. "United have proved that real greatness means much more than a galaxy of star players. It means possessing a thing called spirit. Believe me, I am not being sentimental when I say that I've stood back in proud bewilderment at the fantastic recovery made by these men at Old Trafford. Behind it all, of course, is this incredible man called Jimmy Murphy. A man who has been a rival of mine as a player, as the assistant manager of a rival Lancashire club, and as the manager of a rival national team. This for Jimmy must have been the most remorseless months ever spent by any man behind the scenes of modern sport. Yet it is still a quality greater than even Jimmy Murphy possesses which has prompted the miracle of Manchester. There would have been nothing but sympathy for them if they had announced, "We just cannot see this season through." It would have been a perfectly human reaction. But, now as they fight on, we will see them for what they are. A superhuman club."

As ever, before any major match, Jimmy Murphy took his team away to Blackpool's Norbreck Hydro hotel. For four days they made their plans. Back in the fold from Munich was the winger Ken Morgans. After playing just one game in the reserves against Newcastle, the Welsh teenager scored and looked impressive on his return. Come match day in Birmingham, ticket spivs were cleaning up with United supporters desperate to see their team. Some paying up to ten times the normal price. A massive £2 10s! Fulham may have been only a Second Division club, but they possessed some fantastic players, none more than their maestro inside-forward and Captain Johnny Haynes. He was confident and had no problem letting people know in a

London newspaper article. "I am one of Manchester United's greatest admirers, however, Fulham are determined to hammer them. We know the majority of the country are willing United to win our semi-final, I can assure you that every Fulham player will not be pulling any punches when we meet them because we want to get to Wembley ourselves." A Fulham call to arms from their Captain Johnny Haynes, one which his team mates duly took up.

The Teams.

Manchester United. Gregg, Foulkes, Greaves, Goodwin, Cope, Crowther, Webster, Taylor E, Dawson, Pearson and Charlton.

Fulham. Macedo, Cohen, Langley, Bentley, Stapleton, Lawler, Dwight, Hill, Stevens, Haynes and Chamberlain.

On Saturday 26th March 1958, in front of a 69,745 crowd, Manchester United and Fulham fought out a thrilling 2-2 draw, with all goals scored in the first-half. For United, Bobby Charlton was magnificent, as was Johnny Haynes for the Londoners. Despite being in separate Leagues there was little to choose between the two sides. Charlton fired the reds in front after only twelve-minutes. A half volley smashed home from twenty-yards, the type soon to become Bobby's trademark for both United and England. Almost immediately from the restart Fulham equalised! Their right-winger Arthur Stevens slotting past Gregg from close range. Seven-minutes before half-time they went in front. Jimmy (The chin) Hill storming past Ronnie Cope, before beating Harry Gregg with a fine finish! As the Fulham supporters roared in delight, the Mancunians tried hard to raise their team, for unusually in the FA Cup, they had not turned up. Except for Bobby Charlton, who to the utter relief of his supporters levelled this semi-final once more just two-minutes before the interval. With Fulham down to ten men after their full-back Jimmy Langley had gone off injured in the time added on, Charlton lashed home a rebound. 2-2! Suddenly, as Fulham would be forced to play the second-half with a badly, limping Langley, the scene had been set for Manchester United to take full advantage. But this failed to transpire. With the Craven Cottage men fighting for every ball, and their keeper Tony Macedo excelling. Including two remarkable saves against the on-fire Charlton, they survived to force a replay. The closest United came to a winner was ten-minutes from time, when who else but Bobby Charlton crashed a ferocious effort that smashed against the underside of Macedo's rattling crossbar. Following the full-time whistle the Fulham full back George Cohen and Charlton shared a warm handshake. Two young men in just eight-years' time, who would play integral parts of an England side winning the World Cup. The Manchester United players looked close to exhaustion on leaving the pitch. A horrific season like no other seemed to have finally caught up with them. "United's worst display since Munich," claimed the Daily Mirror's Frank McGhee. It was announced the replay would be played the following Wednesday afternoon at Highbury. Much to the utter disdain of the United supporters. A venue on Fulham's doorstep, a home match. Not to mention the cost and travel arrangements to reach the capital from Manchester. It would have to be a case of taking two days off work which was simply out of the question for so many of them. Then it was announced to huge relief up north that the BBC had agreed with the Football Association to show live coverage of the semi-final replay. An astonishing decision when considering the only football normally shown on television was the final itself and the rare European Cup and England match. Despite all the difficulties involved around ten thousand Manchester United supporters still made it to Highbury and what they witnessed was truly something special.

Highbury. Wednesday 26th March 1958.
With all the problems involved in reaching London from Manchester, plus the BBC live television coverage, a lowly crowd figure of just 38,000 were present at Highbury. When a full house of 68,000 was the expectant number. Instead this turned out to be the lowest Cup semi-final crowd for twenty-nine years. The loss in revenue was cited

at around £5000. A huge amount. One plus amid the chaos was the ticket spivs taking an enormous hit! Back in Manchester, the amount of doctor, dentist appointments and funerals on that Wednesday afternoon were countless! Sadly, for the younger supporters, even though the match was on television, other plans had to be put in place. Otherwise it meant having to race home on a miserable, dark, rainy afternoon to ensure they caught the second-half on the twelve-inch black and white screens. Over to my good friend Roy Cavanagh to tell his tale of how as a 12-year-old schoolboy he saw the entire match!

"Live televised football matches were still an exceedingly rare feature of life in 1958, so when the semi-final replay was announced as being chosen for such an event on the following Wednesday afternoon, I did a rather foolish thing to get off school to see it. I actually stood on a nail which kept me off and laid up on the couch for the midweek afternoon replay!"

Those without televisions gathered in their hundreds in town, and elsewhere outside Rental electrical shops, which had them in the windows, desperate to watch the reds and praying they would not be switched off!

The Teams.

Manchester United. Gregg, Foulkes, Greaves, Goodwin, Cope, Crowther, Webster, Taylor E, Dawson, Charlton and Brennan.

Fulham. Macedo, Cohen, Langley, Bentley, Stapleton, Lawler, Dwight, Hill, Stevens, Haynes and Chamberlain.

The game itself was a classic with Manchester United finally running out 5-3 winners, courtesy of an Alex Dawson hat trick, but only after a truly, compelling contest. A penny for Harry Gregg's thoughts as he entered onto Highbury's heavily sanded pitch. The last time he played there was the 5-4 epic, the Busby Babes last game on English soil. The reds began hard and fast peppering the Fulham goal and winning half a dozen corners. Ronnie Goodwin for one moving up field and hitting the crossbar. The scoring began on fourteen-minutes with a scorching header from 18-year-old Alex Dawson, from a Shay Brennan corner that flew past a hapless Macedo. Any hope United would go on to dominate were swiftly dashed when Arthur Stevens levelled just before the half-hour, after being put clear by the brilliant Johnny Haynes. Fulham's goalkeeping hero of the first semi-final Tony Macedo was to suffer a dreadful game this time around. Roughed up early doors from corners by Dawson, no doubt under orders from Jimmy Murphy, he haunted and bashed Macedo with a barrage of thumping shoulder charges. Dawson gave everything and more to the United cause post-Munich, too much and in time his career at Old Trafford would suffer due to such unbelievable effort. It was he who shot the reds ahead again, although a terrible error from Macedo letting the ball slip through his hands. Still Fulham would not lie down and three-minutes before the interval their left winger Trevor "Tosh' Chamberlain levelled once more after a great run and cross from a now, fit again Langley. Tosh was a huge favourite amongst his supporters and even more so now. With the same scenario as the previous Saturday seemingly set to occur, 2-2 at the interval, Macedo inexplicably erred again letting in Shay Brennan to fire United in front for a third time, after being set up originally by a lovely Ernie Taylor run and pass. Shortly into the second-half Alex Dawson struck again to claim his hat trick! Bobby Charlton raced away down the left wing beating defenders with ease before finding his teammate who made no mistake. 4-2 and surely now the reds were Wembley bound? But yet Fulham refused to give up, and with seventeen-minutes on the Highbury clock showing still to play they made it 4-3! A Steven cross caused havoc in the United penalty area, ending with Dwight dribbling past a stranded Gregg to finish! Suddenly, it came down to what did the men from the Cottage have left? Those Mancunians present and the ones back home watching on television could only hope their boys had enough left in the tank to see it through. Fulham went forward in search of salvation and with four-minutes remaining, their Captain Johnny Haynes charged down a bouncing ball to run through the shattered United rearguard and shoot past Harry Gregg!

4-4! Only, to the Londoners horror for it then to be disallowed for handball. Time ticked forever further down and with just moments left to play, and a thick rolling mist descending fast over Highbury, Bobby Charlton let fly a thunderbolt past Macedo making it 5-3, sending Manchester United to Wembley! The full-time whistle saw an emotional Jimmy Murphy race on the pitch to embrace every United player. A distraught Charlton finished the game in floods of tears and head bowed. Bobby having to be consoled by both his teammates and Fulham players. Heaven knows the thoughts still in the young lad's head after losing so many of his pals at Munich. It was five weeks to the FA Cup final where waiting would be their near neighbours Bolton Wanderers. For a long time Bolton had been United's bogey team, and with no love lost between the supporters it promised to be a typically, no-nonsense northern showdown at the home of English football. For the United party, the return journey by train to Manchester was a quiet affair. More a sense of relief filled the carriages. Many beers were sunk, but there remained too much sadness. There were half smiles, little more. The memories of so many lost killed any sense of party atmosphere. Munich lived on in every orifice of Manchester United Football Club. It was the air that they breathed.

CHAPTER TWENTY SEVEN
THE PITS OF HELL

"Through this holy anointing may the Lord in his love and mercy help you with the grace of the Holy Spirit… May the Lord who frees you from sin save you and raise you up."
This a part of the Holy Sacrament of the Last Rites.

Twice early in his stay at the *Rechts Der Isar* hospital, the devout Catholic Matt Busby was administered the blessing from a Roman Catholic priest. This Last Rite on earth. Busby had suffered horrendous injuries to his chest, lungs and two twisted, badly broken legs. He was placed into an oxygen tent with his breathing assisted by a Trachetomy because of one collapsed left lung and punctured right. Such was Busby's grave, uncertain condition drifting in and out of consciousness, certain surgical procedures had to be performed on him without given anaesthetics in case he never came back round. It was considered by the German doctors treating him that these injuries were far too severe for anyone to survive. An early short hospital statement issued on Busby read: "We do not have much hope of saving him." However, slowly there was noticed minor improvements and enough for Professor Maurer to comment: "Herr Busby's chances are now fifty/fifty." That he recovered was due totally to the magnificent efforts of the hospital's doctors and nurses. They never gave up on Busby, even when at times he appeared to have given up on himself. After Duncan Edwards passed fifteen days on from the crash, Busby still remained totally unaware of who had lived or died. Whilst physically the improvement was visible, psychologically he was a tortured soul racked with guilt. The time finally came after he overheard snippets of conversation for Busby to be told. The doctors had warned against this because they wanted him to get stronger in case the depression turned even deeper, but the decision when to do it hung over his recuperation like a dark, foreboding cloud. His wife Jean told them when the time arose she would tell her husband the grim tidings. Many times when he asked Jean about how his lads were doing, she simply changed the subject. Also, Busby pondered why was there always the same small band of fellow survivors visiting him at his bedside?

Where was Bert Whalley?

Where was Tom Curry?

Where was Duncan?

Where was his Captain Roger Byrne?

Where was the little loveable rascal Eddie Colman?

Why had the others also not called by to say hello?

"It was at a time when I gradually became aware that some of my boys must have been killed. I did not know for certain. I just knew something dreadful had happened. I was in that tent, barely alive myself. Twice I had been given the Last Rites. I just wanted to stay inside the tent and die there, rather than come out and learn the truth. So I prayed for the end to come quickly."

Finally, Busby spoke of the moment when the dreadful news was finally broken to him. "I had drifted in and out of consciousness for days on end. Something when I was awake, told me there had been a terrible accident, but the nuns and doctors said nothing. Then I came to one day and Jean was there, leaning over me. She said nothing either. Jean has always been my strength. I said: "What happened?" She still said nothing. So I began to go through the names. She didn't speak at all. She didn't even look at me. When they were gone she just shook her head."

Jean recalled: "Matt remembered everyone on the plane. Every time he mentioned the name of one of the dead players, I just shook my head. It seemed as if it would never end." Being told only sent him soaring into a deeper spiral of despair. Not just both Busby's body and heart had been broken by the crash, but his soul had also been deeply scarred. Everything he worked and strove for had been ripped away from him in a blazing inferno. A funeral pyre burning the ashes of his boys. Busby's Babes wiped out in Southern Germany and he thought it was all his fault. Busby was close to losing his mind. Ranting and raving in the hospital bed. Why them, why United? A human error or technical and why had he not died with them? What was so special about him to have been allowed to live? "So many times I asked myself whether there was anything I could do, or ought to have done to stop that plane. But you saw how it was. We went back to the terminal building and everything seemed to have been checked. It would have been as pointless for me to ask the pilot if everything was in order, as for him to ask me whether I had picked the best team for Manchester United."

After ten week lying desperately ill, then falling into a deep depression, news came from Munich that Matt Busby had been deemed well enough to head home. Around this time it was also announced that Professor Georg Maurer had been awarded an honorary CBE by the Queen in recognition of his services in the aftermath of the Munich air disaster. This obviously went down wonderfully well with the Manchester United supporters. Their appreciation and gratitude towards this man knew no bounds. Maurer had become a hero amongst them, as had all who worked at the *Rechts Der Isar* that cared for their boys. It was an honour deemed very much deserved for the Professor. Now they awaited eagerly the return of their manager. Matt Busby had travelled with Jean on the Munich to Rotterdam express train, then crossed the North sea by ferry. Before finally on the afternoon of Friday 18th April 1958, arriving back at his Chorlton home on Kings Road. But Busby remained far from well. Both physically and mentally. He had visibly aged. His hair had turned white. As Busby stepped out of a black Humber using crutches, he was clearly struggling. Large crowds of neighbours, well-wishers, newsmen and photographers had turned out to welcome him home. There was cheers and loud applause as he came into sight. Flowers lay propped up against his garage door left by workmen. A little girl ran towards Busby with her own bouquet to welcome the famous neighbour home. Inside the house the hallway lay flooded with flowers from friends. This stretching into their living room. Typical of the man although clearly causing him pain he lent down to accept them and say thank you to the little girl. Busby's smile, if not painted was clearly masking his true inner feelings. A man reeling. ''Are you all right everybody. How have you been while I've been away?'' He forgot to mention in the pits of hell. Busby's convalescence at home remained a painful experience. He was unable to dress himself and stayed mostly at first in bed. Paddy McGrath was amongst the first to visit his old friend. ''When Matt saw me he put his arms around me and broke down.'' Despite all he had gone through Busby's body, if not troubled mind healed relatively fast. Though at first utterly against the idea of going back to Old Trafford to see old faces, he quite literally forced himself to go through with what ultimately proved a harrowing experience. All the club staff were gathered together in the ground's medical room to see the boss, but it was cut short for Busby simply could not hold back the tears, and was led away. ''It was far too early,'' he recalled. ''I felt better for the tears and because I had forced myself to go back.'' As the FA Cup final approached Busby toiled with the notion of whether he should attend. Professor Maurer's advice being to go would be a step too far at this stage of the recovery. He decided otherwise, and made plans to watch his Manchester United attempt to achieve what was being deemed by all a sporting miracle. However, all talk of the possibility Busby might lead out the Manchester United team at Wembley was immediately shot down by the man himself. ''Jimmy will lead the boys out,'' Matt insisted. He more than any other was overjoyed Matt Busby would once more be alongside him at Wembley Stadium. ''People wonder why I've turned down top jobs to stay with Matt, but our association is founded on mutual respect. Matt respects everybody with who he has dealings, all the way down from the boardroom to ground and laundry staff. That is just one of his qualities. The others include wonderful intuition and extreme patience. His foresight was proven when he led English clubs into Europe and when he broke up the 1948 side to give youth a fling. My greatest reward was at Wembley in 1958, when the boss came back from Munich, still a sick man. He said: ''Thank you Jimmy, you've done a wonderful job. I'm proud of you.''

CHAPTER TWENTY EIGHT
ABIDE WITH ME

Jimmy Murphy had by god's grace survived a world war, missed an air crash by a twist of fate, but whether he would be able to live through the traditional Wembley hymn *Abide With Me* was truly debatable. An hour before kick-off and the massed bands of the Grenadier Guards were preparing. 47-years-old, a heart broken, every bone in his body telling him to rest. But that time was still far away. Though shattered, drained and surviving only on pure adrenaline, he just had to keep moving forward. Jimmy never slept, he closed his eyes but then would appear the faces of those lost. He could not afford to dream in case of accidentally slipping off into the darkness and hearing their voices once more. Duncan, Eddie, Tommy, Roger. An open wounds. Just empty seats in the Cliff dressing room and the canteen. Distant echoes of lost voices drifting in the Mancunian air. Red ghosts struggling to find their way beyond the light. Manchester, Salford, Dudley, Yorkshire and Irish accents. The lovely, riotous noise of laughter in the corridor, and the clack, the wonderful clack of football boots. Yet, when Jimmy went to look, no one? No one… Morning broke to reveal a beautiful May morning when the United supporter set off for Wembley from Manchester. As ever seemed the way on Cup Final day, the sun was shining bright. It had been decided the players would be wearing on the left breasts of their shirts an image of a Phoenix to symbolise how the club had rose from the Munich flames, telling the world Manchester United were not going away.

As United's preparations took place in sunny Blackpool, Jimmy finally had the unusual problem for him of who to play and leave out. Normally since the crash his line-up all but picked itself. But now Dennis Viollet had returned from Munich. He had begun training again just before Easter, but it had taken time to get Viollet back into

any kind of match fitness. He did play in the first team for their last game of the season away to Chelsea, that Jimmy used for a Cup Final rehearsal. This had Bobby Charlton at centre-forward with Viollet and Taylor as the inside forwards, and Colin Webster on the left-wing. United lost 2-1. The reds were not great by any means and their forwards at times lacked momentum and cohesion. Players performing out of their normal roles. As for Dennis Viollet, he obviously appeared off the pace and scratchy. All concerned knew it would be a great risk to pick Viollet at Wembley, but such had been his ability to score goals from anywhere, a true match winner? Pre-Munich, Viollet was a master of his craft, however that was then. Since Bobby Charlton had been excelling in his old position, to the extent of earning an England call-up against Scotland in the British Home Championships. ''I don't want to butter you up, Missus, but your son will play for England before he's twenty-one!'' The prophetic words of United's chief scout Joe Armstrong to Bobby's mother Cissie, the first time he saw her son play. On Saturday 19th April, the English won 4-0 at Hampden Park, with Bobby Charlton sensational and scoring a magnificent volley from a cross by Tom Finney. Armstrong later said to Busby when recommending this wonderful boy from the north east, who he had first seen play in a raging blizzard. Who had two great feet, clever footballing intelligence and such beautiful balance. ''If the boy does not become a footballer he would make a fantastic tightrope walker. And a good lad to boot! He does everything with care, almost as if he was sitting at a piano.'' Jimmy Murphy had been given a lot to think about. Viollet himself had no idea whether he was going to play. ''I don't know for sure that I will be in the Wembley side, but I make no secret of the fact that has been my aim and my deeply cherished hope. Some supporters apparently don't share my feelings and have written to say it would be unfair on the lads who battled through after Munich against seemingly hopeless odds.''
Two days before the final Jack Crompton advised Jimmy Murphy after a training session in his opinion, Colin Webster was not fit enough to play in the final. Also that Dennis Viollet remained much

too short of match practice to risk in such an important game for the club. Jimmy agonised over the decision and went with the same all-out attacking team that lost at Stamford bridge. In doing so meant leaving out such post-Munich stalwarts as Mark Pearson and Shay Brennan, but he could ill afford such sympathies despite his love for those lads. Manchester United had to win this game and Jimmy Murphy would have to trust those eleven chosen to win the FA Cup. On the Friday, the team travelled by train from Blackpool to Crewe to pick up the main service to London. On leaving the Norbreck, they were clapped off by the hotel staff and huge crowds of holidaymakers. First helped onto the coach was Matt Busby who smiled politely as several over-enthusiastic supporters made it on board also to shake his hand. All along the journey in astonishing scenes, supporters and neutrals wished them well as the footballers were mobbed like film stars in a sea of goodwill. Jimmy's worries about the pressures on player's privacy being completely vindicated. This was Elvis like! The Norbreck had proved a priceless, temporary oasis away from the reality of Munich. A godsend. Manchester United's Cup Final hotel was based in the peaceful settings of Weymouth, far enough away from any of the prevailing madness that surrounded them, and perfect for just the one night stay. Come the actual coach trip to Wembley, it was incredibly hot and stifling with the unusually, steaming summer weather, but the comforting sight of Matt Busby sat once more at the front with Jimmy Murphy, could only have helped calmed a little of their pre-Cup Final nerves. Theirs's had been an FA Cup run fuelled by a tidal wave of emotion, masterminded and cajoled by Jimmy Murphy, but mostly driven on by a desire not to look back. It was a remarkable effort, but it was simply akin to getting blind drunk at a loved one's wake. United were playing on to numb the pain. Fired up beyond all measure by Jimmy, this patched up team of hired hands, kids and survivors who by some miracle had held itself together since Munich. It is hard to believe *Abide With Me* on Cup Final day had ever been sung before, or since with such profound feeling and heartfelt emotion. The lyrics to this beautiful prayer so apt for what had happened. How they managed to survive what originally felt like an abyss from which there was no comeback. Yet, led by Jimmy Murphy, despite almost vanishing in a sea of grief, the Phoenix had rose to breathe fire and life into Manchester United Football Club. Eighty-six days on from the Munich air disaster, the Red Devils though ravaged by such grief and loss were still alive.

ABIDE WITH ME

…Abide with me; fast falls the even tide;
The darkness deepens; Lord, with me abide;
When other helpers fail and comforts flee,
Help of the helpless, oh, abide with me.

Swift to its close ebbs out life's little day;
Earth's joys grow dim, its glories pass away;
Change and decay in all around I see.
O Thou who changes not, abide with me.

I need Thy presence every passing hour;
What but Thy grace can foil the tempter's pow'r?
Who, like Thyself, my guide and stay can be?
Through cloud and sunshine, Lord, abide with me.

I fear no foe, with Thee at hand to bless;
Ills have no weight, and tears no bitterness;
Where is death's sting? Where, grave, thy victory?
I triumph still, if Thou abide with me.

Hold Thou Thy cross before my closing eyes;
Shine through the gloom and point me to the skies;
heav'n's morning breaks, and earth's vain shadows flee; In life, in death, O Lord, abide with me…

On Saturday 3rd May 1958, Manchester United and Bolton Wanderers stepped out into the blazing Wembley sunlight to compete in the 86th FA Cup final. Led by Jimmy Murphy, the noise from the United supporters on seeing their team appear threatened to tear the roof off the stadium. A proud Jimmy strode purposefully, a brisk walk, behind him his Captain Bill Foulkes. A frail looking, pale-faced Matt Busby on crutches was present, but still too weak to be able to assist in any manner. A smile and a wave for the United supporters on spotting him who roared out his name. He was driven into Wembley via the royal tunnel entrance. Busby's eyes though, like Jimmy's gave the game away, both men remained lost in a fog of grief. Shortly before kick-off at Jimmy's behest, Busby did go into the United dressing room to wish the players well. "Just go out and follow Jimmy's instructions," was all he could manage before breaking down and having to leave. Throughout the final Busby sat in a wicker chair just behind the United front bench after declining a seat in the royal box. The reason being he would struggle badly to climb the steps, but also maybe Busby just wanted to feel close to the action once more. Not be forced to have to endure polite, idle chit-chat. Instead his eyes could stay focused on the game watching Jimmy's Manchester United. Those in red shirts, some familiar, but many were strangers to him. Where had all his own boys gone?

The Teams.

Manchester United. Gregg, Foulkes, Goodwin, Cope, Crowther, Dawson, Taylor E, Charlton, Viollet and Webster.

Bolton Wanderers. Hopkinson, Hartle, Banks, Hennin, Higgins, Edwards, Birch, Stevens, Lofthouse, Parry and Holden.

Through absolutely no fault of their own Bill Ridding's Bolton Wanderers had been written up as the bad guys in the final. The villains of the piece. Geronimo's Indians with bows and arrows to Jimmy Murphy's cowboy's in white Stetsons. Their defender Ray

Hartle had been in the Bolton side hammered 7-2 by the Busby Babes just two weeks before the crash. "They were on another waveband. They were so talented. Most sides have three or four talented players, they had many more." The sheer emotion of the day also took a hold of United's opponents. Hartle recalled the strange atmosphere on travelling to Wembley aboard the team bus. Even some of their own player close to tears on driving past the tens of thousands of United supporters with many wearing the names of the dead players on rosettes. Chanting their names. Bolton had their own reasons for wanting so much to win the Cup. Five years previous they last out in arguably the greatest FA Cup final of them all. The 4-3 defeat after leading 3-1 against Stanley Matthews's Blackpool. Immortalised as the *"Matthews Final"* even though their centre forward Stan Mortensen scored a hat trick! Also, the now United man Ernie Taylor, was said by many that day to have been the unsung hero and true man of the match. This defeat cut deep for the Wanderers and they were desperate for a victory over their bitter rivals. The record over the reds in recent years had been remarkable. It was said the Wanderers had black cat's eyes over Manchester United. Bolton had finished eleventh that season, a good team, ageing, but a well organised defence. A hard running midfield and forwards that could do damage. They epitomised the tough tackling, physical power of the English First Division. None more so than their magnificently powerful and when needed brutal and ruthless centre forward. England's *'Lion of Vienna"*. Nat Lofthouse. Albeit, many thought the Bolton curse had been well and truly broken with the savage 7-2 mauling, the events at Wembley would prove if this was really true. Manchester United were being labelled the *"Nation's team"* and it appeared everyone across the land wanted them to win. A rainbow's end for Jimmy Murphy's brave lads. All except in and around Bolton! They had suffered enough with the *"Magic of the cup"* nonsense against Blackpool. Not again for the Wanderers, there would be sympathy after the match for all their opponent had endured, but during it no mercy and win at all costs.

After being introduced to his Royal Highness Prince Philip, both teams broke away preparing for kick-off. Finally, the referee Mr Jack Sherlock blew his whistle, and as 100,000 crowd roared out the game got under way. Within three-minutes Bolton Wanderers were a goal up and it was their centre-forward who struck. United's offside plan failed miserably and the Bolton warhorse Lofthouse raced in to fire past Harry Gregg. From that moment on United never really played in the first-half. Too young, uncertain, making sloppy mistakes. The early goal appeared to sap their legs as well as confidence. The strain of the day taking hold. Come half-time Jimmy Murphy obviously had torn into them as they came out for the second period, albeit for a while full of their old fire and zest. The United who had glittered and shone during the cup run had returned. Bobby Charlton rattled the Bolton post and the ball bounced back into their goalkeeper, Hopkinson's hands! As hope amongst the Manchester United supporters soared of an equaliser, Nat Lofthouse came lumbering back into the story to win the day for Bolton Wanderers. Close to the hour, their inside-forward Dennis Stevens (Duncan Edwards cousin), lashed a fierce cross into United's six-yard box that Harry Gregg went for but could only palm up. In Lofthouse came crashing like a tank to send both Gregg and the ball backwards over the goal line. An outrageous challenge! As the Bolton supporters erupted to salute going 2-0 in front, United heart's stopped. Gregg had been unusually uncertain throughout with his handling, but surely Mr Sherlock would disallow for a foul? You did not have to be Sherlock Holmes to see the United keeper had been barged into by Lofthouse. No! The referee pointed to the centre-circle. The goal stood and for the second year running, controversial decisions stalked Manchester United goalkeepers in Cup Finals. For Peter McParland now read Nat Lofthouse. It was four-minutes before Gregg was deemed well enough to play on after being treated by not just the United trainer Ted Dalton, but Bolton's also, Bert Sproston. That same summer Mr Sherlock bumped into Jack Crompton whilst on holiday in the Isle of Man, and admitted after watching the incident two or three times on television replays, he had indeed made a mistake. Sherlock apologised to Crompton but the damage had been done. The rest of the game proved a non-event, and it felt as if everyone was just waiting to hear the final-whistle. As for the United players they appeared simply drained of all energy, the final quite simply one game too far. Nat Lofthouse found himself booed every time he touched the ball by the Manchester supporters, but one man's villain is another's hero and in Bolton, already a hero, Lofthouse was set to be given legendary status. "I headed the ball over the line as it came down and before Harry caught it. We went into the final as the "Other Team" and that only gave us greater determination. We are sorry United could not crown their season with a win, football is a game where there can be only one winner, and I am proud to say that was Bolton Wanderers." When questioned also by the press men Harry Gregg refused to complain about the decision. "I remember nothing of the second goal. I had to turn around to catch the ball. All I could see was the crowd. Then something hit me. I don't blame Nat, I would have done the same thing!"

So, no rainbow's end for the reds. It was to be the Wanderer's greatest ever player Nat Lofthouse handed the FA Cup trophy with Bolton colours on it by the Duke of Edinburgh. There followed respectfully, muted celebrations by the players as their opponents quietly slipped away to lick the many wounds. Ray Hartle again, he recalled how celebrating the victory on the pitch was hard, such had been the torrid, emotional atmosphere in the stadium. "We were doing the lap of honour and Tommy Banks turned to me and said: "Shall we go?" I replied we might as well. This is not a happy thing to be doing. As we headed off the pitch our trainer Bert Sproston said: "C'mon lads, this is a trip of a lifetime!" Bert convinced us to complete the lap of honour."

Jimmy Murphy had no argument with the result. "I am still very proud of the way these United boys got to Wembley and the way they performed today. But there is no question that the better side won." Through hellfire and sheer will of strength, post-Munich, Jimmy had kept his promise to Busby of keeping the flag flying. A ninth place finish and FA Cup final runners-up, was in all honesty far more than anyone would have thought possible in those thirteen awful days following the crash. On the train home north every station lay packed with United supporters waving their scarves as they passed. The team may have returned to Manchester without the trophy, but still hundreds of thousands of people were waiting to greet them. A city turned out to say thank you. The players staring down from an open top bus into the massive crowds that lined every pavement ten, twenty deep. Bill Foulkes recalled: "They all seemed to be crying. We came out of the station and I've never seen so many people. You couldn't see a chink of light. When we finally reached The Town Hall in Albert Square, it seemed like a million people just standing there, not moving, no noise. As Captain I had to get up and say a few words, but after that I had to get away." However, defeat at Wembley did not signal the season's end. Since their FA Cup final semi-final replay win over Fulham at the end of March, Manchester United had played twelve games in just over a month. The players were shattered, the management exhausted, the supporters drained, but there remained unfinished business in the European Cup. Despite many heroic performances one player in a red shirt had stood head and shoulders above all. At still just the tender age of 20, Bobby Charlton led the charge back. A magnificent talent had begun to blossom in the darkest of times for United. A two-footed, explosive forward able to play in several positions. Bobby was not playing in paradise anymore, he was in purgatory, but unless you stared deep into his eyes you would struggle to see the difference on a football pitch. He would glide over the mud-spattered surfaces of Old Trafford and beyond. A reminder to the supporters of what had passed, here was still that rarity. Priceless now. A Busby Babe.

CHAPTER TWENTY NINE
UNFINISHED BUSINESS

Extended purgatory.

The grief-stricken period which had engulfed Manchester United since the crash, meant there still remained the small matter of AC Milan in the European Cup to play. The semi-final. A now infamous tournament for Mancunians that had become etched with the blood of those who had perished on that wretched German runway. For the winners a place in the final against the holders Real Madrid in Brussels, Heysel stadium awaited. Fate's hand complicit and forcing supporters to ask the one question those of a red persuasion. "Just what if?" What if that plane had not crashed off the end of Munich runway? What if the Babes had lived? Edwards, Taylor, Colman and all, then United would have started favourites, if not equals against the immensely talented *Rossoneri,* before playing Di Stefano's all conquering Real, with the possibility to gain revenge for the previous season's semi-final defeat. Something that before the crash all Manchester United supporters dreamt about. Just give their boys one more chance against those strutting Spaniards from Madrid. Just one more go and see what happens. The Busby Babes were a year older, wiser. It would have been a game to write songs and glorious tales about, but sadly it was never to be. Of course, come the semi-final and all that had gone before, the reality was few now cared wishing only for Jimmy Murphy's boys to avoid embarrassment, and put to bed what had been and still remains the most diabolical year in the history of Manchester United football club. The city and the club needed lighter days and a summer time to mourn their dead and regroup. To fight again another day, another season. For recent events had proved with their dramatic FA Cup run to Wembley, United were not going away. Oh, they were desperately wounded, but no longer fatally.

The talk of air travel at Old Trafford was forever prevalent, no more so than amongst the survivors. Publicly they said little when asked, but privately all made it clear there was not a chance in hell any would step foot on an airplane for the immediate future. Aware of the feelings within United on this subject, chairman Harold Hardman stated before the semi-final draw: "United do not have any plans to fly to any of the remaining European cup games." Harry Gregg, Bobby Charlton and Bill Foulkes spoke in fearful tones of once more boarding an airplane. Gregg had no inclination whatsoever to fly. "No way I am not ready."

Foulkes was adamant: "To put it bluntly I don't want to fly. What happened at Munich was so terrible to see. How shall I feel in time? I don't know."

Charlton was honest enough to just admit: "I don't fancy it. I don't fancy it one little bit."

However, UEFA acted to ensure such a scenario never occurred by agreeing to all but fix the draw. In an unprecedented move the committee decided overwhelmingly that Manchester United would play the winners of the Borussia Dortmund-AC Milan quarter-final, rather than the more awkward cities to reach in Madrid and Budapest, thus allowing the Mancunians the possibility to travel by land and sea. "We're grateful but never asked for any favours," said Jimmy Murphy on the decision. Back on home soil sympathy for United from their own Footballing Association, like the Football League was in short supply. The decision to allow Stan Crowther to play against Sheffield Wednesday the only semblance of help provided since the crash. Now they insisted on the service of Bobby Charlton for England's meaningless friendly game against Portugal at Wembley the evening before, and away to Yugoslavia the following Sunday, in of all places, Belgrade. (There England were thrashed 5-0 with the home side having another three goals disallowed!) A penny for Bobby thoughts once back in that city. This decision meant United's best player post-Munich would miss both legs of the semi-final. A crippling decision for the reds and one that infuriated Jimmy Murphy, but no longer surprised him, for he was becoming accustomed to his club being kicked when down. So, Just five days on from the huge disappointment of their Cup Final defeat, on Thursday 8th May 1958, at Old Trafford, in front of 45,000 supporters, Manchester United in all white and AC Milan went head to head.

The Teams.

MANCHESTER UNITED. Gregg, Foulkes, Cope, Greaves, Crowther, Goodwin, Webster, Pearson, Morgans, Taylor and Viollet.

AC MILAN. Buffon, Maldini, Radice, Fontana, Lieldholm, Bergamaschi, Beraldo, Schiaffino, Bredesen, Cucchiaroni and Mariani.

Showing no mercy the Milanese began as if they intended to end the tie within the opening quarter of an hour. A makeshift home side was so outclassed that it appeared only a matter of time before the Italians went in front. Arguably Milan's great ever player, the alluring Uruguayan maestro, inside-forward Juan Schiaffino. So pale and slender, he dominated the ball as his snake-charming, left-foot ripped the home defence apart at will. On twenty-four-minutes the *Rossoneri* deservedly took the lead when Stan Crowther, a very decent First Division player, but out of his depth against such a wealth of talent mishit a pass to defender Bill Foulkes. Reacting like a jackal pouncing on a stricken deer, Milan swooped and the lightning, quick Norwegian international Per Bredesen found team mate Schiaffino. With an artist's precision the Uruguayan placed his shot beyond Harry Gregg into the goal. A turkey shoot threatened to ensue as the Italian champions pressed, but duly squandered a host of opportunities to finish off United. An impassioned Jimmy Murphy raged on the touchline, infuriated and helpless as his side were toyed with. Playing in white, United were hardly angelic as they tore into tackles, some legal, others fraught with desperation in an attempt to repel Milan dominance. Whipped into a fury at the sheer injustice and cruel circumstance of the last three months the home crowd erupted in grim defiance. A wall of noise fell over the pitch. Milan rocked, the crescendo dampening their swagger. Harry Gregg hurtled into

Schiaffino to leave him crumpled in a heap! Dazed and more than a little angered by the big Irishman's fierce challenge, the Uruguayan play-maker returned to the fray with a plaster above his cut eye. With Ernie Taylor finding his feet against such esteemed opposition, he began to dictate more on the ball. The decibel level rose even higher five-minutes before half-time, when the normally, impeccable defender Cesare Maldini misdirected a back pass, and was forced to watch in horror when United's Dennis Viollet intercepted. Old Trafford held its collective breath as he raced clear before dispatching with typical aplomb past goalkeeper Lorenzo Buffon to level! After a disappointing Cup Final showing, Viollet at last was starting to show glimpses of his devastating pre-Munich form. They had been outplayed and outmanoeuvred by AC Milan, but with Murphy attempting to re-enact World War Two on the touchline, Manchester United were never outfought. 1-1!

After a dressing room speech by Jimmy Murphy blazing with passion and furore, United returned after the interval on fire, and a second-half blitz orchestrated by the guile of Ernie Taylor had the Italians hanging on. Welshman Colin Webster shot wildly over when it looked easier to score, whilst Taylor himself saw a wickedly hit effort saved supremely by Buffon. The scheming 33-year-old had proved an inspired signing by Murphy, and was swiftly earning himself cult status at Manchester United. Missing the first-half promptings of Schiaffino, Milan fell back. The Uruguayan was a mere shadow of his true self following the collision with Harry Gregg. Knowing another goal was essential to have any hope for the second-leg in Northern Italy, United threw caution to the wind and with just eleven-minutes remaining they received their just reward. Again, it was the impressive Dennis Viollet creating trouble for Cesare Maldini, as he outpaced the Italian to race clear into the penalty area. Struggling to keep up Maldini cut across United's number ten, causing the two men to go down. As Old Trafford screamed for a penalty, the Danish referee Leo Helge pointed to the spot and AC Milan to a man went mad! Maldini collapsed to the turf in mock grief, team mates confronted and surrounded the referee, whilst officials raced from the stands to join in and demand Mr Helge reverse his decision. Finally, calmer heads prevailed and order was restored. Away from the hysteria United's penalty taker Ernie Taylor simply stood, watched and waited for his moment. Once Helge had forced all the irate Italian players back beyond the eighteen-yard line, he motioned Taylor forward. With a stadium uproarious, teeming with emotion, up he came to lash the ball off the underside of the bar with such ferocity past Buffon that it almost broke the stanchion! Ernie Taylor's position in the annals of Manchester United folklore was secured. Despite a cup run scarred with terrible images of broken bodies, blood in the Munich snow and burning wreckage, somehow United remained alive and had earned themselves a fighting chance of reaching the European Cup final when battle recommenced in the Milanese cauldron of the *San Siro*, the following week.

CHAPTER THIRTY
THE SAN SIRO (Part Two)

All concerned with Manchester United were praying for a miracle in the European Cup. Sadly, after all that had occurred few believed in such anymore. Milan in the fifties. A dynamic city of grace and style. Of sophistication, class and beauty. Two magnificent football teams, but one seething, utterly determined to put right what they deemed at Old Trafford a severe injustice. A United side that had travelled overland to Italy were greeted with a hostility not seen in Milan since *Il Duce*, Benito Mussolini and his mistress Clara Petacci were executed and then left to hang upside down in the city's Piazzale Loretto. The travelling Mancunians had left Manchester for London the previous Saturday where they stayed overnight. The Sunday saw them sail to Calais from Dover, then across Europe to arrive in Milan on the Monday. United stayed at the Hotel Principe e Savoia, where they were lauded and treated with great respect by their Italian hosts. However all that changed come the day of the match as 80,000 Milanese gathered at the *San Siro* with the mindset of a baying mob. In a blatant act of gamesmanship United's coach was refused entry at the stadium and the players only made it to the dressing rooms twenty-minutes before kick-off.

The Teams.

AC Milan. Buffon, Fontana, Beraldo, Bergamaschi, Zannier, Radice, Danova, Bredesen, Schiaffino, Liedholm and Cucchiaroni

Manchester United. Gregg, Foulkes, Greaves, Goodwin, Cope, Crowther, Morgans, Taylor E, Webster, Viollet and Pearson

The entrance of the two teams sparked a deafening fervour of flares and fireworks, some thrown directly at the visitors. The vitriol and animosity towards the Mancunians was mind-blowing. As they came into view rotten fruit, cups filled with urine and coins rained down upon their heads. Benvenuto Milano! On the pitch matters were not much different as the German referee Albert Dusch turned a blind eye to the scandalous off the ball antics of the home side. When Herr Dusch dared give a decision in United's favour the entire Milan bench invaded the pitch to remonstrate! Four times this occurred as play was held up, much to Jimmy Murphy's disgust on the touchline. Carnage ensued. Shirts were tugged, elbows flew and punches thrown as United players were hacked down and spat at. Then there was the overacting when any Milan player was tackled that would have shamed a circus clown. Alex Dawson was grabbed around the neck and almost choked whilst Bill Foulkes was thrown over an advertising hoarding! The bile and vitriol even extended to the press box where English journalists found themselves the victims of supporters intent on doing them harm. Many feared being lynched if United actually scored! As thunder rolled across grey Milanese skies, Manchester United were hammered 4-0 and dumped unceremoniously out of the European cup. For amid all the thuggery and cheating AC Milan produced football that glittered. None more than Juan Schiaffino who back on home turf tortured the English. It was his precise, low strike from twelve-yards past Harry Gregg that began the rout after just two minutes. On the half-hour Herr Dusch blew his whistle and stopped play for a minute's silence. The United players appeared staggered for they had not been informed this was to occur! At first the English contingency in the stadium presumed it was for the Munich victims, only later to be informed it was in honour of an Italian FA official who had died earlier that week.

United held on grimly in the first-half, but shortly after the interval Milan scored again when a glorious Schiaffino chip beat Gregg, only for a defender to handball on the line. Up stepped *Il Barone*, the sublime, blond Swedish attacking midfielder Nils Liedholm, to fire past Harry Gregg opening the floodgates. As the *Rossoneri* cut lose a badly outclassed and much intimidated United found themselves handed a thrashing. Further goals from the Milan right-winger Giancarlo Danova twenty-minutes from time, and a last encore from the devilish Schiaffino put paid to Jimmy Murphy's brave, but tortured, exhausted side. Ironically, at the post-match banquet the Milan President gave a speech lauding the merits of "Sportsmanship!" One can only imagine the thoughts of Jimmy as he listened on? And so the most horrific season in Manchester United's history came to an end. Jimmy Murphy had worked miracles since the crash, but defeat at Wembley in the FA Cup final to Bolton and the massacre in the *San Siro,* proved the road back from Munich would inevitably be long and arduous. In that miserable year of 1958, Manchester United really did experience the worst of times.

CHAPTER THIRTY ONE
OUR FRIENDS IN MADRID

It was with a heavy heart that the Real Madrid fixer Don Raimondo Saporta broke the bad tidings of the Munich air crash to Alfredo Di Stefano. On hearing, Saporta telephoned the player at his home. A call which the player would later recall as amongst the "Saddest moments of his life." As news reached Madrid of the horrific, full extent of the disaster, a distressed President Don Santiago Bernabeu spoke solemnly of this great tragedy and of his prayers for the dead and the survivors. None more than so than his great friend Matt Busby, who survived the crash but was hanging on for dear life in the *Rechts Der Isar* hospital in Munich. Of the eleven Manchester United players who originally lined up against the *Madrilenos* in the two-legged semi-final the previous season, five were killed instantly. Roger Byrne, David Pegg, Eddie Colman, Tommy Taylor and Liam Whelan, whilst Duncan Edwards fought on valiantly but lost his battle for life fifteen days later. Edwards' death touched Alfredo Di Stefano immensely and he told of the "Magnificent impression" Duncan Edwards had made on him during the second-leg in Manchester. "Such a strong will to win and power in one so young. None deserved more the fullness of a great career than Duncan." What profoundly moved Bernabeu was being told how in his last ailing days, Edwards had called out for his gold watch he had presented to him in Madrid, following the semi-final first leg. Sadly, in the early hours of Friday 21st February 1958, with his watch close by time was called on a young footballing maestro respected and feared by the *Madrilenos*. Now, six and eight in all of the players lay dead. *Los chicos*, the Busby Babes were gone.

In an act of wonderful generosity, the three times European champions offered to hand the grieving Mancunians the European cup for that season, but whilst stricken in despair United politely refused, thanking in turn the Spaniards for their deep friendship. For this trophy had suddenly become so much more for all concerned with Manchester United, and had to be one fought over and won. Too much blood had already been spilt, too many hearts had been broken to accept such an offer. On a more disturbing note was the Football League's utterly shameful decision to ban them from competing in the 1958-59 European cup competition, after being invited by UEFA as a grateful thank you for their "Service to Football." United accepted this classy offer and found themselves drawn against Swiss champions Young Boys of Berne, only then to be informed that their participation had been denied by the English hierarchy because they were not League champions. Again, another spiteful payback by Hardaker, who even after Munich simply could not help himself. Busby's decision to originally take United into the European Cup against his wishes remained stuck in Hardaker's craw. Instead the reds played Young Boys in two friendlies home and away which they won on aggregate. That same season the Swiss excelled to reach the semi-final stage. As for the English champions Wolverhampton Wanderers? With Manchester United blocked by Hardaker and the Football League, they therefore became England's only representative in the 1958-59 European Cup. Stan Cullis's team received a bye in the first round. Come the second they were drawn against the German champions Schalke 04, who knocked the Wolves out 4-3 on aggregate, after hardly managing to get a football boot in the competition door.

Compare Hardaker's pettiness to the actions of Don Santiago Bernabeu. With the loss of European Cup football, Matt Busby understood how vital it was they retained the experience of playing against the world's best. To stay involved with what was happening on the continent tactically. Therefore, on meeting with the Real President in Madrid he suggested a series of friendly matches between their two clubs. But there was a huge problem first to solve. Manchester United had been vastly under-insured for the crash. In essence they had little money. Real Madrid normally charged a £12,000 appearance fee for the honour of sharing the same pitch as their superstars. Busby explained this to Bernabeu asking if he would consider accepting a smaller fee for the time being. Maybe United could pay them at a later date the full figure owed? To his shock and great surprise a generous Bernabeu insisted that he should pay only what his club could afford. They shook hands and both agreed to treat the games as serious affairs.

Though far from well Matt Busby was back at the helm. After a remarkable 1958-59 season, when Manchester United defied all odds to finish in runners-up position, reality would soon strike like a cold, bitter stinging wind in their faces. Nobody had been more surprised than the manager at coming second. "All I was hoping for was a reasonably safe place in the First Division until we got things sorted out. These boys have played better than I dared hope. But a lot has to be done. It will take years to try and build up again." With what appeared indecent haste Busby wasted little time moving on Stan Crowther and Ernie Taylor. Crowther to Chelsea, Taylor to Sunderland. In came far younger players, Wilf McGuinness at left-half and Warren Bradley, outside-right. Earlier in the season he had also smashed the British transfer record buying Sheffield Wednesday's Albert Quixall for £45.000. A staggering amount but there is an interesting story behind the fee. Sheffield Wednesday's General manager Ernie Taylor said of the Quixall transfer: "The real price should have been £25,000. The other £20,000 was for Mark Jones and David Pegg." Both Yorkshire schoolboys who Wednesday had expected to have a career at Hillsborough and not Old Trafford, where fate's cruel hand clipped their wings far too early. Many supporters were fooled into thinking business as usual and not the nightmare forecasted following Munich. Then a new foul day truly dawned. The Mancunians had begun the 1959-60 campaign in rather, more, manic fashion lying in sixth position at the time of Real Madrid's first visit. The previous Saturday they had been taken apart 4-0 at Preston North End. Inspired by the still magical Tom Finney, the home side were unlucky not to reach double figures. United were terrible as the wheels came off in gruesome style. Whilst dazzling going forward, defensively they were atrocious. Busby was desperate for reinforcements before a bad run morphed into a relegation battle. Fine defenders such as Blackpool's Jimmy Armfield and Rangers Eric Caldow were targeted without success. He also bid for Burnley's creative, Northern Irish midfielder Jimmy McIlroy, much to the anger of United's old foe chairman Bob Lord. Not surprisingly he turned it down with a warning for Busby never to return. Lord not appreciating them attempting to take his best player from Turf Moor. It was the second time Matt Busby had gone for McIlroy, he would not go back again. These were worrying times, at this stage of their recovery, a season where Manchester United veered from the sublime to the ridiculous on a weekly basis was driving supporters to despair. Following United had never been for the faint hearted and that particular period they were capable of anything. Whether it be brilliant or absolutely shocking. A thrilling, goal-laden 6-3 win at Stamford Bridge over Chelsea watched by 66,000 evoked the best of memories pre-Munich. As did a 6-0 home crushing of Leeds. Then, the dark side, a new phenomenon. A humiliating 5-1 drubbing at Old Trafford by Spurs and a feeble 3-0 surrender in the Manchester derby, when City outfought their neighbours was dreadfully hard to stomach. As the inconsistency stretched into October there were many worried brows on the Old Trafford terraces. A new dawn had arrived, this was a new United. The grim expectations that the Munich survivors Bobby Charlton, Harry Gregg, Bill Foulkes, Albert Scanlon and Dennis Viollet would carry the team were huge and unfair, but all had shown incredible bravery and character. Their every waking day must have still been filled with terrible images of friends lost and what they witnessed, yet all carried on. They had kept a red flag flying, albeit painfully in both body and spirit. None more so than Bobby Charlton, on whose slim, young shoulders United fans placed most faith and the pressure was therefore the greatest. His best friends killed, Bobby found from somewhere the courage to not look back. He was regarded as the one who spanned the pre-and post-Munich era. A living and breathing epitaph for the fallen who evoked the spirit of the Babes. With him around the future remained palatable. If their Bobby could go on then they also. In reality Bobby Charlton's heart was broken and would never mend.

It was hoped that the four-times European Champions Real Madrid's imminent arrival, as part of the Bernabeu-Busby pact made in Madrid would provide a welcoming change from the weekly pitfalls of First Division football. Take the pressure off from a gruelling schedule. A friendly match with nothing at stake. Just take a deep breath, relax and enjoy the party tricks of a Real Madrid team who would simply go through the motions and showboat to the crowd. Alas, for the Mancunians it was not to be. President Bernabeu had instructed his team to do as to what he and Matt Busby agreed. Busby warned his players what was heading their way and to be prepared, but despite his procrastinations, United would not know what hit them! So, it was that under orders from their President to perform at full throttle and on a £50 a man win bonus, Real Madrid came to Manchester and cut loose in terrifying manner. In a game shown live on ITV television, United received a dose of cruel reality as they were handed a frightening, footballing lesson. The brutal 6-1 score-line saw them escape lightly and did little justice to the imperious *Madrilenos* that night, as Busby's team were vastly outclassed. Even more formidable than the pre-Munich team, the Spaniards illuminated Old Trafford with an irresistible, unstoppable concoction of European and South American artistry and guile. None more than the irascible Magyar genius, the Hungarian Ferenc Puskas. Rescued from footballing exile by Bernabeu, Puskas' wonderful ability and charm added immensely to a Madrid white storm. Wise as he was talented, the Magyar played the role of loyal Lieutenant to Di Stefano to perfection, preferring to waltz gloriously in the shade of the all-consuming shadow of the great *Blond Arrow*. Also arriving in the Spanish capital to perform alongside the holy trio of Di Stefano, Gento and Puskas was their huge, summer signing, the deceptively languid, but utterly, brilliant Brazilian playmaker Didi. He was joined by fellow countryman Canario and the wickedly, gifted Uruguayan defender Jose Santamaria, who was a marvellous footballer, blessed not just in his ability to play and begin Madrid attacks, but also in the finest tradition of Uruguayan stoppers, willing when necessary to commit atrocities in defence. Christened by my dad as the "Dirtiest greatest defender he has ever seen!"

THE GRAND CHALLENGE MATCH

The Teams.
Manchester United. Gregg, Foulkes, Carolan, Goodwin, Cope, McGuinness, Bradley, Quixall, Viollet, Charlton and Scanlon.

Real Madrid. Dominguez, Lesmes, Marquitos, Santamaria, Ruiz, Santisteban, Gento, Puskas, Di Stefano, Didi and Canario.

With an emotionally, deafening 63,000 crowd roaring them on, United started brightly and Bobby Charlton twice went close with thunderous strikes that the Real goalkeeper Rogelio Dominguez did well to save. Real had their eye on Bobby! A few hints were dropped his way, none more so when on England duty, he ran into Raimondo Saporta at an airport. A grinning Saporta embraced him then asked: "Hey Bobby when are you coming to Madrid?" Much to the young Englishman's huge embarrassment! Then, on seven-minutes, as if annoyed that Bobby Charlton possessed the cheek to attempt a couple of shots the visitors opened the scoring. A delightful through pass by the dazzling Didi to Puskas caused gasps of awe from the terraces. The Hungarian maestro waited for Harry Gregg to commit himself then with great audacity, slipped the ball beyond the big Irishmen into the net. It was all done with the ease of one blessed with genius. After a spell in the wilderness caused by the break-up of the magnificent *Magyars* with the Hungarian revolution, Ferenc Puskas had shed the excess pounds, rolled back the years and was back. The *Galloping Major* was off to gallop some more! It was soon 2-0, when on twenty-five minutes the scintillating, flashing pace of Francisco Gento set up Puskas who once more looked up and flashed a ridiculous, swerving drive past a flailing Gregg into the net. It was bewitching football. On the half-hour it was 3-0. Real were relentless, with what appeared effortless skill, Didi supplied a dagger of a pass into the path of an electric-heeled Alfredo Di Stefano, who without slowing down took the ball in stride before beating a besieged Harry Gregg with ease. Yet the best was still to come when moments before the interval, Di Stefano delivered a moment of wizardry that bamboozled the United defence, and made many in Old Trafford believe they were witnessing something quite unworldly. Standing by a goalpost, he produced an outrageous back flick after trapping the ball with his heel before turning and flicking it past a befuddled Gregg! At 4-0, Madrid left the pitch to huge applause from a home crowd that watched through disbelieving eyes their beauty and majesty. The breathtaking images of those gleaming white figures under the Old Trafford floodlights re-ignited memories of heroes lost. None more than Di Stefano, whose magical piece of artistry for Real's fourth goal earned him a moving reception as he vacated the stage from an adoring, if still grieving audience.

United came out for the second-half determined to save face. Albert Scanlon went close before Bobby Charlton sliced apart the Real Madrid defence allowing winger Warren Bradley to run through from the half-way line and score from a tight angle. A consolation only, but for Bradley, loaned to Manchester United by famed amateurs Bishop Auckland, as they strove to regain their feet after Munich, it was a special moment. Warren Bradley's bravura effort served only to irritate the Spaniards and Real swiftly moved back into top gear. The ball was passed with a tenderness and technique, but kept from United's grasp like a child clutching his favourite toy. On sixty-three minutes, a grateful Puskas accepted Didi's delightful pass before crossing for the unmarked Pepillo to make it 5-1 from close range. Pepillo had signed that same summer from Sevilla and was yet another *Madrileno* superstar in the making. As for Didi, this night, under the hazy glare of the Old Trafford floodlights was arguably his finest hour during a short and turbulent career in Madrid.

Twelve-minutes from time and with United being dangled, toyed and prodded, Francisco Gento suddenly got bored. He exploded past a bedraggled United defence before almost breaking the back of the net, with a ferocious finish past a desolate Harry Gregg. Beaten six times and at fault for none, Gregg was thoroughly fed up and cut a disconsolate figure. Come the full-time whistle Real Madrid gathered in the centre-circle taking the rapturous acclaim of an adoring Mancunian public. The United players also stayed to applaud the *Madrilenos* off the pitch. It had quite simply proved a mis-match. Dennis Viollet spoke to the Manchester Evening News afterwards. "It seems an odd thing to say after losing 6-1, but I have to say I enjoyed that! They were special." Munich had decimated Manchester United and many years would pass before they could resemble a team good enough to give the European champions a real challenge. After the match Matt Busby was brutally honest in his own summing up. "They have walloped us 6-1, and in doing so confirmed what I already know, that we have a long, long way to go to close the gap." The newspaper headlines next day extolled Real Madrid's bravura showing.

The Daily Herald. **"Real Give Greatest Show On Earth!"**

The News Chronicle. **"Shooting Seniors Smack In Six!"**

The Daily Mirror. **"Real Perfection!"**

Whilst in Manchester with a gesture so typical of the man, President Bernabeu took the entire Madrid party to visit Eddie Colman's grave at Weaste cemetery in Salford. There they prayed and laid flowers. It was a touching moment for all. Salford and Archie Street where Eddie lived was half a world away from Madrid, but here they were. Paying tribute to the young lad from across the Trafford swing bridge. The two teams would play four more times over the coming years in friendly matches. Two days later a touch of Di Stefano and Puskas must have rubbed off on Manchester United as 41,000 returned to Old Trafford to witness the Red Devils thrash Leicester City 4-1. Bobby Charlton's opener on five-minutes was followed with a brace from Viollet and another from Albert Quixall. The grim realities of this post-Munich dawn though ever present, if only for a short while numbed a little. On an Old Trafford pitch still sprinkled with

Madrileno gold dust United sent their supporters home smiling. That itself a small miracle in such trying, desperate times.

ESTADIO BERNABEU
Wednesday 11ᵗʰ November 1959.

Six weeks on from the 6-1 massacre at Old Trafford, a return match was staged in Madrid with Manchester United and Matt Busby given the red-carpet treatment by Santiago Bernabeu from the moment they landed until the moment of their departure. A pleasant stay was tinged with real sadness at memories of events only two and a half years before, when the Babes arrived so full of life and captured the hearts of the Madrid public. United went to Spain on the back of a 3-3 draw away to Fulham in which a late Bobby Charlton goal salvaged a draw. Lying in sixth place their league form remained patchy and infuriating. A bookie's dream and a pundit's nightmare. However, on their better days which could never be predicted they remained a match for any team in England. A fact soon to be confirmed with events in the *Bernabeu*. The affection and admiration for Manchester United was obvious amongst the *Madrileno* faithful as they handed the visitors a stirring welcome on entering. As for the game, it turned out to be a remarkable match with United scaring the living daylights out of Real, before finally going down in a 6-5 shootout!

It was Boy's Own football! An 80,000 crowd watched on in astonishment as the visitors raced into an extraordinary, shock two-goal lead after only fifteen-minutes! The first a penalty after Bobby Charlton was cynically chopped down by Jose Santamaria, a man who clearly did not believe in friendlies. The goalkeeper Dominguez saved the initial shot from Albert Quixall, only to lie helpless as the United man got lucky and lashed home the rebound. Sixty-seconds later Albert Scanlon skipped clear of Marquitos and his long searching pass was picked up by Warren Bradley. Racing past the defender Parchin, Bradley let fly and his shot deflected off Santamaria and beat Dominguez to silence the stadium. The Madrid crowd were shocked, and they soon let their heroes know about it.

However, at the opposite end they had no quarrel warmly applauding Harry Gregg, who after his nightmare experience at Real's hands in Manchester was busy banishing ghosts. Two sensational saves by the big Irishman, as the Spaniards turned up the heat from Enrique Mateos and Alfredo Di Stefano brought the *Bernabeu* to its feet. Gregg staging a one man show of defiance. He was finally beaten on twenty-one minutes, but only by a debatable penalty after a very soft handball was alleged against Bill Foulkes. Up stepped Di Stefano to thrash the ball past Gregg and halve the deficit. Immediately, the crowd's spirits were raised and they shook life into a so far listless home side. Game on, but just when it was thought Madrid would switch into overdrive, United struck again. On the half-hour the reds broke out and a four-man-move between Freddie Goodwin, Albert Scanlon, Bobby Charlton and Dennis Viollet, saw the latter sweep the ball past Dominguez from five yards. It was football *Madrilenos* style by the boys from Manchester! A feeling of bemusement filled the *Bernabeu,* for though classed only as a friendly, it was thought unthinkable for Real Madrid to be 3-1 down on home soil. The natives were restless. Gregg's heroics in the United goal hardly helped their mood as he threw himself around in order to keep out a barrage of shots. However, good fortune favoured the Spaniards once more when moments before the interval a clearly offside Mateos was allowed to run through and score. At 3-2 they had been handed a lifeline. It was cruel on the Mancunians who knew they now faced a second-half onslaught from the European champions.

Five-minutes after the break normal service appeared to have been resumed as Real drew level. A brilliant through ball was latched onto by their latest wonder kid, 19-year-old Seville born Manuel Bueno, who fired the equaliser past a diving Harry Gregg. A frustrated Gregg pounded the turf in frustration at being beaten. Bueno was a truly outstanding talent, but due to such riches at the *Bernabeu* his appearances were limited. Now, the *Madrilenos* turned up the gas. They pinned Manchester United back and hardly needed the helping hand of a clearly out of his depth, French referee Monsieur Barberan, who on fifty-four minutes, produced another shocking decision awarding a penalty for an innocuous challenge by Goodwin on Mateos. This proved the last straw for the visitors who blazed in anger at the inept official. After having a quiet word with the United players, Alfredo Di Stefano appeared to gesture an apology to the crowd before purposely hammering his penalty over the bar!

There was class and then Di Stefano.

Two-minutes later United had edged back in front. Albert Scanlon released Bobby Charlton to crash a powerful shot in off the post past Dominguez! Bobby had been wonderful throughout and appeared comfortable playing on such a prestigious stage. He was turning heads in Madrid. Happily for Manchester United supporters Bobby Charlton had no ambition to ply his trade elsewhere and no amount of Spanish gold would tempt him abroad. Madrid clearly had its attractions. The money, the sun, playing alongside Di Stefano and Puskas every week. But it wasn't Old Trafford. The last half-hour saw Real up their game significantly with Alfredo Di Stefano seemingly on a mission to make up for his deliberate penalty miss. The *Blond Arrow* proved unplayable, like a ghostly white wind he flitted across the pitch, impossible to mark and thrusting passes like swords through the United defence. Three times he shredded the thin red line and each was put away with aplomb past Gregg by the sensational Bueno. It was a superb hat trick that left the visitors reeling, Harry Gregg speechless and the match surely safe for the home side. Out came the white handkerchiefs in tribute, a rare moment in the sun for Bueno who acknowledged the crowds chanting his name. But still United came back, refusing to lie down they scored again in the dying embers of the contest. Alec Dawson cutting in from the touchline and smashing a scorching drive past Dominguez making it 6-5! A classic encounter finally ended and despite being light years away from the *Madrilenos* in terms of class, Busby's men had shown a spirit that boded well for the future. Come full-time both teams were cheered to the rafters as the *Bernabeu* showed their appreciation for a memorable spectacle. Di Stefano had been impressed by the United performance. "In many, many ways they were the better team. Certainly, they gave us the biggest fright we've had for many, many home matches. The inside forwards, Quixall, Viollet and Charlton attacked our defence like men with sabres. They cut us to pieces. The young left-half McGuinness is a wonderful prospect too. With players like these and with Matt Busby to inspire them all, Manchester United must be strong again before long."

That evening Santiago Bernabeu spoke at a money raising banquet organised by the Spaniards for the families of those killed at Munich. In a speech the Madrid President revealed once more of his huge respect for the United manager. He told the assembled guests: "Matt Busby is not only the bravest, but the greatest man I have ever met in football." Words spoken from the heart. They would meet again.

OLD TRAFFORD
Wednesday 13ᵗʰ October 1960.

Manchester United were entrenched in a desperate struggle for survival. 1-0 down at Bolton Wanderers with just fifteen-minutes remaining, these were truly, traumatic times for the Old Trafford club. The first three months of the season had proved horrific with only two games won and their First Division survival looking dubious. It was the worst start to a campaign for United since World War Two and the unspoken word was finally being uttered around the club. One since Munich few dared to mention. Relegation. As the Burnden Park hordes rejoiced in the misery of their famous, big city neighbours, an 18-year-old Manchester United debutante called Norbert Stiles stepped forward to save the day. A right-half and former altar boy from the United hotbed of north Manchester, Stiles set up his close friend and team-mate, Irish midfielder Johnny Giles to run on and finish superbly past Bolton goalkeeper Hopkinson. 1-1! A valuable point was earned by two boys brought through United's youth scheme to prove some things at Old Trafford never changed.

Five months on from their historic 7-3 victory over Eintracht Frankfurt at Hampden Park, to win a fifth consecutive European Cup trophy, Real Madrid again took on Manchester United in the latest in a series of friendlies that were starting to take on a life of their own.

The relationship between the two clubs had grown to something quite extraordinary in Munich's shadow. A typical example came when it was thought Alfredo Di Stefano and Ferenc Puskas might not have been fit to travel, Santiago Bernabeu phoned Matt Busby, and asked if he wished to postpone the game until Real's leading lights were fit? However, not wishing to appear ungrateful to the *Madrilenos,* Matt Busby insisted they come anyway. Busby informed the Real President that: "Real Madrid have become like family and whether bearing their most fabulous gifts or not Manchester is eagerly anticipating their visit." On hearing this Bernabeu relayed Busby's message to Di Stefano and Puskas, who then decided to travel and if possible play at least some part of the game!

"You are playing with my money!"
Alfredo Di Stefano

With the *Little Cannonball* and the *Blond Arrow* in the visitor's line up, 50,000 supporters welcomed back Real Madrid to Old Trafford. The match was again televised, but only the second half was covered. However, such was the appeal that the TV Times gave this *Soccer Spectacular* a huge build-up. The dazzling sight of those gleaming white shirts under floodlights was the stuff of dreams. Memories were still fresh of the *Madrilenos* in their absolute pomp ripping apart the unfortunate Germans of Eintracht Frankfurt at an enraptured Hampden Park! Many on the terrace feared total carnage if Madrid were in similar mood, and after just nineteen-minutes a delightful pass from Puskas found Di Stefano, who slammed a wonderful shot past Harry Gregg. Old Trafford held its collective breath then warmly applauded. Lancashire's home sat only within a short walking ground of the football stadium and with a cricket score looking set for the evening, a wag in the crowd joked maybe they should have played the game there! Amid the spellbound masses that night as the *Madrilenos* performed their pre-match warm up routine, was a 15-year-old George Best. The Belfast boy had just arrived in Manchester and felt unable to take his eyes off Francisco Gento as he performed for an awe-struck audience. The Real goalkeeper Vicente dropped kicked the ball to a waiting Gento, twenty-yards away. *El Motorcycle* dragged down the ball in mid-air with a magician's ease. Then, as if passing back to Vicente, Gento's intended hit suddenly stopped on contact with the ground and spun back towards him! Gasps fall down from the terraces as Francisco took a bow. Applause broke out. The greatest footballing show on earth was once again set to descend on Old Trafford.

Like rain falling in Manchester, a goal for Alfredo Di Stefano against United was equally expected. Real appeared in troublesome mood as the ball was moved waspishly across the field. There did however not appear the intent to twist the dagger any deeper into the hospitable Mancunians, the visitors had come to put on a show, display a few tricks and go home. Di Stefano could sense this and began to lose his imperial temper with strutting team mates. He feared complacency. United began to make their own opportunities. Bobby Charlton, who always impressed against the Spaniards, let fly only for Vicente to leap magnificently and tip over the bar. Roused by their Bobby's effort the noise level soared and on thirty-minutes to the utter disgust of Di Stefano, the home side equalised. A Charlton in-swinging corner was headed clear by Jose Santamaria, only for Albert Quixall to launch it back into the penalty area. As Vicente came to meet the ball, Mark Pearson reacted first to flick from six-yards past him into the net. Pearson was a big favourite of Jimmy Murphy's. An inside forward, small but tough and brimming with talent. He had been thrust into the reserves to carry the flag after Munich, and played on that tear-stained night against Sheffield Wednesday. Now, Mark Pearson had rocked the European champions. Suddenly, it was all United as Real Madrid, seemingly stuck in showboat mode were forced back. Again, Bobby Charlton cut a swathe past chasing white shirts, before flashing a shot inches wide and into the side netting. By this time, the *Blond Arrow* was apoplectic with rage! Reacting and probably a little fearful for what awaited them in the half-time interval, the *Madrilenos* upped gears. Ferenc Puskas, who had walked around uninterested for the previous thirty-eight minutes, revived to leave three players on their backsides, before laying off a pass for Jose Maria Vidal to hammer from twenty-five yards past Harry Gregg into the goal!

As the half-time whistle was set to blow a now focused Puskas lashed in a ferocious left-footed shot that Gregg did well to see, never mind save. It was a timely reminder that inside the squat-looking number ten with the oily, greased hair lurked one of the all-time greats. Alfredo Di Stefano wasted no time venting his spleen as he began tearing a strip off a shocked Ferenc Puskas, even before they had reached the privacy of the Old Trafford tunnel. A public dressing down was not appreciated by the Hungarian who appeared to just shrug his shoulders at the irate Argentinian, as if to suggest: "It is just a friendly Alfredo. Why are you getting so wound up?" But an irate Di Stefano was not for softening, and the accusing finger pointed at Puskas was because he knew that Real Madrid could never afford to let down their guard. The same effort must apply in every game, be it a meaningless friendly or a European cup final. The path to ruin lay in complacency and Alfredo Di Stefano was not about to let such happen on his watch. Watching on fascinated was the United youngster Nobby Stiles, who could not believe what he was witnessing as two of the greatest players in the world almost came to blows with so little at stake. But for Stiles it was an important lesson, one he would learn well. For fate had decreed a magnificent career for this unlikely looking hero, a short-sighted youngster from the Collyhurst, Saint Patrick's congregation on Livesey Street, who on the day of the crash had raced home from the ground and into the church where he prayed desperately for the lives of his idols. To let them all return safe, especially Eddie Colman. Only then to be left desolate as Manchester faced the grim realisation that most, including Colman had been killed. Now, as he watched Alfredo Di Stefano, the integrity of such a man to give his best all the time and insist others did similar. Nobby Stiles realised just what separated the mortals from the great. The heated debate continued on in the Real dressing room as Di Stefano turned his considerable wrath on others he deemed not performing to the expected standards. Through the walls shouting could be heard, with one voice above all. Any cynics whoever doubted Real Madrid's professionalism and ambition to treat these matches as ultra-serious affairs would have changed their opinion as Di Stefano was heard yelling and demanding more from his under-performing *compadres*. None dared disagree, others preferred to say nothing and just hope Alfredo's temper blew itself out if the game was won, and the £60-win bonus offer helped soothe matters. Even as the *Madrilenos* re-entered the field arguments were raging with a visibly, fed up Puskas still on the receiving end of a Di Stefano's tongue lashing.

The second-half saw a Real Madrid team with their ears still ringing, intent on proving a point to a certain Argentinian. Francisco Gento, a particular target for Don Alfredo, left the home defender Shay Brennan in a heap before being stopped at the last by the long legs of Bill Foulkes. Brennan's brave attempt to halt Gento as he sprinted clear left him unable to carry on and making his debut, 18-year-old Irish full back Tony Dunne replaced him. Another like Stiles destined for glory in a red shirt. As Madrid looked for a third to kill off United, a defence which had been pilloried all season somehow held firm. It was no longer a friendly as tackles flew and the game's competitive edge was evident by Real's Santamaria, whose challenges if committed off pitch would have seen him spending the night in a Manchester Bootle Street jail cell. On seventy-minutes a fierce, hard-fought encounter was decided in the visitor's favour when the gazelle-like Brazilian Canario sprung to fire past Harry Gregg and seal the result. It could have been 4-1 moments later when Ferenc Puskas, now busy trying to ram Di Stefano's words back down his throat laid on Gento, whose first time cross found the *Blond Arrow*, only for his goal bound shot to be blocked by substitute Tony Dunne on the goal-line. To Manchester United's credit they kept going and despite a series of further Real opportunities, all wastefully scorned, two-minutes from time they grabbed a deserved second. Bobby Charlton tore down the wing and crossed dangerously, only for a Madrid defender to head clear. The ball fell thirty-yards out at the feet of 21-year-old, Belfast born midfielder Jimmy Nicholson. Looking up the Irishman picked his spot and thundered a stunning effort into Vicente's top left-hand corner. It was a goal that electrified Old Trafford! A fitting finale to what had been yet another fascinating clash between two football clubs still seemingly heading in separate directions. However, this had been by far United's best performance of the season. The final-whistle saw the home players form a guard of honour and applaud the *Madrilenos* off stage. Though not before Di Stefano and his *compadres*, all friends again bade *Adios* from the centre-circle to a crowd they never tired of delighting. Once more under the Mancunian stars a special night had occurred. Maybe it was unfair to measure United's progress since the crash against such vaunted opponents, but ever so slowly despite their league showing, Matt Busby felt they were coming back to life. He appreciated more signings would be needed. Fresh blood to go alongside the likes of Bobby Charlton, Nobby Stiles and Tony Dunne, and though not blessed to see into the future, for the first time since Munich, Busby sensed hope as the battle to restore his ravaged club continued unabated.

The following Saturday Manchester United returned to league action at champions Burnley, and despite a Dennis Viollet hat trick went down 6-3. It was a dreadful result which left them second from bottom, facing an uphill task to survive in a hellish season. United had not been out of the bottom four all season and with the referee that day a certain Mr Hemingway, it appeared the bell was tolling for an ailing football club.

OLD TRAFFORD
Wednesday 13ᵗʰ December 1961.

For the first time since these two great clubs came together Real Madrid were no longer European champions. Defeat to Barcelona in the previous season's competition meant some cynics suggested their annual visit to Manchester, though still special, had lost just a smattering of glamour. Yet, such thoughts disappeared as photographer's cameras clicked furiously to create a minor supernova of flashes around the tunnel area, momentarily blinding Spanish eyes, before the crowd's roar welcomed them onto the Old Trafford turf once more. Honouring a promise made in the wake of United's darkest days, the *Madrilenos* had returned to a city in which they remained footballing gods. Coming into this match, Matt Busby's struggling team sat two places from the bottom of the First Division. A disastrous run from early October had seen them incur terrible losses, such as 5-1 at Arsenal, consecutive 4-1 reverses against Ipswich and Burnley, and a gruesome 5-1 slaughter by Everton. After this Busby received anonymous poison pen letters. Early hopes for a decent campaign when they appeared settled in the top six became the bitter memories of a false dawn. The normal full house which had accompanied every Real Madrid visit to Old Trafford was for once not forthcoming, as only 43,000 turned up on a freezing December evening. Home crowds had dipped alarmingly as patience with their underperforming stars and those deemed simply not good enough to wear the red shirt finally snapped. Many stayed away also because they had little wish to see United treated like cannon fodder by the still reigning champions of Spain, if not the continent.

Real Madrid themselves were not in the finest of health. Age more than ailment troubled the *Madrilenos.* Father Time was an enemy that even a side of their calibre could not overcome. Yet, even with Puskas injured so not travelled, the likes of Di Stefano, Gento, Del Sol and Santamaria made the trip to Manchester. All four a class above, Charlton apart, plying their trade at United, so the possibility of a rout remained. Once again free from the stress of their First Division survival battle, the home players relaxed and began against Real in menacing, attacking form. With only fourteen-minutes on the clock two United youngsters combined intelligently to beat the Real rearguard. The beguiling little schemer Johnny Giles setting up his team-mate, the Manchester born inside-forward, 19-year-old Phil Chisnall to race on and hammer past goalkeeper Araquistain. Chisnall was an astute passer of the ball with considerable natural talent, viewed by Busby and Murphy as one with a chance. It was a rare chink of light for United supporters in a season that up until Chisnall's fine strike had drove them mad with frustration. Undeterred by this minor setback Real swiftly regrouped laying siege to the home goal, but with a back four of Brennan, Dunne, Setters and Foulkes, United held their ground. It could not last and three-minutes before the interval, Di Stefano from fully twenty-five yards picked his spot to crash an unstoppable shot into the top corner that reserve goalkeeper David Gaskell never saw! Di Stefano's customary goal on the Old Trafford turf proved a worthy addition to a glittering collection of strikes against the Mancunians. As he made his way back to the half-way line Di Stefano was congratulated by his jubilant *compadres,* yet hardly a smile passed the Argentinian's lips. For this was not so much a personal vendetta, but something splendid for United supporters to remember him by.

Normally a moment such as this would signify a home collapse, but instead it was United who came storming back. Three-minutes into the second-half, a Jimmy Nicholson pass found a recent signing from Arsenal, £35,000 Scottish International David Herd. Herd's United career had begun well before the goals dried up. Tormented by injury and lack of form, the pent-up 27-year old Herd drove a clinical low shot past Araquistain to delight the home crowd, and bring a little solace and light relief to his under-pressure manager Matt Busby. Immediately on the ball hitting the net the Real coach Miguel Munoz appeared to lose interest substituting Alfredo Di Stefano, Francisco Gento and Jose Santamaria, saving their ageing legs for more meaningful contests. Sensing a pivotal moment in the match the Old Trafford masses respected the three's departure from the pitch with a grand ovation, but then switched their attention to roaring their own side on to a morale-boosting victory. The clock ticked on with both teams creating chances. David Herd had what looked like a good effort ruled out for a foul, whilst Johnny Giles fired in a shot that beat Araquistain, but was cleared off the line by Pachin. Real struck back and inside forward Antonio Ruiz sneaked behind Shay Brennan before finishing with ease past Gaskell. Only to raise his hands in disbelief when he was deemed offside. Then, with just ten-minutes remaining Herd scored a deserved second and United's third. Substitute Albert Quixall, who had replaced the injured Giles, split the Madrid defence and the forward gleefully lashed the ball past Araquistain's grasp. Game over and Old Trafford went wild! United rejoiced in the 3-1 scoreline. Finally, at the seventh attempt the spell had been broken. Though the Spaniards were clearly not the team of yesteryear, for Matt Busby and Jimmy Murphy, indeed all associated with Manchester United, it was a moment to cherish. The final whistle bore witness to the fact that Real Madrid handled defeat with the same dignity they treated victory. The *Madrilenos* applauded both the crowd and United players before leaving the stage clear for the victors to receive some much-deserved acclaim. Busby hoped the result would act as a spur for them to take into their league performances.

 Yet, typically, the following Saturday disaster struck once more. A paltry 29,000 turned up at home expecting Manchester United to see off a West Ham side who had not won there since 1935. An early goal from Herd looked to have set the Red Devils on the way to a convincing win, only for two late strikes from the Hammers gifting them the points. As a result United remained only two places off the bottom of Division One, and any good will earned in beating Real evaporated amid a chorus of boos across a half-empty stadium. For Matt Busby, still in considerable pain from the crash, redemption had never felt so far away. Any thoughts of conquering Europe seemed now to be the talk of madmen. This United team on present form were going down.

ESTADIO BERNABEU
Wednesday 19ᵗʰ September 1962.

To honour the thirteen-year career of Real Madrid stalwart Jose Maria Zarraga, Matt Busby took his Manchester United team to Spain, continuing a tradition borne out of tragedy, and one highly valued by both clubs. Despite the arrival of Denis Law for a record fee of £115,000 from Torino, United were enduring a horrid start to their own league campaign. The previous season they had recovered

sufficiently to finish a lowly fifteenth, when at one stage around
Christmas they appeared certainties for the drop. Busby's acquisition
of Law had seen hopes abound in Manchester and the Scot began
in sensational manner by scoring on his home debut. Yet, that goal
became a high watermark in a disastrous run that by September's end
and their arrival in Madrid, saw them languishing in sixteenth place.
Four days earlier they had suffered the embarrassment of a home
derby defeat to Manchester City, when even two goals from the
former Maine Road favourite Law, proved insufficient to save an
appalling day for the red half of Manchester. A crowd of 49,455 had
watched in horror as the blue's new signing Alex Harley crashed
home a winner with the game's last kick.
The match against Real Madrid would as on previous occasions,
provide brief respite from domestic turmoil. A Madrid audience of
80,000, welcomed back Manchester United onto the sacred *Bernabeu*
turf. Both line-ups were shadows of their successful pasts, but the
sheer imagery of *Madrileno* white and Mancunian red still captivated
the Spanish public. It was a footballing romance that shown no signs
of waning. The game began in typical manner with Di Stefano now
more selective in his choice of forward runs, but still dictating all
aspects of the Real performance. Forever demanding the ball, pushing
others into position, telling them where they should run and finding
team-mates with an exquisite range of long and short passing. He was
still an artist who retained a wondrous ability to paint beauty on the
Bernabeu canvas, even if nowadays he was unable to complete it.
Alfredo the great was getting old and it was killing him inside.
Following the *Blond Arrow* wherever he strode was United's Nobby
Stiles. A constant irritant to the Argentinian, the great man struggled
to shake off Stiles' limpet like style. Niggling and harassing, the
Mancunian was no respecter of reputation on the pitch, but away from
the action Nobby Stiles adored Alfredo Di Stefano. He had no bigger
admirer. On it, Stiles, like his idol Eddie Colman seven years before,
was driving Di Stefano to despair! On a torrid, sweltering evening in
the *Bernabeu*, the Collyhurst boy was winning hands down. To such
an extent that Madrid's famed number nine gave up the ghost and lost

interest. With Di Stefano under lock and key, elsewhere Denis Law was causing gasps of wonder from a *Bernabeu* crowd that were normally reserved for their own. Law was at his simmering best, playing on the edge and willing to start a fight or finish a move. Prowling, his slim figure moved into scoring mode as if electrified. Law was a flashing red streak that tormented Real defenders. A predator the likes of which they had rarely faced.

The interval came with no score but the visitors much in the ascendancy. As the second-half began the crowd became increasingly impatient at their team's lack of incoherency. Looking to spark some life and urgency Miguel Munoz brought on four substitutes, only then to find himself a goal down moments later. Mark Pearson picked up a loose pass on the edge of the Real penalty area and hit a first-time, left-footed snapshot that Vicente failed to hold. As the groans from the terraces poured down, the ball bobbled under the goalkeeper's body and into the net. Real supporters screamed abuse at the forlorn Vicente. These were changing times in Madrid. The incredibly, hostile home crowd resembled a baying, howling mob. Incredibly spoilt and incapable of handling what these present *Madrilenos* were serving up, they were reduced to silence with a masterly second United goal. Again, it was the explosive Law who proved impossible for the opposition to handle. The Scot split two home defenders with a deft pass to the feet of Johnny Giles. The little Dubliner had lit up this grand arena all night with his touch and guile. With space and time Giles crossed to perfection for David Herd, whose powerful header slammed into the top right-hand corner of Vicente's goal. 2-0! From that moment people began leaving the stadium in droves. Those left behind stayed only to shout abuse at the unfortunate players they felt were white shirted impostors. The final-whistle brought a polite ripple of applause across the stadium for United's fine showing.

Since Munich, the clubs had grown increasingly close off the pitch and now, significantly, on it, there was little to separate them. A true friendship when most of their domestic rivals had seemed content to let United rot, the Spaniards had shown themselves true champions of honour. Manchester United supporters of that era will never forget such generosity of spirt by Real Madrid, for when their club was at its lowest, ever ebb they came to help.

CHAPTER THIRTY TWO
STRICTLY BUSINESS

Come 1968, ten years on from Munich, Matt Busby had led his team to within touching distance of the European Cup final, and all at Old Trafford eagerly awaited the semi-final draw. Their opponents would come from Juventus, Benfica and Real Madrid. As breaths were held across the continent out popped the Spaniards and Manchester United. The old friends would meet again.

The Teams.
Manchester United. Stepney, Dunne, Burns, Crerand, Sadler, Stiles, Best, Kidd, Charlton, Law and Aston.

Real Madrid. Betancort, Gonzales, Sanchis, Pirri, Zunzunequi, Zoco, Perez, Jose Luis, Grosso, Velazquez and Gento.

Old Trafford. Wednesday 24th April 1968.
European Cup semi-final first-leg.
It was a beautiful, gentle spring evening in Manchester, when 34-four-year-old Francisco Gento stepped out at the head of his team into the Old Trafford late sun. The dazzling all white strip still made the heart race faster for Manchester's football romantics, despite the dose of 1960s pragmatism that Real had arrived with a five-man defensive plan intended to ensnare and strangulate United's attacking flair. It was the modern way. They, like United, knew it was essential to avoid defeat. A draw in Manchester would all but finish off Busby's men and leave them indefensible in the torrid cauldron of the *Estadio Bernabeu*. Then you would see the Real Madrid. The romantics with fond memories of Di Stefano, Puskas, Gento, Edwards, and Taylor would have to wait until the second-leg, for now the *Madrilenos* came baring gifts of flowers and goodwill off the pitch. On it would be

strictly business. For this was the European cup. The absent heroes would have understood.

Real Madrid were in good health. Miguel Munoz's team arrived in Manchester as newly crowned Spanish champions after a 2-1 home victory the previous weekend over Las Palmas. This ensuring an astonishing seventh consecutive league title as the *Madrilenos* dominance on home soil continued unabated. To counteract Manchester United's forwards Munoz had opted for a well-drilled, swift and ruthless when required defensive rearguard; Gonzalez, Zunzunegui, Sanchis, Zoco and Luis. A white cloak, orchestrated, pushed, pulled and ordered into position by the magnificent sweeper Pirri. The full-back Manuel Sanchis was handed the unenviable task of man-marking the genius of George Best. The cunning Munoz had chosen well for this was an electric-heeled player, blessed with great concentration and tactical awareness. He was perfectly suited to his task. Though denied the skill, pace and deadly prowess of his main striker Amaro Amancio through suspension, Munoz remained supremely confident that with the dangerous Velásquez, Grosso and the ageless Gento to counter-attack, they could return to Madrid with a favourable result. For after all was this not their tournament? The white knights of the *Bernabeu* believed they were destined once more to win back their trophy for a seventh time. But first Manchester United, a dear old friend, had to be dealt with.

Only the jarring pain of a cortisone injection and sheer courage allowed Matt Busby to name Denis Law in his line-up, but in all reality a serious knee injury had curtailed Law to the point where he was a mere shadow of his true self. Busby knew a win was essential, he needed at least one goal to take to the *Bernabeu*. Anything less and United would require a miracle in Madrid to get through and Busby no longer believed in miracles. A watching world-wide audience of 150 million and a huge 63,500 Old Trafford crowd held their breath as the two teams came out to do battle. At first glimpse the all-white strip still possessed the charisma to send a cold chill down the spine.

However, any feelings of nostalgia and goodwill towards the *Madrilenos* would be temporarily shelved for ninety minutes, as the home crowd concentrated on helping their team topple the Spaniards from their imperial perch. The songs from the Stretford End both amused and deafened. Chants of "Hand off Gibraltar" and "Franco out, Busby in" resonated loud! A few hundred Madrid followers lay scattered loud and proud in the Cantilever stand, happy to make themselves seen and heard with an impressive array of banners and the traditional mass of white handkerchiefs. United opened brightly when from a superb George Best cross, John Aston powered in a header which was brilliantly turned away by the goalkeeper Betancourt. From the ensuing corner Denis Law set up Paddy Crerand to smash in an effort which crashed against the Madrid post. It was a storming start from the home team but one which soon ran out of steam. Madrid took control, their ball artistry delightful and dangerous. None more than the Captain Francisco Gento, no longer flying, but still capable of wreaking chaos as he showed with a deft defence-splitting pass that sent his *compadre* Miguel Angel Perez clear on goal. With just Alex Stepney to beat the recently signed Argentinian Perez took aim and shot past the goalkeeper to horrify Old Trafford, only for the infamous Russian referee Tofik Bakhramov, forever to be remembered as the linesman who controversially allowed England's third goal by Geoff Hurst in the 1966 World Cup final, to blow for offside. It was an act the Spanish took great exception to but it was also a disturbing reminder for Busby's team. A timely example of what awaited if they dared to switch off. Despite United's two early opportunities, Real retained a strict defensive discipline. There was no air of panic amongst the white shirts despite the wall of noise that emanated from all four corners of the stadium. None were more supreme than Pirri, looking calm and assured. Sublime technique, he was the epitome of a true *Madrileno*. Football's equivalent of a Hollywood superstar.

With Denis Law's injury reducing him to a forlorn straggler, the Old Trafford faithful looked elsewhere for inspiration to break the deadlock. On thirty-six minutes they got their wish when a sweeping

United move ended with Aston jinking past Gonzalez on the left, before squaring for George Best to fire a snapshot past Betancourt into the top corner. It was a stunning finish by Best, hit first time with his left foot showing wonderful technique and with an ease only great players possess. As the terraces erupted a black cat raced the length of the Old Trafford pitch. An omen perhaps? Comrade Bakhramov's whistle blew for half-time and Manchester United had edged in front. But a first-half resembling a chess match had shown beyond doubt there was not a needle's thread between the two sides. The Second-half saw little change with United having the bulk of possession but few opportunities. Munoz's team were proving exceptional at snuffing out any dangers posed. George Best met his match that evening in the form of the limpet-like Manuel Sanchis, who tracked and second guessed the Irishman's every move. It was a remarkable performance by the 25-year-old Valencia born defender and one always remembered by Best who recalled: "Sanchis was amongst the hardest opponents I ever faced."

With United's front four shackled and firmly under lock and key, Real Madrid looked to press forward. An equaliser looked certain when once more Perez went careering through, only for the deputising centre-half, the versatile David Sadler in for the injured Bill Foulkes, to catch him at the last. Sadler was yet another unsung hero but one destined to play a huge part as this epic clash ran its full course over the two-legs. The game finished 1-0 with neither side particularly pleased or disappointed. The final whistle was greeted with muted applause from a knowledgeable Old Trafford crowd whom knew United now faced an awesome task in Madrid to make the final. Matt Busby hid any doubts regarding what was to come in the second-leg and remained bullish in post-match interviews.

"I think we will win through because I am convinced we are the better side." However, many supporters feared the worst for Real had already shown in brief attacking spurts that they possessed enough flair to deeply trouble the Red Devil's defence. In Madrid, the war drums had already began to beat loud as they waited impatiently to end United's torment. For although they wished them well,

Mancunian redemption, an almost absolution of sin would not be allowed to be earned on their turf. They like their forefathers before them stood ready once more to turn out the light on Manchester United. There would be warm embraces for their friends from Manchester. They would speak well of times past. Shed tears at those "Champions of Honour" whom had been taken so cruelly. But once the last toast had been drunk and the *Bernabeu* crowds had gathered baying for blood, the *Madrilenos* would have no choice but to obey. it was nothing personal, this was strictly business.

CHAPTER THIRTY THREE
A TALE OF TWO CITIES

It was the best of times, the worst of times. For the *Madrilenos* an age of unsurpassed glory, for Manchester United an age of unrelenting pain. In Madrid summers of light, in Manchester winters of despair. As Real Madrid swept everything before them, United's Babes lost everything. Now they would clash again. The footballing gods so ironic, determined to milk the last bit of emotion out of a journey that had left Manchester United all but spent. A loss in Madrid would have meant more than simple elimination from the European cup. For the Mancunians would surely have thrown in the towel. They would have one last chance. There would be ghosts present in the *Bernabeu*. Red ghosts. This tale of two cities was almost over.

On Saturday 11th May 1968, a city was divided like never before. Come the final day of the domestic season both Manchester clubs were level at the top of the table, but City slightly ahead on goal difference. With United at home to Sunderland and the blues facing a tough away trip to Newcastle, it was generally regarded that come Full-time the reds of Manchester would be smiling having won another league championship. However, a shocking 2-1 loss at Old Trafford blew a hole in such wishful thinking and cast dark shadows over Manchester's red half, whilst causing untold joy on the blue side. United's defeat and City's dramatic 4-3 victory two hundred miles north meant the First Division title was on its way to Maine Road for the first time since 1937. Already two goals down to the visitors, a lone George Best strike hit early with venom from twenty-yards on the stroke of half-time proved insufficient. This footballing mad city would find itself for once resonating to chants of "Champions" from those of a blue persuasion. A capacity Old Trafford crowd stood stunned. The pubs and bars of Manchester promised to be a painful place for United supporters that evening. Hiding his bitter disappointment, a gracious Matt Busby went straight to the Granada Television studios after the game to offer his congratulations to City manager and close friend Joe Mercer. Then Busby disregarded events on the home front and all thoughts turned to four days' time and a date with destiny in Madrid. No matter how painful it was, they could ill afford to be scarred by losing out to City. Such disappointments had to be put away in a box and forgotten. For a much bigger prize lay at stake.

The Wednesday previously Matt Busby had flown over to Lisbon to watch the other European cup semi-final between Benfica and Juventus. Despite the home side winning 2-0 and almost certainly booking a place in the final, the Portuguese were, in Busby's opinion: "Eminently beatable". Though Eusebio remained a thunderous talent and showed few signs of waning, elsewhere in the *Eagle's* ranks the United manager sensed they no longer soared to past heights. Now a little slower and susceptible to pace, he felt if Real Madrid could be overcome then Benfica's wings on Wembley's wide open spaces could well be clipped. He even admitted as much publicly. "If only we can survive in Madrid then I feel that we have an excellent chance of winning the European cup."

On the Mancunian's arrival in the Spanish capital, Real President, 72-year-old Santiago Bernabeu, welcomed them with a courtesy and charm typical of a man and the football club he proudly represented. "I want Manchester United greeted and treated as the greatest football club in the world. And as our friends for many years nothing must go wrong. If we are beaten by United in the European cup on Wednesday then we shall have lost to a great team. We have met them on many occasions and it is about time their luck changed." They were kind and generous words by Don Santiago, but come the time when battle was most intense, when stakes were raised and tackles flew high and fierce, it was highly unlikely Bernabeu would be so magnanimous. In a concerted effort to remain isolated from the prevailing madness consuming Madrid, the visitors stayed in a mountain retreat thirteen miles outside the city. On the morning of the match the Catholics in the United team went to a local church. There Nobby Stiles, placed a 400 Peseta note into the collection box.

Accompanying Stiles was Paddy Crerand, who immediately blurted out: "Bloody hell Nobby that's bribery!"

The *Estadio Bernabeu* would play host to 125,000 fanatical supporters. Paying £20 for a return flight from Manchester, United also had unparalleled backing for a European away match, around five thousand. But though loud the vastly outnumbered Mancunians would sound like a whisper in a thunderstorm compared to the noise set to erupt from an expectant home crowd. Like gunshots fired across the massed terraces that towered up to the heavens, thousands of firecrackers ignited and banged. The two teams led by captains Bobby Charlton and Francisco Gento looked pensive, the tension etched on the players' faces. Experienced Italian referee Antonio Sbardella led them to the centre-circle, there they broke and gave a quick dramatic wave to the crowds before posing for a final team photo.

The Teams.

Real Madrid. Betancort, Sanchis, Gonzalez, Zunzunegui, Pirri, Zoco, Velazquez. Perez, Gento, Amancio and Grosso.

Manchester United. Stepney, Foulkes, Sadler, Brennan, Dunne, Stiles, Charlton, Crerand, Aston, Best and Kidd.

Real would kick off, their goal scoring superstar Amaro Amancio, back from suspension appearing like a man rushing to make up for lost time. The *Estadio* burned like days of old, Madrid so expectant and demanding. Yet any sentiment that may have resonated from their president's welcoming speech was disregarded as Real Madrid began with a determination to blow their Mancunians *compadres* into kingdom come. A Real line-up containing six of the Spanish national side pressed and probed. A Gonzales corner was headed against the bar by Amancio with Stepney well beaten and then lashed clear by Tony Dunne. United employed their normal defence abroad with a five man rearguard. Bill Foulkes was back from injury to line up alongside the versatile David Sadler, with Nobby Stiles close by to help out. This left Brian Kidd and George Best to forage for scraps up front. They swiftly became isolated as the Spaniards dominated playing in a manner so different from the white shirts seen in Manchester. Back on home soil and with the arrogance of a bullfighter biding his time, it was surely a matter of when not if. Real were superb, Zoco and Grosso highly impressive but it was the darting Amancio who truly stood out. Quick and aggressive, forever looking to run in behind United defenders. He and Nobby Stiles were involved in a ferocious tussle both on and off the ball. Stiles had been handed the task of shackling him, but the Spaniard was proving hard to lock down as his Mancunian jailer attempted to stem Amancio's deadly threat. Stiles snapped and snarled at his heels, always just within the laws, just, but irritating him no end. Amancio raged and implored the referee to intervene. Theirs's would be a battle vital to the game's outcome, one set to become increasingly taut, if at times not downright scandalous.

On the half hour the *Madrilenos* took a deserved lead when Amancio's precise free kick found an unmarked Pirri, who soared above the United defence to head fiercely past Stepney from twelve yards. Matt Busby had warned his team in the dressing room only moments before they took the field: "If they do get an early goal to equalise on aggregate watch yourselves, because for a spell you will think the world has gone absolutely mad!" Well not only their footballers but an entire city went crazy, for now it was advantage Madrid. Their patch, their crowd and for most of the first half, their ball. Real came again, a whirlwind, the confidence now flowing, their football freewheeling and incise, every loose ball picked up by a white shirt. Two minutes before half-time, a Bobby Charlton free- kick was cleared and picked up by the exuberant Velasquez, who immediately attempted to feed Amancio on the wing. However, it was defender Shay Brennan who moved swiftly to intercept, only to miskick horribly allowing Francisco Gento to sweep behind him with a clear run on goal. As one of their favourite's son took aim the *Bernabeu* held its breath. The years and the yards melted away as

Gento sprinted into the penalty area and smashed a low drive past Stepney to put Madrid ahead on aggregate. The stadium went into meltdown, they had them. Manchester United were on the floor. As for Brennan, the boy who became a man during the unforgettable ninety minutes of that strange night against Sheffield Wednesday, ten years before, he was disconsolate with his error. But this was no time for self-doubt as United re-started looking to survive until half-time without conceding further. Yet the fates once more teased the senses, delivering yet another twist in this tale of two cities. Straight from the restart a long, hopeful ball hoisted into the Real box from defender Tony Dunne found unexpected reward. To the home crowd's horror, Ignacio Zoco, who had been arguably Real's best player until that moment, inexplicably sliced an easy clearance spectacularly past Betancourt into the net. The tall, blond haired Zoco cut a despairing figure. Wholly disbelieving his sad misfortune. At 2-2 on aggregate, this semi-final was once more even and despite being hugely outplayed Manchester United remained in the European cup.

As Sbardella prepared to blow for the interval, Real swarmed forward one last time. An astute left-wing cross from the ever-impressive defender Sanchis was met with astonishing technique and a magnificent drive past Stepney's smoking fingers by Amancio to send the home crowd into more raptures! The *Bernabeu* was a scene of utter chaos! An ecstatic Amancio took the salute of an adoring support. His had been daunting shoes to fill and yet as Madrid bowed in awe, Amancio appeared destined to fit the bill of the legendary *Blond Arrow*. It was a cacophony of joy, noise and relief not felt or heard since Enrique Mateos signed off a 3-1 victory over the Mancunians eleven years before. Cornered and on the ropes, United's hopes waned just when they appeared to have regained a fortunate foothold back in the contest. One more blow and it was surely over. As in 1957 to use Matt Busby's dramatic phrase: "The world came tumbling down." The European albatross that hung around Busby's neck weighed heavily once again. The nightmare looked set to go on.

The visitors' dressing room resembled more a morgue. In an attempt to lift his best friend's broken spirits Bobby Charlton offered a kind word, only to be silenced by Shay Brennan, who angrily shot back there could be no excuses. He had erred badly and knew it. No words could ease his pain. The sorry sight of the United players with heads down and sick with disappointment as yet another European campaign (perhaps the final campaign) looked set to end in failure. So badly hurt was Nobby Stiles after a kick out from Amancio that he sat pouring whisky onto an open leg wound. The thought of not carrying on never entering Nobby's head. At the back of everybody's mind was Munich, always Munich. Always........

Busby had to literally scrape them off the floor. He spoke up, telling the players to forget the scoreline. Even at 3-1 down they remained just a goal behind. All was not lost. He recalled: "I told them they were only 3-2 down on aggregate and to go out and play." Paddy Crerand remembers listening on with incredulity: "It could have been five or six in the first half and here was the boss telling us to go out and have a go at them! Well some of the lads were smiling by then. Here we were, having been totally outplayed and this man was telling us to go out and attack them!" To receive such a mauling and remain in with a chance meant anything could yet happen. Real Madrid had played well, brilliantly even but the mindset could now change. It was a dangerous ploy to torture the bull when it still possessed life to lash out. United had been wounded but not finished off. Busby's last words as his team left the dressing room: "Come on boys, remember we are Manchester United. Let's have a go at them."

As the United players headed off back up the tunnel it was obvious by the demeanour of many of their opponents that they already considered the game won. It was a cockiness that riled those in red. Sensing a simmering fuse, the referee pulled aside Nobby Stiles and Amaro Amancio. Smashing his fists down, Sbardella intimated to the two that there were to be no more antics. Both nodded in agreement then rejoined their teammates with the official's warning already forgotten. So, began the second-half with Amancio wasting no time getting in his retaliation first. Knowing Stiles was all but playing on one leg, he went to finish him off. Only then to suffer the irate

Mancunian's wrath when behind Sbardella's back, he was knocked out cold by a right hook. The punch caused howls of derision to sweep down from the terraces. Only to be met by a gentle shrug of the shoulders from the man christened with great irony "Happy" by long suffering teammates. It was a marker laid down by the United man that left his Spanish opponent felled and in great pain on the turf. From that moment Amancio's influence waned and he disappeared as a threat. To further infuriate the masses, Stiles gently tapped the referee on the shoulder and pointed out the distraught Amancio. "He's injured ref!" For his troubles, the Mancunian was hit with a ripe tomato hurled from the crowd and a shoe that missed by an inch! Nobby Stiles would forever be known in these parts as the "Assassin of Madrid."

Real had begun to strut, their "Ole" football not appreciated by Manchester United midfielders Stiles and Crerand, whom ripped into challenges to upset the Spaniards' rhythm. The pace and momentum which had blown away the visitors in that blistering first-half was no more. Suddenly it was United who posed the more potent threat, as a well-struck effort from Paddy Crerand flew narrowly over Betancourt's bar. Then Charlton robbed Perez in midfield before moving forward to unleash a similar effort that the Madrid goalkeeper was happy to see fly inches wide. An anxious air engulfed the *Bernabeu*. All was not yet over. Brian Kidd raced to the goal-line and crossed dangerously, only for Betancourt to save at his near post. On the bench Busby and Jimmy Murphy urged United to keep going forward, for it was clear the sheer enormity of the occasion was affecting their opponents. United pushed on, all was rushed as the clock ticked down. For the Mancunians, the hands of time raced wretchedly fast, while for the Spaniards it appeared to stop. Oh, for a Di Stefano, to tear a strip off those *Madrilenos* who appeared more intent on blaming their own *compadres* rather than ensuring the opponents did not dominate the ball. The stadium was aghast, fraught with nervous exhaustion. For the first time the away supporters could be heard. With twenty-minutes remaining Paddy Crerand urged Bobby Charlton further up field as he raced to take a free kick.

Crerand's lofted chip into the Real penalty area found George Best, who flicked on dangerously to the far post. Arriving late came David Sadler, unmarked from six-yards he forced the ball into the goal and set off in celebration around the back of Madrid's goal to earn the fury of the seething locals! He cared little, for at 3-3 as the game entered its final stage all was set to win or lose. Told to abandon his defensive duties and play upfront by Busby, the 22-year-old boy from Kent had to the abject horror of his Spanish hosts, levelled the tie. With the thought of losing everything at such a late stage simply overwhelming, both teams became pensive in possession. All except one that is. Thirteen minutes remained at the *Bernabeu* when Paddy Crerand's throw in found George Best wide on the right hand touchline. Faced by Zoco and his arch-nemesis Sanchis, the United winger turned and twisted to leave both trailing in his wake, before tearing into the Real penalty area. On reaching the goal-line Best glanced up to deliver a cut back, only then having to look again when he noticed who stood waiting for his pass. The same man who had staggered out of that inferno at the end of a Munich runway. 36-year-old Bill Foulkes had arrived in the penalty area as if urged by his long-lost pals. Best's glorious pass was as close to perfection as possible, but the unlikely figure of Foulkes finishing low past Betancourt with a precision side-foot effort that would have done credit to Denis Law, was out of this world. A despairing Betancourt pounded the turf as Madrid's hearts lay broken. Bill Foulkes, a no nonsense former pit miner from St. Helens, plucked by Busby to play for United, always related the grand tale as if it was yesterday: "The atmosphere was so strange: they were not really playing and we were holding on to what we'd got. Then I shouted to Pat and could see the shock on his face because it was me. I kept running and Pat threw the ball to George. He went past one, then two and I kept moving up. I was only jogging, but I can tell you I was the only red shirt in the box. George feinted to drive it to the near post then flipped a perfect pass for me. I just hit it in the opposite corner."
Normally used to the sight of Foulkes ballooning the ball over the crossbar or screwing a shot haplessly wide, United players watched

astonished as the granite man of their defence kept his cool and scored arguably the most important goal in the history of their Football Club. Paddy Crerand remembers thinking: "What's that big idiot doing up there?"

Bobby Charlton's first reaction was: "Oh no not Bill!" Yet their worries proved unfounded as Foulkes kept his nerve and finished off the *Madrilenos* in their own stadium. Buried in red shirts, Foulkes appeared determined to shrug off the compliments and return to his centre-half position, for there remained sufficient time for it all still to go horribly awry. But Real had gone in mind and spirit, their confidence and belief wiped away in the emotional slipstream of United's dramatic comeback. Yet still they found enough to go to the last. Seconds remained when Velasquez went flying down the United left and fired in a low shot that was deflected and safely cleared. By now few could watch, the tension unbearable. The visitors broke with Brian Kidd setting up George Best to shoot straight at Betancourt. Again, Real swept forward only for Zoco's pass to be picked up by the referee who called proceedings to a halt on an unforgettable night of drama in Madrid! Across the field United players fell to the turf. Exhausted and filled with emotion. None more than Bobby Charlton as the memories of lost friends vividly returned amid the feelings of ecstasy evoked in the Spanish capital.

Onto the pitch streamed hundreds of jubilant United supporters to embrace their heroes. The Madrid police were too stunned and dazed to care. The United players embraced Matt Busby as they left the field. His smile was wide enough to light up the *Bernabeu* as he waited for the team next to the tunnel. For Real Madrid it was a monumental loss and one it would take a generation to recover from. Thirty-one years would pass before Real won the European cup again. A sporting Miguel Munoz sought out the victorious United manager to shake his hand and wish Busby all the best for the forthcoming final against Benfica. Meanwhile, high in the Presidential box Don Santiago Bernabeu applauded the Mancunians' moment of triumph. Though sick with defeat, Bernabeu would later admit: "If it had to be anyone, then I am glad it was them."

The Manchester United dressing room whilst hectic and joyful was also awash with tears of relief and sadness. Matt Busby sat quietly. He was crying. Despite all attempts to console him Busby was heartbroken. "I can't help it," he sobbed. "I just can't help it." Busby was embraced by a similarly distraught Bobby Charlton and Bill Foulkes, three survivors together, now so close to a journey's end that at times had been too painful to bear. The next day, on arriving back in Manchester, Busby was mobbed by the press within moments of disembarking and asked his thoughts on finally reaching the European cup final. A still emotional United manger, his feelings in turmoil but knowing he was expected to deliver a triumphal victory line, declared with a beaming smile: "In the immortal words of the great Satchmo, (Louis Armstrong), it's a wonderful world!"

EPILOGUE

Wembley Stadium. Thursday 29th May 1968.
The European Cup Final.
Manchester United were 3-1 up against Benfica in extra-time. The reds were almost there. On ninety-nine minutes, United roared forward again as Bobby Charlton with socks around his ankles fed a raiding Brian Kidd to sprint down the touchline. Off soared the long-legged youngster before placing a perfect cross onto the right foot of a waiting Charlton. The boy on whose slim shoulders the hopes and dreams of every United supporter had rested since Munich. Bobby swept a majestic effort into the top corner! "That was for Dunc and the boys. My pals," said Bobby afterwards. Manchester United 4-1 Benfica. With such grace and artistry the European cup was won. A beautiful evening under the London stars. "We shall not be moved!" sang the crowd. "We shall not be moved!"
The final whistle. Amid a hub of well-wishers, a beaming Matt Busby strode onto the pitch. Trying desperately to fight away the tears and keep his composure, Busby headed towards the centre circle to sportingly shake hands with the forlorn Benfica players. However, his path was cut short when a crying Bobby Charlton fell into his arms

and the pair embraced. No words were necessary. The best of times. Avoiding the mad huddle of cameras and flashlights exploding all around walked Jimmy Murphy. Never one for the spotlight, this proud Welshman stood content in the knowledge that it had really not all been for nothing. Munich would never go away, but for one night the pain would ease, his boys could salute a job done well. A victory earned the Manchester United way. First you raise spirits, then you break hearts. Then you rise again and prevail. A wink to the stars and the fallen, and Jimmy Murphy vacated the stage.

So the time came for the presentation and the United players, Paddy Crerand foremost amongst them, tried desperately to persuade Matt Busby to go and raise the famous trophy high. However, all efforts were in vain as Busby refused point-blank and instead insisted his Captain Bobby Charlton be first up the Wembley steps to collect the Holy Grail. On being handed the trophy a smiling Charlton lifted it into the air and Wembley stadium erupted! Looking drained and close to collapse he made his weary way back down. This for his dear friends lost in the crash. To them went the glory and spoils of victory. In the celebrations that followed one of the first telegrams arriving to congratulate Matt Busby and United on finally winning the European cup came from an old friend. It was post-marked Madrid.

...To a wonderful football man and club. Real Madrid toast your great success. Don Santiago Bernabeu...

As for Busby it is only apt to end with a line from the novel on whose title this chapter has gratefully borrowed.

"I wish you to know that you have been the last dream of my soul."
A Tale Of Two Cities.

CHAPTER THIRTY FOUR
(SIR BOBBY CHARLTON TRILOGY)
FULL OF GRACE

A very humble ordinary man who did extraordinary things. The news broke around four o'clock yesterday that Sir Bobby had passed. My first thought was how sad that a man who had lived such an incredible life had been robbed at the end of his memories. Dementia is a curse of old age, and seemingly these days, not so old. Past footballers being struck down by this thief in the night that shows no mercy taking everything away. In life, Sir Bobby stood for everything that Manchester United should be about. A gentleman footballer, a gentleman off the pitch. If Hollywood had been sent the script of his United career it would have been deemed ridiculous and passed for another Avengers movie. ''What? This guy survived an air crash where all his buddies were killed. He then won the soccer World Cup for England and then, ten years on from Munich, the European Cup? Get out of here!''

Sir Bobby like all survivors and those connected with Manchester United in that period hardly ever spoke about Munich. If asked there always appeared a far-away stare and a tear also not so far away forming in his eyes. Sir Bobby's best mates in the team were killed at the end of that runway. Notably Duncan Edwards and Eddie Colman. There were others later he grow incredibly close to. Men like Nobby Stiles and Wilf McGuinness. Both who also fell victim to the curse. Nobby now passed. They say the Bobby Charlton who boarded that aircraft, a happy, go lucky, smiling young boy who had the football world at his feet, was never the same afterwards. The pain and the shock of what he witnessed lived forever with him. A dark angel on his shoulders. But there was one place where Sir Bobby found solace. Where for ninety-minutes at least the faces, the laughter, the voices faded away as the game took over. There he was simply

Bobby Charton the footballer. Full of grace, two footed, gliding
across the pitch, forever on the move and when the opportunity arose,
Bobby's shooting was like a grenade exploding. Ferocious! There
appeared no back lift, like a ballerina but then bang! 1-0 the reds!
The Mexicans at Wembley in the 1966 World Cup. Sliding into
position for a thirty-yard thunderbolt to ignite England's World Cup
charge. Wembley, 1968. Manchester United, two wonderful goals to
win the European Cup. For Duncan, for Eddie, for all of them. A
flashing header as United in blue rid themselves at least for one night
only the strangling albatross of Munich. Then the goal in extra time.
Brian Kidd's run and cross for Bobby to sweep the ball home past the
Benfica goalkeeper. 4-1! Typically, it roared into the top of the net.
Was there really any other place for it to go?
There will be a book of condolence today, no doubt each page will be
drenched in Mancunian tears. As the days go on, tears from further
afar will appear. Sir Bobby Charlton was a decent man off the pitch. I
don't believe the horrors of Munich never really left him, but he lived
a life full. He lived it well and good. On the pitch, there really is only
one word to describe him. Full of grace.

RED GHOSTS

I took a ride on the tram down to Old Trafford today to sign Sir
Bobby's book of condolence. It was a bright morning, a slight nip in
the air. Hardly blue skies, Monday grey. Manchester's new
skyscrapers reaching ever higher. They used to say about this city that
whenever there was a spare gap they would build or open a bar.
Now it's skyscrapers.
"The next stop will be Old Trafford" we were informed over the
Tannoy. The sight of Lancashire Cricket club looming large next to
the tram stop. Then the trek up to Chester Road, Lou Macari's
evergreen, immortal chippy appears into view. Blimey this whole area
feels lost in time. The surroundings have changed, but somehow the

walk down Sir Matt Busby way, over the railway bridge, just feels like you're surrounded by red ghosts of the past. You can't hear or see them, but they're around. Drawn back, their hopes and dreams as real as yours' or mine. They're all here today for the same reason I am. To pay their respect to the greatest Manchester United and English footballer of all time. A man who made dreams come true.

A man called Sir Bobby Charlton.

Sir Bobby was the last to die from that Busby Babes line-up, before the game against Red Star Belgrade, on 5th February 1958. A long, gone winter's day behind the Iron Curtain. A pitch full of snow but melting fast. A touch of spring in the Yugoslav air. The day before Munich...

The statue of the Holy Trinity looks beautiful. There's a scarf been placed lovingly around Sir Bobby's neck. Below a sea of flowers and tributes. Red and white. People are having their photographs taken alongside it. Nobody is speaking much, it's all very solemn. Older supporters stand transfixed looking at the statue. Sir Bobby and George gone now, Denis, please god. Look after yourself Lawman. Himself diagnosed with the dreaded affliction that takes away memories, leaving in its rotten wake, nothing. Just a confusion and heartbreaking, hopelessness. I see one old chap of a certain vintage wiping tears away. I go across. "Are you okay mate?"

"Yes son thanks. I just had to come today and pay my respects. Sir Bobby was my hero." We chat for a few moments. He was at Sir Bobby's debut against Charlton Athletic at Old Trafford, this place, when he scored twice. "He was fantastic," said my new mate called Ray. 'But you had to be every week to play for Matt Busby and Jimmy Murphy." Together we went to sign our names in the Book of Condolences. To be fair the club had set everything up with dignity and style. A rarity these days. But I'm not going there. Not today. After saying goodbye to Ray, I had a walk around the ground. I remembered my first game with dad. 30th December 1978. Manchester United 3-5 West Bromwich Albion. I Was nine. I'm not nine anymore. Far from it. United have always been a huge part of my

life. Sometimes I've cared too much. "It's just a game," people would say. "Just a silly game. Do you think they care?" I believe the lads that were killed at Munich cared. Duncan Edwards travelling to Old Trafford on a bike! Eddie Colman whistling, with his boots in a bag strutting over the bridge. The Dirty Old Town behind him. These boys were Sir Bobby's best friends. These boys died at Munich.
Still the red ghosts file into the forecourt. Thousands and thousands. Bowler hats, flat caps, baseball caps. This is Manchester United's travelling support that never really died. Our mum's dad's brothers, sisters from another time. Today, alongside the living they are paying tribute to a man who is undoubtedly, Mr Manchester United.
A certain ten red ghosts are present. Their faces familiar. The lads from the Belgrade line-up are there at the front. All together again. Gregg, Foulkes, Byrne, Colman, Jones, Edwards, Morgan, Taylor, Viollet, Scanlon…And their Bobby.

THE BELLS OF THIS FAIR CITY

Sleep well Sir Bobby.
I hate funerals, fifty-fifty whether I turn up for my own. In life I know come the finishing line, there's no such thing as a happy ending. We all close our eyes at the final whistle. I got a tram into Manchester today. The bloody weather was awful. Manchester, now a booming, European, world-wide city. The city of cranes which is a good thing because it creates jobs and puts money in everyone's pocket. When Sir Bobby arrived in Manchester as a young boy from the north-east, it remained still a bombed-out shell recovering from the Second World War blitz. The Luftwaffe hit us hard, they hit everyone hard, but Manchester was turned into a firestorm. So many warehouses ignited around Piccadilly. Leaping flames careering high. The skies turned blood red. Hundred died, thousands were injured. For years after the war the ashes simmered and you could smell the charred wood. The remnants of the bombs evident everywhere. Vast mounds of rubble set between buildings that survived the initial blitz, but in time succumbed to the sheer shock caused to their foundations.

Now when you get off the Metrolink tram at Exchange Square, Manchester, with the Christmas fair ready to come alive, and everywhere you look there's towering new skyscrapers blocking out the past. Although look carefully, you can still see the history, but mostly this is a city now racing forever onwards. Manchester Cathedral, such a fitting setting to say goodbye to Sir Bobby. A man whose heart was broken at Munich, and who became more of a Mancunian than those actually born here. He adored this city. The people, their ways, their attitudes to life, their families and their football teams. And nobody loved Manchester United more than Sir Bobby Charlton. His birth right may have been Ashington, but he truly belonged to Manchester. I caught a glance of the coffin gently being taken from the hearse. It was quiet, the click of cameras, the distant hum of traffic, the near silence of a whispering tram. Sir Bobby's last journey watched by grim faces, a sea of black and dark colours. A thousand mourners inside the cathedral, but millions more across the world in spirit. Once the service was over the bells of the cathedral rang out for the boy who became a man in the midst of losing all his best pals at Munich. Now back amongst them. It always felt with Sir Bobby as if he could never believe friends such as Duncan Edwards and Eddie Colman had left him. Happily no longer, and I'm sure that pain in his eyes has gone now. It's a bloody miserable day, I'm not hanging around. I just wanted to be here when the great man was laid to rest surrounded by so much love. And hear the bells of this fair city ring out loud and proud for one of their favourite sons.

CHAPTER THIRTY FIVE
NICKY WELSH (Taken from My United Road)
UNCLE MATT

Every birthday, Christmas or Easter celebration I'd meet Sir Matt. They became known to me as Uncle Matt and his daughter, auntie Sheenagh, yet still I'd stare across, utterly blown away that I was sat at the same table with a living legend of my football club. He just had this presence, one coming only from greatness. We got on so well, but saying that it was impossible not to. Sir Matt had a warm and calming presence about him–an aura. A man of few words maybe, though everyone spoken I cherished. To this day as I write, I remember fondly his laugh. Strange, I never, ever, once spoke football with him, even though I ached to. It simply never felt the right time to mention it. I'd wait for him but nothing. United, especially Munich just never came up in conversation, and I had far too much respect and love for the man to even approach the subject. If I'm truly honest, he was to me more Saint Matt than Uncle Matt, who loved his whiskey, in moderation of course! He'd always say: "A nice healthy dram was good for you before going to bed." Always telling me wee stories of him going home back up to Glasgow, and on one particularly night at a house party, his Mum telling him off! "Matthew, you're drunk! Whatever will you be doing next?"

He laughed saying: "Nick, I was twenty-two years of age!"

Sir Matt's son Sandy was another Busby diamond, a chip off the old block, who I also got to know well over this time. Once at the Haydock races when Sir Alex Ferguson was in our group, he turned to me and said quietly: "You know what Nick, it's frightening when I sit and listen to Alex. It might as well be my Dad talking." When you look at both characters though they do share some remarkable resemblances. Neither took the step straight into football, whereas Matt went down the Orbiston coal pits for a while, Sir Alex was an apprentice tool maker in the Govan shipyards. These times in their lives undoubtedly shaped them as people, and I don't think they ever forgot the working man's mentality and principals. Simple, old fashioned customs and values that were instilled in them both for life. The only other man who I've met who gave off the same aura as Sir Matt, you won't be surprised to know is Sir Alex. A breed apart these Scottish men of granite, morals and huge hearts.

On Thursday 20th January 1994, Sir Matt Busby, age 84, passed away quietly at the Alexandra hospital in Cheadle, Stockport. He was surrounded at the end by loved ones and would finally get to meet again his lovely wife Jean and the lads he'd lost on that Munich runway, a lifetime ago, all whom had never left his heart. Though heart-breaking, it wasn't such a sudden shock, for we knew he'd been very poorly. Uncle Matt was gravely ill for some time, yet there was always a part of you that thought, due to what he was forced to endure during the late fifties, and had come through it. Plus, a stroke suffered back in 1980, many, like me thought this remarkable old gentleman would live forever. Sadly, no one does and as the news was released Manchester fell deep into mourning.

Outside Old Trafford, people swiftly gathered and a sea of flowers spread fast over the forecourt. Flags, scarves, teddy bears, private messages to the father of our football team. Denis Law was interviewed by ITV new and broke down in tears, whilst Bobby Charlton simply couldn't speak through being so choked up. United were due to play Everton at home the following Saturday and I invited my then father-in-law Pete to have one of the family season tickets. He was one of Sir Matt's closest friends for many years and it was simply the right thing to do. Come the Saturday afternoon at ten minutes to three, a lone piper led the two teams out from the tunnel into a veil of tears. Old Trafford stood silent, the pipes resonating across the packed terraces full of solemn tear-stained faces. The television cameras cut to an inconsolable George Best clutching a tissue. He wasn't alone. Black ribbons had been placed on Sir Matt's seat, the sight of that enough to break any red heart. After a period of silence where the only sound you could hear was hearts breaking, the referee blew his whistle and the crowd exploded in noise. A gigantic release of emotional that I swear could be heard above in heaven and far away on that Munich runway so shaped Sir Matt Busby's life, and where the souls of so many of his babe's souls departed this earth. A special mention to the Everton fans present that day as they acted with wonderful class, and respected what was for my Manchester United, in all essence a funeral without a body. We'd lost our Sir Matt....

Finally, the game began, and fittingly United played exceptionally well, the football free-flowing, with undoubtedly the star man being a young winger full of tricks, light as a feather and rapier quick. Ryan Giggs led the Everton defence a merry dance throughout, and it was his headed goal that handed the reds a 1-0 win, though in reality it could and should've been a rout. Yet, on that late, cold January afternoon under a mourning, black Mancunian sky, Giggs had warmed the hearts of supporters, and handed them the gift of being able to smile through what had been truly a sad day, as Old Trafford bade goodbye to the boss.

After the game I dropped Peter off at his house in Hale named Lynwood after his good lady, and he asked me in to have a drink. They'd a nice bar within that Peter had built himself. Already sat at it was auntie Sheenagh. I walked over and gave her a huge hug. The tears I'd fought against all day finally falling. Sheenagh drove her dad everywhere, and she and her three daughters not surprisingly were United daft. I pulled a stool up alongside Sheenagh and we began to talk. I told her about what Old Trafford had been like as the piper appeared, and the sheer emotion in the old place. How proud her dad would've been. She'd wanted to go, but felt it wasn't right until Sir Matt had been laid to rest.

"Can I tell you something Nick?" she asked.

She then revealed to me something that left me with chills running down my back and an emotional wreck. Late the previous evening, Sheenagh's door-bell had rung and she'd gone to answer it. Stood there ashen-faced was Harry Gregg. He apologised for calling unannounced at such an awkward hour, but had flown in earlier that evening from his home in Ireland, and just wanted to see Matt's body and pay his respects. This was no problem for Sheenagh, and she warmly welcomed him inside. They settled down and got talking over a bottle of whiskey about a man who meant the absolutely world to them both. Then, Harry started to open up. He told her: ''I've never told this story to anyone, friends, family or obviously the press, but on the night of the crash I found myself out on the runway. I looked over, and I saw your dad across the tarmac lay on his back. Now, your dad Sheenagh love, never swore, but he said to me, ''I've broken my bastard back, leave me be, and go and check for others in that plane.'' 'Harry stopped for a moment to regain his composure, but then continued on. ''I always did whatever your dad asked, we all did, so I crawled back into that burning aeroplane. Everyone always calls me a hero, and that upsets me, because I was just doing what the boss, your dad told me to do.''

The rest is history. I sat listening to Sheenagh tell this remarkable story. One that to this day, I feel compelled to say chokes me whenever I think about it.

Thursday 27th January 1994, was the day of the funeral, and it wouldn't surprise you to know that Manchester was crying rain. Endless drizzle. The service was at Our Lady and Saint John's in Chorlton. Local flower shops ran out of roses swiftly as the roads and street that the funeral cortege would take became lined with people. On the hearse carrying Sir Matt's coffin was a huge red and white floral tribute inscribed simply with the words THE BOSS. I remember a full primary school, every age group stood on the road in the pouring rain on our short trip from Chorlton to Old Trafford. My friend Ron Woods dad, Ken, stood drenched head to toe outside by the forecourt on Warwick Road. Thousands stood in silent tribute as the Cortege stopped for a minute outside the ground, and then a miracle occurred. The rain momentarily stopped! As we headed off to Southern cemetery people began applauding. Faces etched with tears. Again, on the return leg, the pavements remained full, yet so deadly

quiet. Heads bowed. If such a thing was truly possible then a city's
heart lay ripped.

Later that day at Sir Matt's wake, everyone remained so solemn.
Drained by the emotions and obviously deeply upset. What caused me
to do it, I'd no idea, but I just thought Uncle Matt wouldn't want this.
I got up from my chair and began to sing. 'Hello, hello we are the
Busby Boys!' Soon, everyone was joining. I continued on 'Forever
and ever' and we had a good old singsong. Sir Matt always used to
claim after a few drams that he belonged to Glasgow, well, it also has
to be said, this wonderful old man, the father of our football team.
He belonged to us also.
Manchester United.
Rest in wonderful forever peace Alexander Matthew Busby.

Post Note:
Through love and despair Manchester United football club have
always been there. Twenty minutes remained of the 1994 FA Cup
final between United and Chelsea and we were three up. The title had
already been retained and the reds stood on the verge of our first ever
Double. Here in London town the weather was typical Mancunian as
the rain poured down endlessly, and I was soaked to the skin. Before
the match I cried listening to ''Abide with Me'' for it reminded me of
a kindly old man taken from us only a few months previous. Then, I
filled up once more as suddenly thousands of United fans around me
launched into a rousing: ''There's only one Matt Busby!''

CHAPTER THIRTY SIX
PAUL McGUINNESS (Son of Wilf)
THE LAST OF THE BABES

My dad kept lots of photos. He had them in a mini suitcase. When I was a kid I would look through them all. Of course I asked loads of questions and he would tell me. Nobody else connected with Manchester United ever really spoke much about the crash. It was like we don't quite mention it, although it was always there. But for me, it made me feel looking at all these photos of them all. Young guys at the top of their game. They had won the Youth Cup together five times in a row. He told me all about that. We had the best players from all over the UK and Ireland. Dad talked about going on a trip to Ireland, Bray Wicklow, with Duncan Edwards and Jimmy Murphy. They were both England Schholboy Captains a couple of years apart. Basically, the trip was supposed to be for scouting or visiting a club, but it really was all about bonding. They were so clever in pioneering, that was Busby and Murphy. To do things together. They had the Youth Cup to get them used to winning, hardly ever losing a game. So every generation coming up felt invincible. Obviously, they then started getting in the first team at 17,18 and 19. All young players that won the First Division twice. But still Matt Busby and Jimmy Murphy were pioneering. They would take under-20 teams to the Blue Star tournament in Switzerland. There United played against the Italians using *Catenaccio* or German and Spanish sides with their own varying styles. Busby and Murphy also made sure they travelled, for most of their lads had already played in the first team, and the genius of these two was they were preparing Manchester United for when they might well be playing in the European Cup. Again, so ahead of their time. All these lads were having shared experiences so you just got that feeling from what my dad said that the bond they shared coming through the ranks was unbelievable.

They would be out and about in town together! The Kardomah, the Plaza, the Continental, the coffee cafes. It all just sounded so romantic. Like young cavaliers and because they were winning so much they felt fearless. Oh, my dad would have been so cocky it would not have been true! They all had these blazers and would go around town wearing them. My mum would say it was so embarrassing walking straight to the front of the queue at the pictures and getting in for nothing. Dad would've been like a peacock with that! They would also all have these free trilby's on! It just sounded and felt to me like a Frank Sinatra film from the fifties and they all looked like movie stars! The dogs bollocks! I could just imagine them around town feeling fantastic. Again, to me it was so romantic!
Later, I would talk to the players about how good Duncan Edwards was? Then Bobby with his shooting. Tommy Taylor with his goals. Billy Whelan went to mass every day but what a player he was. Eddie Colman, a cheeky chappie. The talk about them all felt for me like I was actually inside a Hollywood movie and I was related to it. Obviously, afterwards, it was Uncle Bobby when he came to our house. Uncle Gordon, the goalkeeper Gordon Clayton was my Godfather. Gordon was so handsome like Richard Burton. Six-feet tall, big hands. He said they were all just so confident having the time of their lives. To me it felt like they would have gone on to rule the world. So you have all that romance, then all of a sudden...
BANG.
Tragedy. My dad talking about it. He saw something on the news stand in town and went to one of the newspaper offices to find out what had gone on. Then it all started coming out. Dad was injured so never went on the trip. He ended up going to every funeral so you can imagine the toll, how it all felt. All that brightness and then darkness comes along. But the strength of that light before, that core family feeling is what resurrected the club. It was Jimmy Murphy who brought it all together, but you had lads like Shay Brennan brought in from the cold. A reserve youth player. We lost for the first time in the Youth Cup that year in the semi-finals, but that was mainly because the centre forward Alex Dawson had been promoted to the first team.

Dawson scored a hat trick against Fulham in the FA Cup semi-final to get us to Wembley. This achievement just showed the power of that family feeling for me What I'm really proud of is when you look back the next season, United finished second in the League.

There's a nice passage in Bobby's book that says if there was anybody who epitomised the spirit at United back then it was my dad. "There was Wilf covering every blade of grass." I can imagine. Just imagine, if you had lost all your mates, every game the next year you're trying to make up for it. You're playing for them. Dad would've given everything, I'm absolutely certain of that. So, all of this feeling. That darkness and the resurrection. Then with Georgie Best, Nobby Stiles, David Sadler, John Aston and Brian Kidd, they finally won the European Cup. They won it with youth which was unheard of so the whole sort of tragedy and romance thing comes back again.

When I was a youth coach at Manchester United, I would be preaching this to the players every year. I wanted them to feel just one per cent of what I felt, because I knew it would lift them to play for United. Sometimes, when I was talking to them about it I'd be nearly crying. I would try and hold it back but it would choke me. But it wasn't just me. You had Tony Whelan who had been there and would do the same thing, There's still people steeped in it. Jimmy Ryan, Jimmy Curran, John Cooke, Mark Dempsey, Danny Keough, Jack Fallows, Tommy O'Neil, so many others. United to their very core. After Sir Alex left someone came from outside. He asked me what was so special about Manchester United then? You're trying to think because he probably looked at it and thought, well I can see other clubs doing lots of different things, you've not got this or that. But I said it's a feeling that you belong to something special. An identity and you're a guardian of that. You're passing it on so United players of the future play and feel the same way about the club.

To close, my dad is defined by this identity. He's defined by being a Bubsy Babe. Dad was so effervescent, so flamboyant, having a good time, but always able to recover from setbacks. The injuries of a broken leg. Recovering from getting the sack, from losing his hair. All these things and he's never moaned once. I think he couldn't moan, he wouldn't moan, because how could he moan about something as trivial as getting the sack or losing your hair when all his friends had died. That's how I see his identity. Dad has dementia now. He's Struggling, but if you put anything in front of him with United on then dad is there. A Busby Babe.

RED MEMORIES

ROY CAVANAGH MBE

In 1955, when I first went to watch Manchester United, I was nearly 7. I lived in Salford in what was a slum, but everyone lived alike and I knew nothing different. Rationing till 1954 and life was very colourless. To me Old Trafford became the "Theatre of Colour". The Old Gold of Wolves, the blue of Everton, the coloured stripes of West Brom and the red of United. Then there was green grass, not much of that around Salford. I first saw the players who would be dubbed "The Busby Babes" in a youth tie against Plymouth Argyle. Colman, Edwards, McGuinness, Charlton, Brennan. Three weeks later Duncan made his England debut. The 1956 FA Youth Cup final versus Chesterfield, Bobby Charlton at number nine for United, Gordon Banks in goal for Chesterfield. Ten years later they both won the World Cup for England. Also in 1956, United won the title and did it again in 1957. Those "Busby Babes" were all over the show, they were my team. One or two bumps and changes, by 1958 I was at the Ipswich game when five would never play again at Old Trafford, then the following week at the reserves, where another five would appear at home for the last time. On 5th February, United were through to the European Cup semi-final for the second season running. The day after about 4.30, I was coming back from school having done some extra lessons for the 11 plus (failed|!) when I caught up with some mates. A news billboard screamed "United in Plane Crash". The 6.00.pm news confirmed the Munich air disaster, many killed they said. No social media, it was the day after when enormity hit home. I was devasted, I could not go to Old Trafford again until the following September. They were my team, my life.
They were gone for ever.

ROD McCAIN

Ten years after the Munich Air Disaster, Matt Busby achieved his life's dream, the burning ambition that had driven him and all those young lads on to make that ill-fated journey to freezing Belgrade in the first place. At Wembley, Manchester United became Champions of Europe, the first English side ever to achieve that feat. I'm sure that even on that famous night in North London, Matt's thoughts were never far from his lost boys. His team that evening contained Bobby Charlton and Bill Foulkes, two men who knew only too well what the triumph had cost their manager. All that has followed on since 6th February 1958, in terms of glory for the Red Devils has been achieved under the all-encompassing shadow of that fateful day. If you become a supporter of Manchester United, you will inevitably get taught to know the history of the club. A history that will always reverberate around the events of February 1958, just as it should. "The Flowers of Manchester" will live on forever in our hearts, even though the majority of us who now solemnly remember them every 6th February, were not yet born into this world when they took their untimely leave of it. We'll keep the Red Flag flying high, because, for us, they will never die.

PATRICK BURNS

When I think of the Busby Babes I have an abundance of thoughts. Pride. Passion. Heart. Courage. Pioneers. Unfulfilled potential. Tragedy. Legends. Icons. The DNA of MUFC. Heroes. The greatest team Manchester United ever fielded. These thoughts often overwhelm me to be honest. I think of the eight boys who died, the two who never played again and those who fortunately did. I think of their families, many of whom I know personally, and their friends. We ceased to be a mere football club on 6th February 1958 and became a global institution.

The Babes are why I became a Red.

They are why I set up the Charity, the MMMF, to give back to the Club and to preserve and enhance, where possible, their historical status for future generations. Working in their name in Manchester, Munich and Belgrade has brought me a greater understanding of just how magnificent they really were. How close they came to dethroning Real Madrid and how their loss affected England in the 58 and 62 World Cups. The greatest honour has been to organise and deliver the memorial services in Munich from 2018 - 2023 (60th to 65th) inclusive and to commemorate the 65th anniversary in Belgrade. Standing in front of your fellow red brothers and sisters, your peers, and delivering a service worthy of their memory when your heart is breaking inside, is quite simply humbling and precious. To be a small part of something to sacred and special to Reds has been an honour and a privilege. I hope I've been able to do my bit in remembering the Babes in the right way and for the right reasons.

PHILIP BROWN

Manchester United is a love affair, my first love and like many others, I am in it for life. In sickness and in health, for richer or poorer, till death do us part. Like any love affair, it is filled with incredible highs and excruciating lows. As you start to learn about Utd it doesn't take long before you're confronted with the Munich air disaster, a story of heartbreaking tragedy, heroism and resurrection. As I have aged through my life, Munich has often been a reference point, when I need to find inspiration to overcome a difficult challenge, I think about Sir Matt who was twice led the last rights. Despite losing eight of his wonderful young team, just a decade later he would lead another brilliant young Utd side to the summit of European football. Who knows what the counter factual would be had Munich not have happened? You inevitably ruminate on all the things that could have been, that should have been and what those young men were deprived off. The present always defines the past and as you learn more about life, in a cruel twist of fate, it brings everything into clarity in a way you sometimes wish it wouldn't. I wish Munich had never happened but it did and the greatest way to honour the legacy of the Babes is to use it in such way that brings about positive change in your own life, in doing so, their spirit will never die.

DANNY LOVELOCK

As a middle-aged man, born in the early 70's, I hadn't the chance to see The Busby Babes live. Like most United fans of that era all we had was stories told to us by our parents, uncles, aunties. I think apart from the tales of how good these players were, one thing that stuck out to me and still does to this day is the fact that they belong to everyone, not just you and your brother etc, but to your mam, your sister, your nana. That's the effect that mystical legendary team has on any one who follows United. Most people will think of the football they played, the dynamism of youth, but for me, it's about more than football, it's about belonging to something more than just football, it's about a team that don't just belong to Manchester United, it's about a team that belong to everyone. The Busby Babes.

BILL LEVER

The Busby Babes are the heartbeat of our history, our club, the reason we sing about them at every game; the age of the players, that still continues today with academy players featuring. Matt's foresight in finding young talent from all points of the country. Ashington, Barnsley, Ireland, Dudley, Salford, and moulding them into what would have become The Greatest Team ever. Unbelievable that hundreds of people travel every year to Munich to celebrate the Busby Babes, the way other clubs reacted to the tragedy, Bayern, Real, and others, shows how special they were. What could they have achieved in later years if this tragedy had not happened? Such a young team, with most of them going to play on for years and form the basis of a team that could have been enhanced by Law and Best, we would have won titles and cups, and European Cups for years! The memory of the Babes lives on every year, we tell the story of Busby's bouncing Babes at every game, we will never die!

TONY WHITTAKER

The bleakest day in our history occurred on 6ᵗʰ February 1958. I was brought up knowing all about that day and the sadness it brought, my dad often spoke about it and telling me about the great players who perished. The one who always came up was the great Duncan Edwards, my dad always maintained the greatest ever, I have travelled to Munich on many occasions to mark the anniversary. The football world possibly lost arguably the greatest club side ever, unfortunately we will never know if that was the case. I visit Glasnevin cemetery every February to lay flowers at Liam Whelan's grave and the bridge named in his honour, the man from St. Attracta Road has a special place in my heart. Sir Matt and Jimmy Murphy deserve enormous credit for steering the club through the darkest of times, in my opinion nobody comes close to them. To sum up The babes will always be enshrined in our history, February 6ᵗʰ 1958 will always be the darkest of all days. God bless the Flowers of Manchester.

M

Back in the day, I used to jib off school to go to the ground on the 6ᵗʰ February, just to stand silently with a few like-minded souls. Nodding to the regulars, the men in overalls on a break from grafting in Trafford Park, the two elderly ladies who had been a couple of Eddie Colman's girlfriends, babes in arms brought by dads or grandads to shiver in the Mancunian chill, the older chaps with the team they had witnessed in the flesh still playing in their memory. All drawn together to quietly pay respects to our lost legends, without fanfare and seemingly without recognition from the club if the date didn't fall close to a home match. A true fans' tribute with tales from a sepia-coated Manchester, Salford & Stretford End, shared in the minutes after the silence, in hushed tones under the plaque that bore the names of the fallen. In 1998, when we played Bayern in the group stages, a couple of us took the time to venture to Trudering-Reim. The old control tower was still standing with the departure lounge still intact though locked prior to its redevelopment. We wrote the 8 names in marker on the door as the wind whipped grit around the bleak site and took a moment to gaze down the runway with teary eyes in tribute. We have returned many times since. In those days, it felt that Munich was sometimes invoked more by the opposition to provoke United fans, rather than something owned by us. It is amazing that now so many make the pilgrimage to Bavaria and that the club permits the gathering on the forecourt after so long avoiding their responsibilities. The team belonged to the fans and lives on in our hearts.

KEV THE RED

I was just 4 when I was taken to see them play by a cousin who was a pro himself, and knew Tommy Taylor quite well from Barnsley. A 3-1 loss to Wolves on 28th September 1957 at Molineux. I don't remember it, just the bus journey there. In the following year, I came home from school, or playing outside in the cold weather, (I can't remember which). My mom was stood at the kitchen sink, peeling spuds I reckon, as we always had sausage and chips on a Thursday. She was crying, and I said: "what's up mom?"
Her reply still haunts me now. "Those poor boys, those poor boys."
That was my first, my abiding memory of The Busby Babes.
The rest, as they say, is history. It was 6th February 1958.

ALAN POPE

It's a strange thing Munich to somebody of my age. I'm 50, and never saw any of them play, yet it still somehow has a profound emotional effect on me. I've been brought up on stories of the Babes and their names trip off my tongue. My Dad adored them, Duncan Edwards in particular. They were his benchmark for every United team. My Dad was a tough bloke, but I could occasionally hear his voice quiver or see a tear when he talked about them or Munich came on the TV. That love of United and the Babes passed on to me. So, when I see the old grainy footage of Kenneth Kendall, breaking the news, or the coffins returning to Manchester, it still punches me in the guts and can reduce me to tears. It also fills me with pride when I see the match programme with no names on the team sheet and Bill Foulkes somehow leading the team out against Sheffield Wednesday. When I was younger , I thought about Munich in terms of how many Leagues and Cups United missed out on, but now older, wiser and with children of my own. I think of the human cost. Young boys robbed of life. Munich is the defining point for any United supporter irrespective of their age. We will never die. Keep the red flag flying high.

JAMES COOPER

The famous Busby Babes, the symbol of our great club's history and it's traditions, the promise of so much unfulfilled. The real story of what should have been as the years go by sees the legend of Busby and his Babes grow. In an era of sterile premiership football with its superstars who earn a king's ransom yet have very little in the way of personality, and who seem to have nothing in common with the fans who idolise them, the Babes stand out as a team from us and for all of us who dared to dream of wearing the glorious red of our beloved Manchester United, To wear the shirt with a certain style and panache. Like the city of Manchester, never boastful, just certain in the knowledge it's being done in a certain way, the proper way, the Busby way. Time will see if we ever produce another crop of youth, it's been done twice, but in all fairness the first time we did it was like getting a glimpse of paradise. Maybe it was just too much for us mere mortals to take in. God bless the Babes.

JOHN DUFFY

My Munich memories are quite vague. I was born July 55, so was only two years, seven months old, but my older siblings and cousins never stopped talking about the Babes, and what a side they were and more appropriately, what they would have gone on to become. I'm the second youngest of eight kids and the age gap between me and my eldest brother Seamus was fifteen years. He indeed could have been a Babe himself, Seamus was that good and at 16, Jimmy Murphy tried to sign him, but he was indentured to the Daily mirror and earning fabulous money even then. So being a major breadwinner in the family Seamus stayed at the Mirror. The rest is history as they say. Five days after the crash he was asked along with a friend, Richard Larkin, to a trial at Old Trafford, as they were so desperate for players. They played a young Celtic side who'd been sent down from Glasgow to try and help the cause. So, you can imagine the legacy Munich left on me and my family. Sir Matt was also revered in our house. His Irish heritage was always mentioned. He was by far in my opinion the greatest of all time. To climb out of a hospital bed, win an FA Cup, two League titles and a European cup after losing virtually a whole team just ten years later. Wow, that's some achievement.

NICOLE DEANS

I remember them in February,
I remember them when I hear the calypso.
I remember them as forever legendary,
I remember them in every football high and low.
Without them, we wouldn't be us. A reminder of fragility, of how precious life is. A reminder of what Manchester United truly means yesterday, today and tomorrow. They will always be. In a flicker of an old film, of vintage pictures few, your heart stops as you see the flowers of Manchester. Our Busby Babes who gave it all, yet could have given so much more if fate would have allowed.
They represent the heart and soul of the club I fell in love with. They are etched into every kick off and every full time whistle. And will never stop paving the way for future players, those of which I implore to look back to find and make a path forward. May they always rest in peace and eternally stay in the minds and hearts of the fans who will never ever forget them. What do they mean to me? Absolutely everything we stand for.

DARREN WEBB

Watching all the videos of the terrible accident makes me still cry to this day. My mum used to tell me how brilliant the Busby Babes were, and how they would have ruled England and Europe for many years. I just wish I had born to watch this team live. If we ever go on holiday and someone spots my shorts when by the pool they always mention the Busby Babes, whatever part of the world I'm in. That says it all to me.

NEZ BAKER

Munich still weighs heavy on my heart. It really is for me what United are all about. As a teenage Stretford Ender and then United Road, with older lads, I loved it, but I always knew there was something magnetic about this club. Enter the BBC VHS videos. 101 great goals being my first purchase. Then the history of Manchester United narrated by John Motson. There's a clip in there of Stan Pearson talking about Duncan Edwards, he had a tear in his eye as it showed you a clip of Duncan training. I was 17, as they say, the rest is history. From that day on and every game I've attended, I've always thought about the Babes, always. It's hard to explain because as a teenager you went to Old Trafford to sing your heart out, but I knew in my heart it was deeper than that. I've seen it all and only missed one game away in 1999, Lodz. United is the most magical thing. But in hindsight this would have never happened if not for Matt Busby and more importantly Jimmy Murphy. I will die a happy man.

RAY MORGAN

My first memories of Munich were getting off the 42 bus from Xaverian college to Piccadilly, to catch the 55 to Church Lane. I walked through Lewis' arcade at the end of which news vendors were shouting about United plane crash with many casualties. I stood

in silence listening to the comments from people which left me stunned initially, then a deep sense of loss at what had happened to our team. I caught the bus home and all the conversation was about the crash. My mum and dad got home from work and we watched the news on BBC. No instant reports in those days but grainy black and white news film exposed the scale of the disaster while the number of deaths among the players staff and reporters was announced. City legend Frank Swift among them, which always makes the City fans arm waving Munich songs very ironic. The next few days were passed in a blur with me and my dad talking about our games together, including the 7-2 hammering of Bolton, which was our last sight of so many of the Babes. One thing that struck me during this period and when the caskets started arriving home was that it never seemed to get light with permanent drizzle as though the heavens were crying. We were among thousands who watched the Babes return, but never in our worst nightmare did we expect their return in such a heartbreaking manner. The sense of loss was atmospheric and palpable. The grief like a physical force to all there. Among the survivors, Sir Bob, Bill Foulkes and Harry Gregg would return and play sooner than expected. The injured survivors remained in Munich and included Sir Matt and the mighty Dunc which was a light at the end of a very dark tunnel. That light was all but extinguished when the Big Man eventually succumbed to his fatal injuries, while Sir Matt and the remainder recovered, although some never to play again.
"Man United will never die" was the call then and since.

RAVI TEJA ANDAPAKA

To me personally, the Busby Babes are not just a distant memory or a chapter in a book. They are an integral part of our footballing consciousness, a timeless testament to the human spirit's ability to triumph over tragedy. Time may not age those lads, but in the hearts of fans like me and many, their legacy remains forever young and eternally inspiring. Unruffled and untroubled, may your celebratory sleep last lads. I remain grateful and faithful to the ''Gospel'' I call Manchester United.

DR. GARRETT McGOVERN

Being an Irish lad from Dublin, "Cross Channel" football was a huge lure for all of us. In those early, largely trophy barren, years I was keenly aware of the history of this great club. I learnt about the crash at Munich through football annuals, newspaper cuttings and the oft repeated *Pathe* News footage of the 1968 European Cup final win over Benfica. The pictures of Matt coming on to the pitch at the final whistle, being hugged by the jubilant players, ten years after losing most of his team on a snowy Munich runway, are so poignant. History changed on 6th February 1958. We didn't just lose most of our great team but we lost a chunk of history. This great bunch of players, most of them barely out of their teens were beginning to challenge the great Real Madrid side Sadly, this was never to be. Possibly one of the greatest rivalries in football never happened. One player stands above the others amongst the Babes of that era. When the late, great Sir Bobby Charlton says that Duncan Edwards was the only player who made him feel inferior, you realise how good this lad was. An England regular by the time of the crash and he was only 21. I'll finish with a little tale about Duncan. Manchester United. Many years ago I travelled to Manchester for a midweek European tie and was on a train talking to a couple of mates about the great George Best. As the train pulled into Piccadilly station, a frail elderly lady pulled me by the arm and said. "I've been following United since 1948 and let me tell you, I've seen many great players in that time, but none of them have come anywhere close to Duncan Edwards." That was enough for me.

TREVOR DWYER-LYNCH

I was born in June 1958, four months after The Munich air disaster. My Mam was from Salford and she knew Eddie Colman well as both families lived in Ordsall. She and my Gran told me how the community converged on Old Trafford when news spread of the catastrophe. This date holds immense significance for me as a

Manchester United fan and the millions around the world as it represents not just a football tragedy, but a profound loss within the club's history. The resilience shown in the aftermath and the eventual rebuilding of the team under manager Matt Busby and Jimmy Murphy contribute to the emotional connection fans have with the events on 6th February symbolizing the club's spirit, passion and unity. As a player it's expected you exercise those very same values when you walk onto that Old Trafford pitch. THIS IS MAN UNITED NOT THE DOG & DUCK pub team. Play for the shirt, play for the fans, play for those who died paving the way for you to belong to the greatest Club in The World!

SEAN BONES

I wasn't fortunate to be born early enough to see the Busby Babes play and grace the hallowed Old Trafford turf. I was lucky enough to be good friends with Tom Clare. Tom could almost put you back in those Incredible times in United's history. Those young lads played without fear, their style of football was mesmerising, they played attacking football at pace with an incredible beauty and a precision. Enchanting the football world. When they crossed the white line onto the field, at such a young age it would have been easy for them to have been intimidated, but this was a very special group of lads. This wonderful, young United team well on their way to the summit of European football. Then the tragedy of Munich struck. The whole future of Manchester Utd flickered in the cold and darkness of those times. The great Jimmy Murphy somehow through the pain and devastation that engulfed him, from losing so many of the lads he loved and worshiped. Jimmy didn't give up and from deep within found the energy to lift the football club on his shoulders and carry on in the memory of the boys he had lost. As supporters, each year on the 6th February at 3.04.pm, we gather at Old Trafford, remembering and praying for the players and passengers who lost lives and their families and loved ones. We are also so thankful to the doctors and nurses in Munich who saved the life of Sir Matt Busby. He once

Said: ''Manchester United football club is at its best when it comes together as a family.'' There is no more greater testament of that than when United supporters gather under the Munich clock each 6th February, to remember those who perished and to sing the ''Flower Of Manchester'' together as Reds.

CHRIS ROBERTS

Munich and The Busby Babes are about many things: the last line-up, the forgotten game in Belgrade, the darkness then the light; grainy runway images of wreckage and snow; players in hospital; coffins; funerals; the grief of Manchester; the guilt of Busby; the nameless team sheet; Jimmy Murphy; the clock (3.04); the anniversaries; the eternal flame; Bobby of '58, '68' 08 (Moscow); the players who survived but were never the same again; Wembley ten years on. My thoughts are bookended by one man, Duncan Edwards and a question. What if? What if Arsenal players had gained revenge for an injury to one of their players by injuring Duncan Edwards during United's 5-4 win in their last game in England before Munich. He wouldn't have travelled, wouldn't have played, wouldn't have died. In 1958, most recognised Duncan as far and away the best player, some say he would have been the England captain of the '66 World Cup winning team. My thoughts begin with that last game against Arsenal, what Duncan had achieved already at such a young age and what he could have achieved if he lived. My thoughts end with a personal final chapter relating to Duncan. I feel great emotion reading a book written by my father (The Team That Wouldn't Die) that was sent to relatives of the players who died at Munich prior to publication. Sarah Ann Edwards, Duncan's mother, sent a hand-written letter saying thank you for the book and that they will give it pride of place with Duncan's other things in his cabinet and will always treasure it. I will be forever touched by Munich, a place that took so much away, yet in some ways is seen as the start of the history of the modern Manchester United.

PETE MOLYNEUX

I was born in 1954, Manchester United became my team after the FA Cup Final win over Leicester City, nine years later. I became fascinated, then eventually addicted to following this club. Before my Dad would take me to actual matches around September 1964. I would read voraciously about ANYTHING to do with Manchester United's history. Like many, I was particularly drawn-in by the morbid fascination of the Munich Air crash. Only four when it happened, I knew nothing about it. So I read anything I could. At Christmas family get togethers I'd ask my uncles about what they knew. Few words were forthcoming, it was still raw, too soon to talk about. My research taught me how wonderful the Babes had been, how Busby dreamed of United taking on the best sides in Europe and his adopted city conquering this continent's finest. His young team played with derring-do, going forward with power and pace to try and win the game in style. This was the "United way". "Football played by Matt Busby" as the song goes. Over the next four years I witnessed United conquer their Everest, sweeping aside Real Madrid and Benfica to become the first English team to lift the European Cup in May 1968. The driving force behind this achievement was forged by the triumph of the Babes plus the tragedy that robbed them of their rightful place in football history. The crucible was Old Trafford; the welders were Busby and Jimmy Murphy. They perfected the template for all Manchester United sides since, and for all those who wear our shirt in future.

PAUL BOOTH

I wasn't around at the time of the Munich air disaster, but my late mother was. She was 13-years-old and the family had a newsagent's in Stretford. So my memories of Munich come from her. Every once in a while in her later years we would rest a while longer at the dinner table when my children had gone off to play, and pour an extra glass of wine and talk. Sometimes this led to memories of her youth and

Munich was a subject painted vividly. Her story was not of watching the news of events - it was of selling it. And by her accounts the shop floor was covered in the tears of their customers as they took their papers and wept. So the disaster for me brings thoughts of the suffering of that young girl, the community the shop served and those poor young men who were lost and hurt so cruelly, and whose faces I know despite our lives not coinciding. It also brings thoughts of resilience, rebirth and new life, of how the club went marching on, always retaining their hopes of glory and keeping those Babes in our hearts.

ROSE MILLS

Like many an Irish man of his generation my da went over to England for work, he settled in Birmingham and worked as a labourer before meeting my mother and returning to Dublin in 1959, a great man for a yarn, his whole face would light up telling about the time he saw the Babes playing against Villa, majestic was one of the words he would use. How proud he was as a Dublin man of Liam Whelan and the shock of hearing the news of the crash and the sadness of the loss of the Babes. My mother had six brothers most of whom were sporty, and she always spoke about some of them crying like babies at the news of Munich. I was born in late 1966 but it's like I've always know about Munich and the Busby Babes. I never fail to walk through the Munich tunnel when I'm visiting Old Trafford, Match days or not and say a wee prayer for the dream that died.

TONY STREET

The Busby Babes, apart from the wonderful footballing skills, the first thought is Munich. I was a junior player at Manchester United in the Babes era and in complete awe of these wonderful footballers. First reports suggested casualties but little detail, then more information. Players and journalists among the dead. At first I simply couldn't absorb this information, refused to believe it. Back at Old Trafford I turned up for a training session to be told, "you may as well go home Tony we'll be in touch regarding the situation." If I remember correctly, Mujacs. B and A teams didn't play for a fortnight, all efforts concentrating on the first team. I'm 83 now but still shed a tear every anniversary. God bless all who perished.

BEN ALLEN

Growing up in Dublin, I was always very aware of the Babes. My Dad saw them in Dublin in 57, and the loss of Liam Whelan is still felt. He'd wax lyrical about the team. Edwards and "Snake Hips" Colman in particular and Roger Byrne. By 77/78 I had become besotted with United and remember the entire family (mother included) watching in silence the 20th anniversary BBC programme on the crash. I couldn't process the fact they played thirteen days later against Sheffield Wednesday, nor the run to Wembley. The bravery of Gregg, the bravery, defiance of the club. And the tragedy of it all. In 68, I was just 4, but I always remember my Dad and brother watching the final and me peeping from upstairs. The cheers, the celebrations in extra time. Winning it for those who died. The miracle of the club rising from the ashes was often discussed. To this day, The Team that Wouldn't Die (I got it in 78) remains a prized possession. Extraordinary really that from across the water, such a (in those days) distant event could seem so close and impact our lives in the way it did.

SEAN BRETT

When I first left school I worked in an Insurance brokers in Chorlton. Sir Matt Busby was a Director, when he called in I used to brew up for him. We had a mutual friend called Tommy Fallon, who I played snooker with four times a week. Tommy would always talk about "The crash". He was at Sir Matt's house the night before that fateful trip. Whenever he spoke about it he cried like a child, something I never forgot. How such a terrible thing could make a man weep in an instant, and he wasn't alone in that. An indelible stain in the history of our club, and our city that will be honoured forever more.

CAROLINE D'ARCY

It was the newsreel footage that did it for me. All in black and white, of course. A tough Northern city in the February cold. Dark streets lined with white-faced people under headscarves and hats and caps, crammed silently together as they watched their team come home from Munich. Fit young athletes who used to go to training and matches on the bus or on their bikes, coming home to Old Trafford in a convoy of sleek black funeral cars. Even years later, it's all but unbearable to watch. The voiceover in that long gone staccato BBC accent, crisply narrating something almost incomprehensible in its devastation: "Great players….. were borne in the slow cortège. Along the route to the club ground, one hundred thousand people stood in homage." One hundred thousand people. It's easy, in these days of the half a million quid a week footballer, to dismiss or misunderstand what Manchester United meant then and what it still means today. Munich was dreams and guts and blood and a million tears. It shaped my football club and my allegiance to it. Never forgotten.

VINNY THOMPSON

What do the babes and Busby mean to me? Someone once said ya win nowt with kids. In my honest opinion these kids,(average age 22), would have won the lot. Robert Nestah Marley spoke of a "natural mystic" well Matt Busby, although adopted, was our Manc Mystic. My dad loved the bones off him and consequently so did I. Matt and the Babes were both unique and legendary. The team, Jimmy Murphy and Sir Matt set the template for how things would be at this club in the future. To paraphrase The Stone Roses they were "The Resurrection and the light". They carried the torch of Mancunian defiance and graft afraid of nothing and no one. After the crash those left didn't just get on with it, but took the spirit of the Babes to go on to be world beaters. As a kid in the Stretty and a teenager among naughtiness in the Scoreboard, we sang: "You'll never die, we'll keep the red flag flying high." The significance of those words and that song only came with age. God bless Matt, Jimmy and the Babes who inspired the future red shirted heroes to keep that red flag flying high.

ROGER@UiNeillAD371

Munich. I wasn't born. As a child I didn't understand what it meant. I mean, I was just a kid. To me football was United, United and George Best. As I got older, I grew to know what Munich was. The players, the people, the club. A tragedy What could have been. Trailblazers. Dreamers. People like you and me. Proud. Manchester United. Living the dream. United are everything but in that moment it meant nothing to the families, relatives, fans, oh what they must have felt. I still get emotional but it is different to other tragedies. The journey, the love affair continues, we dream, we remember, we celebrate. As Fergie said: "Football, eh."

JOHN STEPNEY

Hearing the words "Munich' 'and "Busby" generally make me stop whatever I'm doing, the importance of these words is somehow ingrained in me. Being United daft since a kid in the early 70's, I knew about Matt Busby and the devastating plane crash back in 1958. I knew that in a way, what happened kind of built United, the world mourned, fans of every team were stunned. For me, words can't really explain what was taken from the club in the crash, my lack of words is probably my way of showing respect as it's just way too sad and overwhelming, it means too much. My dad played for United under Matt Busby and I got to meet the great man many times, Matt always remembered my name, always. For me, Busby was a leader of men in the very best way, he led with strength, honesty and by trusting his players. My dad's voice, when he's asked about Busby, goes a notch lower. I'm not sure he knows he does it, but I've noticed. It means a lot to me to hear that. Sir Matt Busby was, in my humble opinion, the greatest football manager ever. His achievement of winning the English league title followed by the European cup just ten years after Munich is unmatched.

WASSIM KABBANI

So what impact did Munich have on myself? Initially not a lot, I was aware of the songs mocking the disaster, but I hadn't realised how much of an impact the disaster had on not just Manchester United, but English football as a whole. A documentary as part of the 25th year anniversary was shown on TV, explaining how this team of young talent nurtured by Sir Matt and Jimmy Murphy sweeping all before them domestically, and well on the way to doing the same in Europe, had been decimated. That sparked an interest in me to learn more about this team. At the time, there was no internet so, it was books and newspaper articles that were my only source of info. From time to time I allow myself to drift off and imagine what might have occurred if Munich never happened. In Europe, the famed Real Madrid team would still have won the European Cup, but certainly not five years in a row. In '58 United weren't far away and I'm convinced that they would have won two, maybe three European Cups. George Best would have complemented a side that was outstanding already and with his added talent…So, what does Munich now mean to me? It means that the lads who passed away, left a blueprint for all those that have followed. Breath taking football, full of speed, skill and desire. A club that will always give its own a chance to go and play for the shirt. The red flag will always be kept high and Man United will never die.

DAVE COLEMAN

I was born on 7th May 1958, just three months after the Munich Tragedy. My paternal grandfather was an Irish immigrant worker with LY&R, my father was born in Denton. I had four older sisters and an older brother all dyed in the wool reds. My father saw the Babes play at Burnden Park but couldn't go to a United match again after the air crash. My eldest sister and her boyfriend were at Old Trafford for the first match after the crash. My brother had a framed print of the MEN picture of the Babes on the wall. My father taught me all the names of the Babes so he would say the first name, l would say the surname all this before I was 2! It was drummed into me that these boys gave their lives for the club my family loved and we should never let them be forgotten. They are the heart of Manchester United, the epitome of the "United Way." The Busby Babes are everything l want Manchester United to be. To be famous for and be remembered for.

KATH PARKER

The Busby Babes, like many of my generation is how my United journey began. My dad moved to Manchester from Ireland in 1948, when our Captain was Johnny Carey, a fellow Cork man. He began going to games and after he moved to Oxford in the early 50's he continued to follow the team when they played in London and the midlands. His favourite players were Bill Foulkes and Duncan Edwards. My mum said that the only time she saw my dad cry was on 6th February 1958, when the news came through. More tears followed when Duncan finally gave in to the terrible injuries he suffered. I grew up on these stories and it can't help but bind you to the club in a very unique and special way. I met Bill Foulkes walking to Wembley in 1994, and it remains one of my very special days.

YASMIN GOVENDER

When I think of The Babes, I feel the rush of an era passed. The goosebumps on my skin remind me that giants walked among us. The likes of players of their calibre may never be seen again. This team was the foundation our great club was built on. The Flowers Of Manchester. Eight lives lost so tragically. Their sweet fragrance snuffed out before the world could fully appreciate their remarkable scent. Diamonds in the rough, picked up and polished to perfection. A team like no other, they won when the odds were stacked against them. When they lost, they'd come back fighting. A resilience that spoke volumes to the working class fans who packed stadiums to cheer them on. They left to conquer in Europe and sadly not all returned. Survivors left with emotional scars that were carried throughout their lives. Sir Matt Busby, Sir Bobby Charlton, Bill Foulkes, Ray Wood and the ultimate hero to me, in Harry Gregg, who went back into the wreckage to save his teammates and civilians, one of whom was a baby. I can't remember The Babes without all of this running through my mind. A team who epitomised the meaning of determination, grit, blood, sweat and tears. As the anniversary of this tragic disaster looms, may we never forget that they were unsung heroes, giants of men, courageous and honourable. Boys who became legends, yet never to become men. May their beautiful talented souls forever Rest In Peace.

DONNA HINDLEY

Growing up and understanding what it meant to be a United fan, the Busby Babes were always there. You knew, you just sensed, that there was a history, a gravitas behind the team that had come from the trauma of what happened in Munich. My nana would get teary eyed still when describing the final journey of the "boys" into Old Trafford, and we would sit watching grainy footage but it was too hard to imagine what it must have been like. How it must have felt back then when Bobby would get the bus with the fans and Eddie Colman was a regular sighting on the Salford streets. They were their boys. Just imagine.

HASSAN MOHAMMAD

The Busby Babes to most United fans abroad are ghostly figures who paid the ultimate price for the badge, in a grim twist of fate they were taken in their prime. Very few know the details of the story and the men beyond the names and pictures. it takes more effort to know them better and I'm happy I did go the extra mile, through reading, and watching docs and match highlights. it broke my heart to learn how so many good lads, and so much talent was taken away at the end of that runway. How a City was consumed by grief for a bunch of young lads in red shirts. to me they're the martyrs of United, the ones through whom the soul and the legend of Manchester United manifested giving faces and names to what this club stands for, its standards and how to play "the United way". It also became a matter of what-ifs, what if they survived? What if big Dunc was spared? What would they have accomplished had they played with Best and Law? So many if's, but one truth, forged by their legend, rises above all. United will always rise from the ashes.

ADAM MARSHALL

I feel I understand just what Munich means to the very essence of Manchester United. My father greatly admired the Reds, his favourite player was Eddie 'Snakehips' 'Colman, one of those to tragically lose his life in the disaster. Although a Londoner, the strength of his love for the club grew even stronger after 1958, and they were always going to be the team he supported. Of course, he passed that on to me and ensured I knew all about Munich and the devastating impact it had. I wondered just how good Duncan Edwards would have become, particularly when my dad told me the surgeon examining his body after the crash said he was the fittest human specimen he had ever come across. I'd attended Munich tributes before and been in the crowd for the 50th anniversary against City, which was beautifully orchestrated. Yet nothing could come close to how I felt ten years later, when I was in Belgrade with Nicky Butt's Under-19s for a UEFA Youth League game. After visiting the stadium where Busby's boys drew 3-3 with Red Star, we attended the Majestic Hotel. This was the scene of the Babes' last meal together and the menus were still on display from that night. It was an eerie place to visit, and one where I could literally feel the emotion charging through me and almost a ghostly presence. I'd never felt more connected to Munich and the club, and it only emphasised just how utterly privileged I am to work for United because of how much it means to me.

MIKE GASKELL

I was less than 2-years-old on 6th February 1958, but ten years later I was voraciously reading a copy of the late David Meek's great book on the crash at Munich Airport. Born and brought up in St Helens and living within earshot of the old Knowsley Road ground on the other side of Taylor Park, my sporting starting point was Rugby League, but my older sister started covering her Alice in Wonderland wallpaper with pictures of Denis Law, Bobby Charlton, David Herd and Paddy Crerand which started my journey towards United. At first I had leaned towards Everton, enthralled by the stories told on the bus to junior school by a lady who caught the Number 7 into town with me, my mum and younger brothers at the same time each school day. But in the end, mum declared that Matt Busby was "a good Catholic" so we should support United. Then my dad said that Bill Foulkes who had survived the crash was from St Helens and that his mum lived across the street from us. That did it for me. I spent hours and hours reading David Meek's book from cover to cover. It made a deep impression, from the heroism of Harry Gregg and Bill Foulkes to the deep sadness of the deaths of many, particularly Duncan Edwards. In short, the Busby Babes, Busby, Munich and the aftermath through the 1960s are the reasons why I have been and will remain a supporter.

STEVE GRAINGER

When I think of the 6th February, the Darkest Day in United's History, I am often overcome with a tidal wave of emotions!

Pain-The loss of eight of the greatest players the British game has ever produced. And we cannot forget Walter Crickmer, Tom Curry and Bert Whalley also lost their lives. Johnny Berry and Jack Blanchflower who fortunately survived the crash, never played again. The Busby Babes had illuminated both domestic and European football, and would have continued to do so for many years if not for that fateful day in Munich.

Sorrow-There is so many 'If's and But's' surely if not for the tragic plane crash the famous Busby Babes would've have conquered Europe long before 1968. Sir Bobby stated, England would have probably won the World Cup in 62, 66 and 70, and the great Duncan Edwards would've been the captain. One thing is for certain, the tragic loss of life at Munich not only threw a dark shadow over English football, but world football.

Pride-Amazingly, the club came back from The Ashes of that Munich runway and Sir Matt and Jimmy Murphy, built a third great United team that eventually conquered Europe.

Faith-The Busby Babes will live in our hearts forever. I was in Munich for the 65th commemoration and I was comforted to see so many young United supporters there. And just as it happened at Old Trafford, five years earlier, just after 3.00.pm on the 6th at Manchesterplatz, a flurry of snow fell over us. A sign that past players, managers and staff were with us? Because of the Flowers of Manchester, We Will Keep the Red Flag Flying High, And Man United Will Never Die.

JOHN DORWARD

I don't know when or how it came about, but I remember my dad telling me about the Busby Babes and the Munich disaster. I remember him telling me about all these young players, players I had never seen play, never known, and a Scottish manager who had risen again like a Phoenix. Then how the club had recovered years later to become kings of Europe. This football team was different to any other team I had known or heard about. This team, this club felt mythical. From that moment on, United was etched in my conscious as a team I had to follow, a team I had to see play, a team I wanted to be part of. It took me a long time to get to Old Trafford, but as soon as I saw the stadium, the hairs on the back of my neck stood up, and I could hear my dad's voice telling me that same story again. I was about to be part of the myth and magic that is Manchester United.

SHANE WILLIAMS

I wasn't lucky enough to witness the Babes first hand but have been blessed to spend time in the company of some who did. From their memories, and from the precious footage that exists, I've always felt great pride that Busby's youthful side pioneered English football's foray into Europe with such style. Then even prouder that their spirit lived on in the rebuilding of a team that went on to win a European Cup ten years later. We can talk about league titles, European Cups and trebles but the Babes reign above all that. And then in the aftermath of tragedy, putting a side out versus Sheffield Wednesday less than two weeks after the crash, and somehow going on to reach the FA Cup final that same season, for me sits above any achievement since. Munich defined the MUFC I fell in love with. Those who died always remembered and respected, and no more so than in Trudering where I am always moved by how the locals have looked after the lovely memorials at Manchesterplatz. But from that tragedy rose a remarkable spirit, to not just continue but to go on to reach unimaginable successes. We owe it all to them.

PATRICK NICHOLL

Silence is deafening. I was only 15, but I still felt the intense anxiety in the air in the lead up to the match and the huge significance of what that day meant. It was February 2008, United v City, a derby day that just happened to fall around the 50th anniversary of the Munich Air Disaster. I went with my cousin Mike, only 17 himself. We had a usual routine at Old Trafford-get into the ground and wolf down a jumbo sausage roll, while Mike tried to get someone to buy us a pint, if he couldn't get served himself. But then when we got to our seats there was nothing "usual" about the scene. Red, black and white scarves adorned every single one, so many yet untouched like an immaculate graveside memorial. "The Flowers of Manchester" played just before the teams walked out, replacing the usual "This Is The One" by The Stone Roses. The entire crowd deafeningly sang "We'll

Never Die" around the ground as 75,000 plus scarves were held aloft in unison, while the pipers played. And then…SILENCE. And it was the silence that broke me. The thought of the dreams of those lads hit me like a tidal wave of emotion. Tears streamed down my face. They were ALL one of us. It made me realise that the history of your community, and the people in it, transcends your age and the passage of time. And of course, life itself always transcends football. I'm not sure I've ever felt anything as powerful as that at a match again, or ever will. I made a short film in 2017 called 'The Spirit of '58' (set in 1999) symbolically recalls the strength of those lads, our Busby Babes, in the search for inspiration in the lead character's struggles. They were bigger than football. They were every single one of us that has ever strived for a dream.

ANNEMARIE DRAY

The Munich air disaster of 1958 is the darkest day in Manchester United's history, and the loss of eight footballers among the twenty-three that perished in the German snow is a loss so enormous it still resonates today. To pause and think of goalkeeper Harry Gregg pulling his teammates out of the wreckage of a burning plane in the midst of a blizzard, or the manager Sir Matt Busby being administered the last rites when doctors didn't think he would survive his injuries is imagery so heavy it would catch in your chest. The tragedy robbed the world of the Busby Babes and young footballers like 21-year-old Duncan Edwards. Edwards was a player portrayed as being so perfect and so complete a player that it's difficult to imagine he ever really existed at all. I've often felt envious pangs at those that were blessed to watch this almost mythical footballer Sir Bobby Charlton described as "colossal" live. Whenever things have become a little tough on the pitch and in the moments the football hasn't been so easy on the eye in the last decade, I always remind myself that this football club has been through unimaginable tragedy and still refused to die. And that the bravery of the men surviving a burning plane forever shaped Manchester United.

TONY McCORMICK

Born in the Pit village of Ferryhill, County Durham, I am quite often asked: "How come you support Man U?" I used to give them the honest answer of watching Match Of The Day with my Dad and asking him: "Who is the baldy man with the hard shot and who is the man who doesn't pass to anyone?" As my love for the greatest club in the world grew, including the 1974-75 season, history to me wasn't what they attempted to teach you at St Johns Comprehensive School in Bishop Auckland, County Durham, it was finding out for myself why I loved Manchester United, when I was expected to find a team from the North East, as United were now in the second tier. Newcastle and Sunderland? Not bloody likely! My dear father, Bill was a 'Boro fan but not a fan the way I was with United. Dad was more like, well, he just liked to see them doing well. History research led me to discover the tragedy of Munich and desperate loss of life including a number of the Busby Babes. I got my first library book out 'The Manchester United Book No.4' by the much-missed David Meek. It was released in 1969 and covered the European Cup win and how it evolved from a broken aeroplane ten years earlier with the loss of eight first team players. Knowledge is Googled these days, but wisdom has to be acquired and Sir Matt Busby was one of the wisest men of football who passed on princely amounts of what he knew to those with ears to hear. God bless the Busby Babes.

BARBARA MILLS

Born in 1940, my dad took me to see United in the winter and Lancashire in the summer, a real Manchester thing to do. I was about 15-years-old when I was allowed to watch the home team play, I wasn't allowed to go to away games, but that didn't matter as the reserves were superb, and of course became The Busby Babes! My heart throbs were David Pegg and Duncan Edwards and I was distraught at their deaths. Sadly, I never had any personal encounters with the Babes, after all they were gods in our eyes ,and the impact the crash had was huge. I learnt of it at school from the teachers and we were so upset that the school closed early as we were all in shock. A few days later my friend Sheila and I made our way to the airport to wait for the dead to come home. This was long before social media and mobile phones! The crowds were huge and most were in tears, including us and we tried not very successfully to talk about United and our times at Old Trafford. It was pouring with rain but the players and journalists were, in our minds, our friends and so we waited for hours until the hearses drove slowly past us and we could pay our respects and then we, along with the sodden crowds, left for home, which they would never do again. At the first match back, United v Sheffield Wednesday in the FA Cup, we were all silent, very sad and numb with shock, as it was the equivalent of several members of our family dying. The young reserves soon had us cheering and made Manchester United come alive once again as they won 3-0. I felt very proud to be there and be a very small cog in a giant wheel of United fans.

PETE MARTIN

I arrived home from school so it must have been about 4.00.pm. Me mam said there had been something about Manchester United in a plane crash. My immediate thought was that me mam surely wouldn't joke about something like that, so it must be true. The next news on the wireless wasn't till six o'clock, we didn't have a television. 6.00.pm, horror struck, this wasn't a play on the wireless, it was true, the plane had crashed at Munich airport. The news said that the plane had caught fire after take-off and some players, known as the Busby Babes, had lost their lives. I'm from a big family and somebody in the family must have known somebody who worked for the Manchester Evening Chronicle because we received phone calls giving us updates through the night, bad news that was confirmed when the nine o'clock news came on. Some of the victims were named by this time but they are lost to me now. At school, the next morning I heard lurid stories from other 9-10 year olds about the condition of some of the victims. I had never witnessed this atmosphere before – total shock and horror!

Looking back now I am so very grateful for the survivors. Harry, every inch a hero (I wrote a song with that title), Bobby, the supreme footballer (another song about Bobby). The names are all there and the memories come flooding back, seeing photos in the newspaper of crowds lining the streets as hearses drove past carrying our broken superstars. Now, on every anniversary of this most shocking days, we hold a memorial service under the Munich plaque outside Old Trafford to pay tribute to all the victims, those who died and those who survived. We strive to keep alive the memory of this great loss to our community.

MARK GILLIGAN

The Munich Air Disaster is my earliest recollection of anything in life. We lived off the dock road near to The Boro picture house on London Street. I was upstairs in my bedroom and I vividly recall my dad coming up sobbing, and he came to me and hugged me. His father had just died and it was the day of the plane crash. Obviously, I wasn't fully aware but I cried too. My next recollection is standing with him on the dock road, holding dad's hand. It was silent but there must have been thousands lining the route. The sound of horses hooves broke the silence and people began crying as one of the Babes was being taken to the cemetery. Everyone was in tears. I have never forgotten it. Fast forward to Sir Matt's passing and I too did exactly the same with my son as his coffin passed by Old Trafford. I wrote about it (I am a pro photographer and writer) and it was used in the United magazine. My team my love.

DEREK MANTON

I worked at A & S Walkers in King Street, just off Albert Square. They were a stationers and printing shop. I was 15, (1952), when I started in a six-year apprenticeship as a compositor. The printing section was in the cellar, well below street level. On 6th February 1958. At 4.30.pm, the foreman came to me and said that the United plane had crashed. I said that if this is going to be a joke I didn't think it was funny. He said no, and there had been some deaths. We didn't get much news for the rest of the day. The next morning my Dad came to wake me up to go to work. He had been listening to the radio and started naming the known dead. I just rolled over and sobbed and sobbed.

PAUL HOLMES

My dad was an avid United supporter, following them home and away with his mates. He was 24 in 1958 and worked in Manchester as an accountant, I was born two years later and it would be when I was 9 or 10 that he'd tell me about how he felt about the Busby Babes and the disaster. Dad was heading home from work to catch the bus to Unsworth (near Whitefield) and he saw people with sad faces and tearful shocked looks. Passing a news stand he caught the headline United Flight Crashed, and then discovered the terrible news of the Munich air disaster. Dad was heartbroken that his heroes were dead or badly injured, he would listen to the radio for updates on Matt Busby's condition and got the sad news of Duncan Edwards passing days later. He would tell me how good the team was and the expectation of what could be achieved. I can only relate to how we felt when the class of 92 came through, how proud I felt seeing our young boys breaking into the first team and winning multiple titles.

JOHN

My uncle Dennis(winter) played for United juniors 59-61. On his first training session he could see everyone was a bit anxious waiting for the trainer. He didn't think much of it until the trainer arrived with the kit in a bucket. Everyone started scrambling for the kit and when he asked why? A fellow player said: "Nobody wants Duncan's number, it's seen as bad luck." He later told me a whole load of emotions went through him at that moment, the main ones being anger, and ultimately deep sadness.

GARY HOGAN

Of all the people and players involved in that great team and their untimely demise, I always think of three in particular. Billy Whelan, Duncan Edwards and Jimmy Murphy. Like me, Billy was a native of Dublin and lived my dream of heading to Manchester from Ireland to pull on the red shirt. It makes me heartsick to think of his poor family back home in Cabra receiving the news from Germany. Obviously, there are his stats, old newsreel footage and anecdotal evidence of just how good he was. It sounds like he was the kind of natural finisher that would've scored goals in any era. He died at just 22, with the potential to be mentioned alongside Giles, Keane, Brady and McGrath as the greatest Irish players of all time. Such a huge loss for his family, Utd and Ireland. My late father in-law was a huge fan of Duncan Edwards, who remained his favourite player. He didn't mind admitting that he cried the day he died. When I think of Duncan, I think of him. Seeing photos of Duncan and reading about his exploits, it seems like he was a combination of Robson and Keane! Can you imagine? Jimmy Murphy is the reason Manchester United exist as a football club today, it's as simple as that. His ceaseless dedication to keeping the club going forward following the disaster, against all odds, mark him out as one of the most important figures in the club's history. They will never be forgotten. RIP.

HUGH OBRIEN

As a young lad growing up in Manchester in the 1960's, the shadow of the Munich Air Disaster never left us. The emergence of another great side from 1965 brought hope and a sense of expectation to the supporters after the disaster. My Father was an Irish immigrant and we lived in Levenshulme, most of the Irish kids I knew were reds. He talked to me about the great United side who were devastated by the tragedy and how it impacted on the nation, not only Manchester. He said Manchester was in mourning and it took years to shake off the memories of the loss of such great footballers. He would make reference to the great Real Madrid side winning five European Cups in a row, and say it wouldn't have happened without the disaster as United were an exceptional team who were going to dominate both the English league and Europe. We watched the final versus Benfica on a black and white tv and I was swept up in the joy of the win and the celebration outside on the streets is stuck in my memory. I was a 7-year-old lad watching the game with my Dad, who had seen the great Busby Babes play many times, I remember him saying this is for the lads who will never be forgotten. I have embraced the United rollercoaster ever since those days with many great occasions. I still think Barcelona 99 has taken a couple of years of my life.

ROBERT BOLTON

I was only 2-years-old when possibly the greatest ever Utd team were decimated, but when I first saw Best, Law and Charlton play at the age of 9/10, I became obsessed with the club and its history, thanks to my Dad (RIP), and his newspaper collection. (some of which I still have) I learnt about the events of that fateful day, the heroics of Harry Gregg and the terrible sadness of the entire nation. This had quite an effect on me and prompted my obsession with collecting anything Utd related. Every year on the anniversary I take a minute to remember them and still do to this day. If I was ever at Old Trafford on the relevant date, I would always spend a little time in front of the memorial. To me Sir Matt and the Babes will always epitomise everything about Utd and the ethos of the club. To sum up, whenever I hear or read that yet another academy player has made the first team it always reminds me what Sir Matt started all those years ago, and that is the Legacy of the Busby Babes

MICHAEL JORDAN

Growing up in Moston in the 1970s my brother and I were privileged to be brought up as United fans. It was such a thrilling time to be taken by my Dad at the age of 6 to my first game in 1976 to see Tommy Doc's side. I followed them religiously either in person or more likely live on Piccadilly Radio or watching highlights on The Kick-Off Match. I considered myself to be so close to that team, and the ones that came later. Dad would listen to me talk about Coppell, Buchan and Macari and I asked him who he thought was best. Without any doubt in his mind, he always told me the greatest player that ever lived was Duncan Edwards. He used to smile as he remembered those magical days when Big Dunc won games from defence, midfield or attack and the pure joy The Babes gave to him as a teenager. He was convinced United would conquer Europe as Real Madrid had recently done. I always noticed that at this point of the conversation the smile left his face and was replaced by tears. The tragic event on that Munich runway took the heart of United's side and I believe the heart of Dad too. The 6th February 1958 was Dad's 18th birthday. The Babes weren't just a great side, they were young lads who fans knew and loved. Dad taught me about the team and players, and I became aware that although I felt close to my United team, it was nothing close to how Dad felt. To him, it seemed that not only had United's future been torn apart, but also his own. With the recent passing of Bobby, I just hope we don't start forgetting about United's greatest side.

PAUL COOK

As a United fan and a match going red you are very aware of Munich and The Busby Babes. Nobody sits you down and tells you what happened, it is like you learn by osmosis, it is just the very essence of the club. What do the Babes and Munich mean to Utd fans? Everything, they mean everything to us. They are outside the ground, the clock, the plaques and statues. They are inside the ground, with the songs that we sing and the banners around the stadium. They truly "will never die" We want our teams to be like them, great young footballers, some home grown, others not. All with a talent for playing fast, exciting, attacking football. Because of the Babes, the least we expect is that our teams wear the shirt with pride and dignity, no badge kissing just being united for United. We were always going to be a global club, after Sir Matt insisted on us playing in Europe, however I believe, sadly, the tragedy escalated that massively. I remember my dad, a Wolves fan from Dudley (like Duncan) who had his own heroes at that time, talking about the Babes with pride, passion and sadness in his voice. I think that says a lot, they really did touch all generations. We will never forget them. Every time an Academy player makes a first team debut, we are all buzzing and that is because of Sir Matt and the Babes. Keep the red flag flying high.

EMMA JACKSON

The Busby Babes will always hold a special place in every Manchester United supporters hearts. Although I wasn't alive at the time I was brought up with the history reading books and watching old footage in awe of what they achieved and the devastation of the lives that were lost I couldn't imagine if it happened in today world. Sir Matt and the Busby Babes spirit still runs through the club they are an inspiration. My love for Manchester United comes from them.

KAUSTUBH PANDEY

To me as a fan who supports United from afar but has lived in Salford in the past, the Busby Babes represent this image of footballing romance in an era which didn't have too much of it. They weren't just entrenched in the working class ethic of Manchester, but they played in a way which set them apart from the rest and they did that at such a young age. To me, what Sir Matt Busby created with that team is something so many managers struggle to do even in 2024. It is incredibly rare to see bunch of players who came through the club play a brand of football that lifts you off the seat, wins accolades and challenge the biggest teams in the world. It would still represent a dream scenario for so many managers out there and it is unlikely someone replicates it. What happened later shouldn't take away the fact that the Busby Babes were ahead of their time and while history could've been very different if the ill-fated disaster never happened, but the fact that they're still a model for the club to follow says a lot about how great they were and forever will be.

ASHLEY SHAW

My father, Peter Shaw, was born in 1934 so spent his formative years with the country at all-out war: rationing dictated what little food was available and an air raid siren seemed to go off every other day meaning long spells in an Anderson shelter in the back garden. To make matters worse his father, my grandad Arthur, was off around the world fighting the Axis powers in a jaunt that eventually saw him stationed in Singapore after the war. He wouldn't return to Manchester until 1948. When Arthur did return they bonded over football. From letters written by my dad as a child it's clear he grew up a City fan, but all that changed once Arthur came home and he guided him to the correct path and so the pair of them watched that great post-war team assembled by Matt Busby which packed out Maine Road and converted many a blue into a red. Mild-mannered Stan Pearson was my dad's favourite as the team won the FA Cup in '48 and the league title at the last knockings in '52.

If the '48 team had arrived fully formed then the Busby Babes were drip-fed to supporters as each season saw a new starlet blooded into the first team before they stormed to the title and then into Europe on foreign adventures. The Babes stood for modernity, optimism, a future free of rationing and Anderson Shelters. By the time I came along and started going to football my father had very much fallen out of love with the game - the hooliganism off the pitch and gamesmanship on it was completely alien to him. Tactics were for chess, he would say! But more than anything else he never recovered from the disaster. He wouldn't really talk about it and, although he kept going through the 60s and acquired a new hero in Denis Law, he abruptly gave it up after '68, job done. To sum up The Babes were football to my dad and he simply never got over that loss.

KATHERINE McDERMOTT

I remember the tears. They welled and bubbled. There were no words, not for a while anyway. There was an uneasy silence as I watched him cry. I thought he had lost someone close. A family member, or a friend. I thought I had done something wrong. I was only 5 at the time, so I probably had done. Then my dad softly said: "So much hope gone. They were so young and full of hope." All so young and not to be seen again. He then clutched his beloved Manchester United scarf, as if he was clutching to the last bit of hope. As if his life depended on it. You have to hold on to something, whether it's a memory or a scarf. Anything to hold on to and keep going. Hope is all he had then and all he had at the time the Busby Babes died. Hope is all many people had during the fifties. "They could've been great, Katherine. They were electric. Speed, magic, passion. They had it all. They never gave up." Happiness lit up in his eyes, like a flame in the tears. They made my dad feel they had something to look forward to. We all need that, don't we? " We carried on. That's what you must do. Never give up." It was a lesson for life and one I've never forgotten. I didn't understand it at the time, but I soon learnt the importance of it. My dad never met the Busby Babes. He didn't have to for them to mean something to him. They brought joy and hope. A light in the gloom. A fire on a cold and bitter day in Manchester. It was the loss of what was, what could've been. They brought people together. There was a beating heart of collective joy whenever they played, and a beating heart of solemness whenever they were remembered.

RAED ALDROUBI

Being a devoted Manchester United fan is more than a choice; it's a profound connection to a legacy, a passion ignited by the club's triumphs and the indomitable spirit embodied by the legendary Sir Matt Busby. For me, supporting United goes beyond wins and losses; it's a commitment to a rich history, a tapestry woven with moments of glory and resilience. Sir Matt Busby isn't just a name from the past;

he's a beacon of inspiration, a symbol of unwavering dedication to the Red Devils. The love for Busby is rooted in the genuine admiration for a man who not only led the team but also nurtured a philosophy of attacking football and youth development. As a fan, the mention of Sir Matt Busby stirs a deep sense of pride and nostalgia. His legacy transcends generations, connecting us to a time when the "Busby Babes" played with unbridled enthusiasm. The Munich air disaster wasn't just a tragedy; it became a testament to Busby's resilience as he rebuilt the team, showcasing a strength of character that resonates with every true supporter. In the ups and downs of United's journey, the love for the club and Sir Matt Busby remains unwavering. It's a sentiment that transcends the pitch, uniting fans globally in a shared passion. Sir Matt Busby's legacy lives on in the hearts of fans, an eternal flame that continues to illuminate the path for the Red Army.

SARKIS KHALOYAN

United, a team that never dies. Like the phoenix that rose from the ashes of Munich and never said impossible under any circumstance. United always finds a way to turn things around as they did throughout the history. I can only imagine what would have the Busby babes done and won trophies if that doomed day never happened, I wonder of Duncan Edwards how many times would have won the Ballon d'Or, how long we would have dominated in England even in Europe. Times are difficult again, but I believe we will rise again from the ashes one more time and as many times needed, because this is what Manchester United is made of and is. They always come back. Manchester United is more than a football team, it is a way of life. We eat, drink and breathe United. It is more than 90 minutes on the field, it is a whole lifetime. Once again, the spirit of the Busby babes is needed to help the team stand on its feet, to spread fear across England and Europe and the whole world. Once again, the Busby babes' determination is needed to keep working hard and push ourselves to the limit. We owe them a lot and must not give up on our team in these situations, because the Busby babes never did. Rest in peace Busby heroes, Manchester United will never die.

TRACEY MALONE

Since I was a kid I've always known about the Busby Babes. My dad was a bit of a lad in his day he loved Manchester United with a passion that was infectious. He went to every game, home, away, friendly he was there, I grew up on tales of the Babes. He had this record (LP) in the house, black and white by the spinners and that's the first time I heard the song the Flowers of Manchester. I was probably about 4/5 years old. He loved that song and I loved my dad so I played it over and over until I had memorised it. From that moment whenever we were in a pub with more than two United fans my dad would pull out a stool and say "Tracey. Flowers" and I would sing it. Never a dry eye in the house, it became my trademark, when I started going to the game myself, I started to realise the importance of this piece of our history and singing it became more personal for me. I used to get up on tables all over the country and my mates would send an ashtray round, years later to be asked to go and sing it at the crash site on the 60th anniversary was one of the proudest moments of my life. It was so special that year, I vividly remember being stood on the stage and as I started to sing it started to snow, I just about made it to the end of the song before my voice broke and the crowd helped with the last couple of lines. The last time when I was there for the 65th again so special, the German people put flags out of their houses to show support. I went back to the memorial site later that night and again the next morning when the crowds had gone to just reflect, all the flowers that had been laid were frozen, suspended in time and it made me cry. My generation never saw them play but I will always keep the memory alive and passed on to my son and his kids after. We will never die.

ROY TAYLOR

I was too young, and too far away from Manchester, to have seen the Babes. My father, a proud Scot, moved down to England after WW2 and he supported United, chiefly, because of the style of football plus it helped that Matt Busby was the manager. Dad regularly attended England v Scotland matches. His allegiance to a team (Scotland or United) was fierce but he always appreciated top players in the opposition ranks. He was in awe of Duncan Edwards. Our house, no television, always had the radio on. Home Service or the Light programme were continually in the background and listening to the news was a prerequisite, presumably a remnant/habit from the war. I dimly remember the feeling in the house when news of the Munich crash was first heard and subsequent bulletins were awaited with a mixture of dread and disbelief. However, nothing outside family bereavement ever approached the emotion I saw in my parents, when Duncan Edwards death was announced. Both subdued and quiet there was a deep sadness and grief, almost like a blanket, around the family house. I can trace my own "conscious" United journey back to that point in time. Even now, I can close my eyes and feel the sadness of that cold, February, 1950's house, clearly as I can feel the hairs on the back of my neck still rise, whenever Solskjaer's goal is replayed, and I'm transported back to Barcelona. From then on it was about United rising up as a football club. Words are totally inadequate when it comes to explaining the feelings experienced by both Dad and I, standing together at Wembley in '68. I'm sure, in my own mind, the Babes were also present that night.

JOSEPH TEDESCO

I was born in 1971. My father was a big Man Utd supporter and his passion for this football club filtered in my blood as I grew up in not such a great decade for the Red Devils. The first time I heard the story about a tragedy which took the lives of so many people in Munich it sort of got me very much intrigued. I wanted to know what happened, how, why…but there was no internet to help out. Hence, I started to look in books and encyclopaedias in local libraries, slowly capturing a sequence of events, reading about Busby, the FA, the babes, the 3 flight attempts, the ice on the wings…then the crash! I was so captivated by all this that I compiled the story in a scrap book, using pictures from pages I sneaked from those publications. I grew older and got involved with the Manchester United Supporters Club in Malta where I have been serving as a committee member for 27 years and counting, 14 years of which I have had the honour to preside. Ever since I got the grips of what 6th February was all about, every year that day is for me a day dedicated to meditation. In 2018, my very good friend Joe Glanville took me with him to Munich for the 60th anniversary of the darkest day in the history of our beloved United. This was my first trip to Tudering-Riem, my first glimpse of the monuments which commemorate so much pain and devastation. What I felt that day is inexplicable in words. You have to live it to understand. Nowadays it has become my annual pilgrimage and we are preaching it to all…last year we took a group of 40 for the 65th anniversary. Munich and the Babes are for me the baptism of my Man Utd religion.

RUTH DENTON

The darkest day in Manchester United's history happened 22 years before I was born, which seemed an eternity when I was growing up, but in reality more time has since passed since May 1999. I also mention that night as I truly believe Sir Matt was there at the Nou camp exercising divine intervention. As a very young child my grandad and dad told me about the devastating events of the 6th February 1958, the sheer acts of bravery, and the miracles surrounding those who survived. I was also made aware of how the whole of Manchester, red or blue were broken and devastated and in true Mancunian style, were United in grief. As a life-long Manchester United supporter the perpetual feeling of sadness for the souls we lost

that day is something that will never disappear, and the Flowers of Manchester will always live on in honour of those lost souls.
I'll always play my part to keep the red flag flying high.

RAMAN PAUL

When I think of Munich and the Busby Babes, I still get a cold feeling, one that is filled with complete sadness and heartache. Questions run through my mind, of which the answers cannot be completed, such as "why did they need to make another attempt to fly on the icy and treacherous runway?" And "what if Munich never happened, just how much the Busby Babes could've achieved, winning further silverware and winning the hearts and minds of many more football fans throughout the country?" Munich will always have a special place for all Reds, a place where thousands descend to pay their respects at ManchesterPlatz. To talk about the Busby Babes would take another entire book to write. So much could be written about the swashbuckling style in which they completely dominated the FA Youth Cup in its inception. Moving into the first team, the way they continued to play without fear, coached and managed by the inseparable Jimmy Murphy & Sir Matt Busby. The three pillars that defined the Busby Babes: Youth. Courage. Success. Each Busby Babe brought something different but each played with exactly the same passion and enthusiasm expected. Whilst I have a cold feeling thinking about Munich, I have a warm feeling when I think about the Busby Babes and the joy that they brought to thousands of Manchester United and indeed football fans throughout the world.
I am always filled with pride when I think about the Babes, and that they played a significant part in our beloved clubs glorious history.
My prayers and thoughts are always with those affected by the tragic events in Munich 1958.

DAVID HAWKES

A lad of just over 8 ½ years old came home from school on February 6th, 1958, to find his Mum sitting on the floor in floods of tears. She was a Red from Miles Platting and she'd heard the awful news on the radio. From then on the lad was Red and he can still remember that scene in the house. That lad was me and I've been a Red ever since and am proud to be so. Watching United is so special to me and it all comes from what was taken away on that dreadful day. It's an integral part of who and what I am and what I'll always be!

FLOSSY

The 6th February 1958 is a date etched in, not just mine, but every single Manchester United supporter's heart. Indeed, the darkest day for our club's history, but it fills me with so much pride to see the respect from fans every year on the anniversary. The ever increasing media coverage is integral to our memories and has been filtered down through generations in my own family. Yes, Munich will always resonate painful memories but the legendary joy and courage of the Busby Babes and those 24 lives will never be forgotten. The youth policy implemented during that era has aided our club to dominate for decades and I for one will never forget that.

JAY MOTTY

Following United over the years has been an emotional rollercoaster, with far more highs than lows but enough twists and turns to fill you with either pride or sadness. One match watching United that felt different to the usual highs and lows you experience seeing them win, lose or draw, was the time I was in Munich for the Champions League quarter final away leg in 2014. During the day of the game, like many Reds my friends and I made our way to the site of the Munich air crash, to see the memorial and pay our respects to the Flowers of Manchester, who perished there that fateful day in February

1958. The site of the crash is no longer near an airport but miles away from the main city and it added to the sense of sadness knowing that many of British football's brightest ever lights were extinguished in such a desolate place. Standing there at Manchesterplatz reflecting, reminded me of just how big a part of United's history the Busby Babes and their fate will always be. Bigger than any cup final, or trophy, the loss of that team, the way Sir Matt Busby and Jimmy Murphy were able to rebuild not just the side but the club itself and take us to the very top of world football is something that other fans will never fully understand. It's what makes United different, the club has been through more than just bad results, has risen from it to heights others can only dream of and standing there on the outskirts of Munich, filled me with not just an immeasurable sense of sadness, but also one of pride that we as a club were able recover from such an overwhelming loss.

ALEX BARNETT

My hero was Bryan Robson as a kid growing up in the 80s watching United, When I think of the Busby Babes and that awful night on a runway in Munich I think of my Dad. They were his heroes. The first United team he remembered. I always think of the devastating impact Munich would have had on the club and the player's families but also on a 14 year old supporter from Manchester. One day you are watching a team with some of the best players in the world set to possibly dominate European football and the next day many of your heroes are sadly gone. My Dad is a quiet man of little words unless it is about United and even then he doesn't go overboard praising players. I do recall that whenever the Busby Babes were mentioned in his conversation with my uncle when walking to games when I started going to United then he would come alive. It usually ended up with him trying to explain to me about Duncan Edwards. I think it was fair to say that it was firmly established in my mind from the age of nine that this Edwards chap was superhuman, could probably have played in any position and had teammates who were some of the best players around as well. Munich is very sad. It is a story of what could have been for great players taken in their prime but it is also the story of a team that were so good that they left memories on the pitch that those of my Dad's generation will never forget. I try and think of the joy the Busby Babes gave to my dad watching them and lifelong love for United they left him with which he then passed on to me. In that sense the Busby Babes always live on.

DARREN HAZELL

When I first think about the Busby Babes it's not Edwards, Charlton, Murphy or even Sir Matt himself I think of, it's my Nan. My Nan who grew up in Collyhurst before relocating South during the war. My nan who first told me about the Busby Babes and shared books and cigarette cards of the players with me. My Nan who pre mobile phones came though the switchboard at my first job to ask I be pulled out of a meeting and bought to the phone - fearing the worse as my Grandad was ill, I picked up the receiver to be told that Andy Cole had signed for United! My Nan who religiously bought me back the Pink sports pages whenever she went to Manchester. As a teenager I remember devouring one all about the first batch of Fergie's Fledglings - including Giuliano Maiorana, Tony Gill and Russell Beardsmore (who I loved and could dream it was me playing so brilliantly alongside my hero Robson) and hoping they could be my generations "Babes." Since then I've read a lot about the Busby Babes and I'm left wondering how good they could have been (for England as well as United) , shaking my head at the attitude of the FA and admiring the class and respect shown by Real Madrid in the days that followed. Having read the Lost Babes book I wish the club did much more for those injured or widowed. But most of all though I marvel at the resilience of those left behind - those who played on, the ingenuity and fortitude of Jimmy Murphy and Sir Matt (plus all the hidden figures behind the scenes who's stories are not told) .

PAUL MURPHY (Jimmy's Grandson)

As I write this I'm on a coach travelling to Bishop Auckland with a coach load of united fanatics, to thank them for their contribution after Munich. One of the greatest teams in history perished on a snowy 6th February 1958. Grandad took the reins and kept the flag flying. Paying my respects at Munich every year just seems to be something I have to do. A vocation you might say, remembering the Busby Babes…Of what we lost and what could have been.

THE FLOWERS OF MANCHESTER

"One cold and bitter Thursday in Munich, Germany,
Eight great football stalwarts conceded victory.
Eight men will never play again who met destruction there,
The flowers of English football, the flowers of Manchester.

Matt Busby's boys were flying, returning from Belgrade,
This great United family, all masters of their trade:
The pilot of the aircraft, the skipper Captain Thain,
Three times he tried to take off and twice turned back again.

The third time down the runway disaster followed close:
There was a slush upon the runway and the aircraft never rose.
It ploughed into the marshy ground, it broke, it overturned.
And eight of the team were killed as the blazing wreckage burned.

Roger Byrne and Tommy Taylor, who played for England's side,
And Ireland's Billy Whelan and England's Geoff Bent died.
Mark Jones and Eddie Colman, and David Pegg also,
They all lost their lives as it ploughed on through the snow.

Big Duncan he went to, with an injury to his frame,
And Ireland's Jackie Blanchflower will never play again.

The great Matt Busby lay there, the father of his team:
Three long months passed by before he saw his team again.

The trainer, coach and secretary, and a member of the crew,
Also eight sporting journalists who with United flew.
And one of them was Big Swifty, who we will n'er forget,
The finest English keeper that ever graced their net.

Oh, England's finest football team its record truly great,
Its proud successes mocked by a cruel twist of fate.
Eight men will never play again who met destruction there,
The flowers of English football, the flowers of Manchester."

THE END

355